THE BOOK OF

IVYBRIDGE

River, Mills and Moorland

IVOR MARTIN

HALSGROVE

First published in Great Britain in 2009

British Library Cataloguing-in-Publication Data
A CIP record for this title is available from the British Library

ISBN 978 1 84114 947 9

HALSGROVE
Halsgrove House,
Ryelands Industrial Estate,
Bagley Road, Wellington, Somerset TA21 9PZ
Tel: 01823 653777 Fax: 01823 216796
email: sales@halsgrove.com

Part of the Halsgrove group of companies
Information on all Halsgrove titles is available at: www.halsgrove.com

Frontispiece photograph: *Members of the Pearce family of Ivybridge.*

Printed in Great Britain by CPI Antony Rowe Ltd, Wiltshire

Foreword

Ivybridge is really a new area; now a town in its own right. The first mention of the 'bridge' was in 1284, before which there would have been a crossing for the monks travelling between the abbeys at Tavistock, Plympton and Buckfast and Ashburton, probably by stepping stones or even clapper bridge.

That the area was inhabited or visited by Stone-Age man is evidenced in the tools, knifes, arrow-heads and scrapers left behind. We know for a fact they were at Harford because of the hut circles there.

For many years the village just plodded along, mainly engaged in agriculture, and then the services were connected and a little clay works started up at Red Lake and Westlake. The village really grew because of the paper mill and London Hotel in the 1780s, both built by William Dunsterville. The mill has passed through many hands since then and at the time of writing is partly owned by French company Arjo Wiggins, producing specialised paper for lottery tickets, etc. At one time the mill produced paper for the old white £5 notes – hence a local Ivybridge medal being named the 'Ivy Fiver'.

As we are such a young town, all our churches and larger buildings date back only to the 1700s and 1800s. Neighbouring communities of Harford, Cornwood, Ugborough and Ermington are much older, but their boundaries all meet at the bridge, which crosses the River Erme. We still hold the annual bridge ceremony, at which Ermington challenges us to pay a toll allowing us to cross the bridge for one year, the toll being a duck from the Erme, a ream of paper from the mill and a red rose.

As a town our claim to fame is that we were once the fastest growing town in Europe; we were also the only place to claim Prime Minister Ted Heath's offer of £400 to celebrate joining the Common Market in 1973, and thus the only place the BBC could find to film such a celebration!

The population of Ivybridge was steady from 1850 to 1950, growing dramatically with the increase in building in the 1960s; we seem to be mainly a dormitory town for Plymouth, and the larger population has made it difficult to maintain the community spirit that existed in earlier days.

The Erme in flood near Waterside House.

During the Second World War we were host to 2,500 American soldiers training to take part in the D-Day landings, from which many never returned.

Although the last cattle market was held in the 1950s, Ivybridge was a market town from 1793 – we even had our own town cryer. There was also a race-course here, built by Sir Frederick Leman Rogers in 1786 on Henlake Down, but which was closed before 1800. So you can see there was plenty to entertain the people of Ivybridge in times past!

Ivor Martin

In 1983 the late C.F. Hankin wrote the following notes on Ivybridge for the benefit of newcomers to our town:

All available historical evidence points to 'Ivy Bridge' having been the commonly used name for an undefined district centred on a crossing of the River Erme long before any settlement of people numerous enough to be a village had established itself here. The earliest known documentary mention of 'Ivy Bridge' (in its Latin equivalent) in AD*1280 comes at a time when community life under the ancient parish system had become centred at the Parish Church, and it is highly probable that the four parishes of Cornwood, Ermington, Harford and Ugborough already had their common boundary at the bridge. The parish system continued, with some changes, until well into the nineteenth century, and it is in the records of the 'four parishes' that the history of Ivybridge from the eleventh to the nineteenth century must be sought.*

Notes on the prehistoric periods prior to the Roman colonisation of Britain are necessarily of an archaeological nature, and may appear to concentrate on sites on Dartmoor. This is not meant to suggest that in prehistoric times there were settlements only on the moor. Relics of occupation have survived there partly because of its almost total abandonment by the time the Romans arrived, after which time a large part of the moor has been left undisturbed, and partly because there was a plentiful supply of surface stone, a durable material, with which to build habitations, tombs, ceremonial monuments and land boundaries. Only a few artefacts, such as stone tools or flints, have been picked up in the Ivybridge four parishes, and no archaeological excavation using modern techniques has been undertaken. Limited excavation has taken place on other parts of the southern moor in recent years, and surface investigations have been made at the estuaries bordering on Dartmoor. A clearer understanding of the prehistoric man's activities in South Devon may gradually emerge.

C.F. Hankin
Ivybridge, 1983

The late Charles Hankin, historian.

CONTENTS

The Newcombe family of Ivybridge.

'Crying over spilt milk', a staged photograph of a young boy at a cottage door, weeping over a broken jug of milk lying at his feet. One of many photographs held in Ivybridge Museum.

The History of Ivybridge

Ivybridge in Prehistoric Times: Neolithic (c.4000–2000BC)

Two miles north-east of Ivybridge, where Dartmoor meets the enclosed farmland above Bittaford, there stands a group of stones abut six feet high which bear witness to the earliest known occupation by man of the Ivybridge area. This monument, on the hill known as Cuckoo Ball, is believed to be the remains of a 'chamber tomb' belonging to the late Neolithic (late Stone Age) period which terminated at around 2000BC. It is one of five such tombs so far recorded on and around Dartmoor; one of them, a short distance north of the Cuckoo Ball, was first recognised in 1973, whilst another is the well-known monument at Corringdon, four miles to the north-east of Ivybridge in South Brent parish. The remaining two sites are both in the Chagford area of north-east Dartmoor, and an unconfirmed but possible sixth chamber tomb was found on Gidleigh common, which is also not far from Chagford.

The Dartmoor type of Neolithic chamber tomb was built in the form of a short gallery or passage, with walls and roof formed by large blocks of granite, and with perhaps recesses built into the side walls to accommodate a succession of inhumations. Earth and small stones were heaped over the tomb to make either a round or an oval-shaped mound, called a 'long barrow', and the entrance at one end was closed by more large granite blocks. It is the large blocks of stone that enable archaeologists to recognise the tombs, since the mound at some sites has almost, if not completely, disappeared, and the acid soil has destroyed all human remains.

The Neolithic people were semi-nomadic pastoralists who were beginning to lead a more settled life by cutting down woodlands in order to practise some sort of farming and cultivation of the soil. They probably moved from place to place when the soil was exhausted, and returned when the ground had regenerated. This would help to explain why few traces of their dwellings have been found: those known near Dartmoor, such as the site at Haldon, near Exeter, and the one at Hazard Hill, three miles west of Totnes, are hilltop settlements away from the moor. The people were content with houses of non-durable materials, such as wood and turf, with thatch of heather and reeds; but for their dead, or some of them, they built long-lasting resting-places in stone. There may have been a religious reason for this, or possibly it was a sign of respect for the chieftain's family, for it appears likely from the few discovered that not every Neolithic corpse was given a stone tomb. They appear to have had a particular liking for moving large blocks of stone about, and they are believed to be the first people in Britain to do this. The well-known stone row on Stalldown, west of the Erme valley opposite Piles Corpse, is built on large granite blocks, and although this monument is seen in its restored state, it is clearly different in character from most other stone rows on the south part of Dartmoor, which are believed to date from a later period. The Stalldown stone row may be a monument erected on Dartmoor in the Neolithic period, and so too may be the enigmatic double stone row that crosses Piles Hill from east to west and has a total length of nearly 1,000 yards. Many of the large stones in this double row, some of which are up to seven feet long, lie flat on the ground in a north-south direction, and it is an interesting question whether this is a destroyed stone row, or one that was planned and for some unknown reason was abandoned before erection.

Although it is evident that quite a lot of human activity was going on around Ivybridge about 4,000 years ago, today we see only a few traces of what was done. Moreover, most questions regarding the meaning of what we see remain unanswered. For those interested in our local prehistory there is still plenty of scope, not only for making new discoveries, but also for coming to a better understanding of what is revealed.

The Bronze Age

The people who inhabited the South West of England during the second millenium BC (2000–1000BC) are usually known by the nature of their surviving artefacts. Following the last of the Stone-Age people, with their chamber tombs and large stone monuments, there came to Dartmoor the 'beaker' people, so called after the nature of the pottery they left behind. Specimens of their work have been found in the Chagford area, and there have been possible finds in the Plym Valley. These people had already acquired the skill of mixing molten tin with copper to make bronze, and thereby had increased the lethal power of their weapons as well as enjoying a greater variety of domestic appliances and articles of personal adornment. It used to be thought that the beaker and Bronze-Age people had moved into Devon from the mainland of Europe, bringing their skills with them, but a more accurate dating of articles found in the South West has led some archaeologists to believe that perhaps our local folk were competent to develop the skills themselves, although at the same time they were trading with the mainland via the Dartmoor river estuaries.

By the middle of the millenium, around 1500BC, the part of Dartmoor above Ivybridge must have been quite thickly populated. As far into the moor as Erme pound and at over 1,300ft above sea level, their occupation sites occur in considerable numbers. They take the form of stone-walled enclosures of the land of various shapes and sizes with which are associated stone and earth built 'houses' or huts, settled in groups of one or two or up to 30 and more 'hut circles', as they are now called, on one site. No evidence has yet been found to tell us whether the people here at such an early period actually got their tin from the River Erme and its tributaries, the Butter Brook and Lud Brook, although they certainly lived close to these streams from which tin at some time has been taken.

Quite a lot of evidence has been collected regarding the agricultural pursuits of the Dartmoor Bronze-Age people. At many of the hut circle sites their field systems have been traced, and over Harford and Ugborough Moors, as well as on other Dartmoor commons, land divisions of a much larger area demarcated by stone and earth banks called 'reaves' have been investigated in depth. All the evidence suggests that there was a well-organised degree of farming and stock rearing, providing meat and cereals for food, and hides and skins for clothing. It would seem that the reaves, which appear to be in no way defensive, could only have operated within an organised community having a civil discipline sufficiently strong to accept peacefully these land divisions.

Natural conditions which made this occupation of Dartmoor possible were a warmer climate than we ourselves endure, and woodland cover to a much higher attitude than presently exists. The full extent of the woodland and its later decline on Dartmoor are not yet entirely understood, but it is probable that a deterioration in the climate during the next millenium (1000–0BC) was matched by man's destruction of the trees, and that there slowly came into existence the 'great waste' of Dartmoor that we so much enjoy today.

In support of the belief that the Bronze-Age people were of a different ethnic origin from the earlier Stone-Age inhabitants, we see the changes that occurred in the funerary practices of the second millenium BC. Instead of the chamber tomb there is the 'kistvaen' or 'cist', a granite-lined pit large enough to take a single inhumation in a crouched position, or one or more cremated bodies, surrounded by a circle of stone and covered with a mound of earth and stones to complete the monument. There are also the numerous large 'cairns' or 'barrows' which are great heaps of stones placed on or near hill tops and often visible from miles around. When excavated, these mounds sometimes reveal a cist below the heap of stones. Many smaller burial mounds and some cists are associated with stone rows, and it may be assumed that these rows date from the same period as the burial mounds. Recent excavations on Shaugh Moor have dated some cairns there at about 2000–1500BC. The stone rows attributed to this period are usually built of small stones, and as seen now sometimes only just protrude above the ground surface. A number of 'alignments' of this type can be seen on the moor above Ivybridge: there is one on Butterdon Hall which is over a mile long, and the Stall Moor stone row on the west side of the River Erme extends for more than two miles. In spite of many interesting theories put forward to explain the stone rows, there is still no more convincing explanation for their construction.

Ivybridge in Celtic Times: the Iron Age

The period known as the Bronze Age continued into the middle of the first millenium BC, when, at around 700-500BC, there is known to have been a widespread movement of people westward and southward throughout Europe. Existing trade connections between Britain and the mainland may have encouraged the migration across the sea to Britain of groups who came with the intention of settling here. They were already known to the Greeks as the 'Keltoi', and at least one group came to Devon and Cornwall, whilst yet another group, speaking another language, found itself in Ireland.

The Celts brought with them the use of forged iron, a metal easier to work than cast or beaten bronze. Having learned their agriculture in the forests and river valleys of Europe, the Celts who came to Devon were not likely to be attracted to a life on Dartmoor where, it is believed, the conditions were becoming harder even for the people already living there. But it seems that the Celts mixed quite well with the rest of the population, and there is one record of their coming to the Ivybridge area in the place name 'penguin' ('at the need of the wood') now in Remington parish, which is wholly Celtic (Hoskins, *Devon* p.393). Celtic weapons, helmets and shields that have survived, both in iron and bronze, suggest that they were of a warlike nature, and they established, or as archaeologists have now discovered, elaborated on, an existing system of hilltop 'forts', but not all of the sites make much sense as places of defence: our local earthwork on Henlake Down above the Erme, for instance, the antiquity of which has been disputed, and the one at Turtley above Glazebrook on the Avon, are more likely to be places where cattle and other stock were temporarily impounded, perhaps where the lowland farmers met and marketed with the Dartmoor stock-raisers.

It is not known when the high moor ceased to be populated. The withdrawal may have been gradual, and some families may have remained on the perimeter of the moor farming the land which, when it was resettled by the Saxons a few centuries later, acquired the Saxon '-worthy' names. These farms are often found to be close to prehistoric field systems. Stock from a wide area would probably continue to be driven to the open for summer pasture, and its return to the farm for the winter months would account for the small 'closes' of irregular shape bounded by the old earth bank hedges which are still a characteristic of the field pattern in South Devon, and can be seen at Filham and other parts of Ugborough, where they are usually associated with

SoWe Don't Get Snow in Ivybridge

Ivybridge Station in winter.

Bittaford in deep snow.

So We Don't Get Snow in Ivybridge

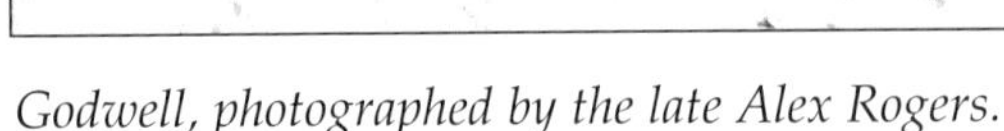

Godwell, photographed by the late Alex Rogers.

The Lower Mill leat, probably in March 1981 at the time of the great blizzard.

Top and above: *The Erme in winter.*

Luson Cross, 1928. The photograph was taken by Mr Close, headmaster of the village school.

ancient 'droves' leading to the moor.

The Roman colonisation of 'Britannia' during the first four centuries AD did not spread west of Exeter, although there is ever-growing evidence of Roman penetration into both Devon and Cornwall. But the Roman road system and constant communication with Rome opened up the whole of Britain, including the South West, to several cultural changes. Christianity was in Britain in the fourth century. The Welsh and Irish monks were great travellers, and it was they who were responsible for the spread of the Christian religion and for the dissemination of Latin literacy. They could also tell the British how agriculture was being practised in other countries they had visited.

At Fardel, in Cornwood, a Christian memorial stone of the sixth century was found in the nineteenth century and it is now in the British Museum. Three Irish names are inscribed in Latin, and there is also an inscription in the Southern Irish 'ogham' alphabet of the third to fourth century. In some form the Irish influence must have reached the Ivybridge area. Whether the connection was with the followers of Saint Petroc, a sixth-century Welshman who had studied in Ireland before coming to Devon, is not known, but there are two parish churches in the neighbourhood, one at Harford and the other at South Brent, which bear his name.

The political and economic collapse that followed the Roman withdrawal from Britain in AD410 had its effect on Devon. Saxons were already in other parts of the country as mercenaries, and the disruption caused by their revolt in AD441 affected the whole of Britain. Arthur, who had strong attachment to the South West, is credited with keeping the central government together, but after his death in c.515 the country was split up into small belligerent kingships, with Cornwall, Devon and part of Somerset becoming the kingdom of Dumnonia. Many people who could move out did so, including the monks, and crossed the Channel to western France. The small proportion of Celtic placenames surviving in Devon could be the result of a considerable depopulation, so that even when the Saxons moved westward by conquest in the second half of the seventh century they had virtually to resettle the land.

Ivybridge in the Anglo-Saxon Period

The defeat of the British by the west Saxons at Penselwood (near Mere on the A303 in Wiltshire) in AD658 opened up the kingdom of Dumnonia to invasion from the east, and after a second defeat in 682, probably somewhere in Somerset, there was nothing to stop a larger scale movement of Saxons into the South West. It is likely that East Devon, including Exeter, was in their possession before 690, and place-name evidence points to a rapid penetration of the whole territory. It is probable that by 722 the Saxon occupation of Devon was complete.

The incomers chose to call themselves 'Angles', although the surviving British knew them as 'Saxon'. Their economy was based on the land, and at first they probably kept to the traditional preference for living in small communities – the 'tun' (basically 'fence') which we now know as the 'village' was compact, and perhaps if there was still in the neighbourhood a British settlement which had survived the conquest, as at Penquit in Ermington, the village name may record this, and 'Ermington' – 'the village of the Erme people' – is one of some 20 'Ermington' parish names in Devon. Where security was a consideration in the choice of a site, it was customary to build a defensive earthwork, a 'burgh', round the settlement, and it is thought that this may have happened at Ugborough, a village known to have existed in AD847.

Independent men of means, 'freemen', subject to no lord below the king, created new farms or resettled old farmland abandoned by the Britons. These farms sometimes took the name of the settler followed by the element '-worthy'. There are a number of farm names not far from Ivybridge, on and around Dartmoor, which may have this origin; Trowlesworthy near Cadover Bridge (at one time there was a Cadworthy), Blachford (blaycheworthy) in 1520, the spellings change through the ages, are familiar to most Ivybridge people. Sometimes enterprising young Saxons who were not freemen were allowed to set up small fenced farmsteads on their own, and these, too, might take the name of the farmer, such as 'Uppaton' and 'Dinnaton' in Cornwood. Ugborough has a few '-tun' names. Ermington has Caton (or Keaton), Upton, Burraton (the farm of a freed slave) and others.

In early British times, the family and its close association with the village was the basis of social and political organisation. Central government under the king was organised through the hundred, an area of administration whose origin is lost in time, but believed to have been at first a community of 100 families burdened with the customary service to the king, including that of providing 100 fighting men. The hundred held its monthly council in the open air, sometimes at a bend in a river where there was a land boundary of some sort. The Old English word for 'council, meeting-place' (basically secret) is 'rune', and it may be that the Ermington hundred met at 'the Runs', where there are now the Erme playing-fields. There is also 'Stert Runs' on the Piall River at the Cornwood–old Plympton boundary. Towards the end of the ninth century, when King Alfred felt it was time he did something about the marauding Danes, able-bodied men of the Ivybridge area in Ermington hundred would do their military service at the earthwork fabrication at Halwell.

The early English were not great road builders, and in South Devon communication between the villagers and the outside world was still mainly along the ridgeways which for the centuries had given access to the estuaries. All along the several ridgeways near Ivybridge there are entrances to narrow tracks, each one leading to an isolated farm set down under the shelter of the higher ground. It was left to the individual family to trace its own way from the homestead to its arable land and pasture, which it did by avoiding bad ground and natural obstacles, and by going round land under cultivation, regardless of the extra distance this added to the journey. So were formed the 'winding Devon lanes' which with centuries of use and weathering have sometimes become the sunken roads or 'hollow ways' that early travellers remark upon. The already ancient use of summer grazing on Dartmoor explains the tendency for lanes around Ivybridge to lead northwards to the moor, and it is possible that the east-west crossing of the Erme at Ivybridge came much later and for other reasons, there being little call for a road across the Erme between the ford at Keaton and the ford at Harford where the bridge now stands.

Anglo-Saxon possession of the land in Devon lasted for 350 years, ending with the coming of the Normans in 1066. In the absence of Saxon cemeteries with their 'grave goods', and of contemporary buildings, the main evidence of their occupation rests with place-names. Only a small number of Celtic names have survived, yet the Domesday survey shows that most of the Devon villages and hamlets were in existence in 1086 (Hoskins), and many farms today have names of Saxon origin. A strip-field system may still be seen at Ugborough on the hill towards Bittaford, and there is another at Lutton in Cornwood. Harford church possesses a font which has been said to be 'early English'. But it was probably not until some time after the Norman redistribution of land, towards the end of the eleventh century, that a new river crossing gave identity to the place which came to be known as 'Ivy Bridge'.

(The notes on place-names come from various sources, but the ground is extremely treacherous and their application to the Ivybridge area is wholly a personal one. For the derivation of 'Ermington', Bill Best Harris, formerly Plymouth City Librarian, appears to prefer the Old English word 'iermen' – 'principal' or 'great' – followed by the '-tun' element, so meaning 'the principal farm' of the area (*Western Morning News*, February 1983.)

Ivybridge after the Norman Conquest

The Norman conquest in 1066 would not have immediately disturbed the ordinary 'man in the field' living in the Ivybridge area. William's intention on taking over his new kingdom was to let the traditional English way of life continue, and at first many high-ranking Englishmen of Saxon descent were able to keep their lands and power, and govern alongside the Norman barons. The English revolts in 1069, in which the men of Devon took part, upset all this, for in a country now always prepared for war, it was no longer possible for English lords to retain land, the possession of which carried the obligation to provide the trained, mounted men-at-arms, the 'knights', who were an essential part of the Norman military system. An analysis of the Domesday survey has shown that by 1086, through dispossession, natural wastage and some emigration, only 8 per cent of the land remained in English hands (L. & J. Laing, 1979).

It was probably reward for 'knight's service' more than any other single cause that brought into existence many of the small estates which are still a characteristics of the South West. Reward for service would be made by grant of land, and the chief lords to whom the land was distributed after the Battle of Hastings or perhaps after the revolts three years later, soon had to divide and let out their possessions to others of lower rank who could provide the service required under the law. Judhael of Totnes, for instance, the largest landowner in South Devon, had to find no fewer than 70 knights. This system lasted in practice well into the thirteenth century, and in law into the reign of Charles II, and it is possible that many of the estates which make up the Ivybridge area today came into existence during the 300 years following the Conquest.

The land to the south of Dartmoor had probably been extensively cleared for farming by the Saxon English, and, as 'leighs' (cleared land), would be ripe for further development. The present-day farmsteads of Challonsleigh, Strashleigh and Cadleigh, west of Ivybridge, and Leigh at Bittaford to the east, could all be post-Conquest farms which replaced earlier Saxon settlements. At Strashleigh there are some 'long-S' shaped field banks which, enclosed, became the '-hams', such as Langham (the enclosure at the boundary) and Filham (the hay enclosure). Rutt, a farm on the edge of the moor in Ugborough, is named from the Anglo-Saxon for 'rubbish for burning' or 'underwood', and there is still a wood, predominantly oak, just above the farmhouse.

Post-Conquest development along the southern edge of Dartmoor would call for road communication with the sea at Plympton and the lord's castle that had recently been built there. When Plympton Priory (founded in 1121) was granted land at Wrangaton in 1160, valued at 'one tenth of a knight's fee', there would have been more need for a road and probably for a new crossing of the river Erme. That a bridge was in existence and known as 'Ivy Bridge' before 1280 is evidenced by a deed of that year whereby John Peverel, Lord of Ermington, granted rights to property in Harford and along the River Erme as far as 'Ponte Ederoso', to his daughter Iseult. Risdon, writing in 1630, tells us that Ivybridge was granted to Alfred de Ponte Hedera by Sir John Peverell's father, and Alfred de Ponte turns up again in 1332 as a substantial taxpayer in Ermington and with a small property in Harford. The use of the Latin in the deed in 1280 suggests that 'Ivy Bridge' was descriptive of a landmark or area rather than of a settlement or village, and it is likely that the Peverells, who then owned Harford and had owned Ermington since the time of Henry I (1100–35), had built the first bridge at this place some time around the year 1200.

To our ancestors of the fifteenth century and even of the eighteenth century a bridge appeared as 'an exception to the common course of things, coming into existence as a result of some extraordinary private benevolence or religious zeal'.

In the early part of the fifteenth century the road from Ivybridge to Plympton had become important enough for Bishop Staffod, in January 1411, to spend penance money on repairs to the road 'near Challonsleigh' (that would be somewhere near Lee Mill), and in the summer of 1436 Bishop Lacy made similar payments for repairs and maintenance along the same road. It is unlikely, however, that the road, which in places must have been over low-lying wet ground, would have reduced the attraction of the older and higher road running east from Plympton to places beyond Ivybridge, which went through Cornwood to the Erme at Harford and thence over the open moor to South Brent, a route that continued in use well into the eighteenth century (Donn's map of Devon, 1765). Whichever way was chosen in the fifteenth century it seems that not very much would be expected of it, for it was written at the end of the following century that:

> *... roads of this district [Devon] were exceedingly bad... Painful for man and horse, as they can best witness who have made trial thereof. For be they never so well mounted upon horses out of other countries, when they have travelled one journey in these parts, they can, in respect of ease of travel forbear a second.*
>
> (Hooker, c.1598, quoted by Risdon, 1810 edition)

Since the eighth century the 'parish' under the patronage of a lay nobleman had been the basis of organisation of the church in rural areas. The system continued, and the proliferation of estates after the Conquest brought many incentives for the Norman lord to build a Parish Church within his domains. This would be done perhaps as a mark of family prestige, or possibly as a penance for sins committed, such as having killed men in battle. There would also be a need for clearer definition of estate and parish boundaries than had previously been necessary. Early boundary marks were usually widely spaced but easily recognised natural or man-made features, often a stream or spring, or objects such as 'stones' put up for the purpose, or perhaps a ditch. The boundary between Ugborough and North Huish had already been established in a Saxon charter of AD962, and the ancient ridgeway above Higher Ludbrook provided a ready-made boundary between Ermington and Modbury, as well as between Ugborough and Modbury Ermington's northern boundary with Cornwood, significantly at Langham, the 'boundary enclosure'. At some period it was evidently agreed that the river crossing at Ivybridge should be the common boundary for the four parishes of Ermington, Cornwood, Harford (with Stowford) and Ugborough, a site then most likely set amidst steep-sloping, boulder-strewn 'waste' which would be convenient to all parties. Distant about two miles from Cornwood and Ugborough, the bridge must have been a notable landmark on what had become an important thoroughfare, and it is not surprising that Ivybridge became the recognised focal point for naming the whole area radiating from the bridge into the four parishes. Several centuries were to pass, however, before conditions were right for a settlement of village proportions to grow up along the banks of the river Erme.

Ivybridge from the Twelfth Century to the Seventeenth Century

It is fairly certain that at the end of the thirteenth century Ivybridge had become a recognised 'place on the map', but that its spread into four parishes would have prevented any sort of village community from growing up here. The Saxon 'vill' had become very much a parish community, and whoever lived at Ivybridge would consider himself a member of the parish in which he lived; he would attend its church regardless of distance, and eventually he would be buried there. In secular matters the landless farm worker and his family lived under the discipline of the so-called 'manorial system', which was also of Saxon origin, doing service on the lord's land and looking for protection, as well as accepting penalties at the lord's manorial court. The landed proprietor would himself be under a higher legal authority, particularly for taxation, an authority which descended from the king through the chief lord or baron, down to the locally based lord of the manor. At all levels of society, wealth, social status and power depended on land ownership, and the history of a rural area such as Ivybridge is largely a record of who was in possession of the land.

From the twelfth century to its dissolution in 1538 Plympton Priory held a lot of land in Ermington, particularly on the high ground north-west of Ivybridge. The estate of Cleeve, Worthele and Swainstone all contributed land to the priory at some time, and Wrangaton in Ugborough had been granted to the priory in 1160, so that Ivybridge people must have been constantly reminded of the presence and power of the Church. During the 24 years Edmund Stafford was Bishop of Exeter, 1395–1419, no fewer than six families living within a mile and a half of Ivybridge were granted licence to hold divine service in their house or private chapel;

Filham in Ugborough, Penquit at that time in Modbury parish, Worthele, Woodland and Ivybridge itself in Ermington, Stowford in Harford. The ruins of Filham chapel may still be seen in the grounds of the present house.

Another powerful group of landowners in the twelfth and thirteenth centuries were the Knights Templar, members of a religious order founded to assist the Crusaders. At one time they owned vast amounts of land in England and throughout Europe. On field name evidence it is interesting to speculate on whether the Templars had any connection with Ugborough. Land known as 'Temple Pike' is recorded in 1614 and again in 1833, situated east of the lane leading to the moor at Davey's Cross, and on the west side of the same lane there is land known as 'Pallace' (the spelling is variable), possibly a contraction of 'Palestine', which is still with us in the form of 'Pallace Cottages'.

The growth of towns and markets in the fourteenth century encouraged the replacement of the service economy in rural areas by a wages economy, and the epidemic of the Black Death (1348–49), with its effect on population and the value of labour, probably speeded up this change. It became easier for men of humble origin to be 'freeholders' (free of most services to the lord), and in the sixteenth and seventeenth centuries a 'yeoman' class of farmer, working his own land, figures frequently in the buying and selling of land in the four parishes with which Ivybridge is concerned. Harford manor, which in Risdon's time (1630) 'consisteth most of freeholders', had five named freeholders in 1428.

As well as in farming, Ivybridge must have been active in two other great industries associated with the Dartmoor environment – wool and tin. There is not much evidence to tell how deeply Ivybridge was involved in the wool industry, but its neighbour Modbury was very much a wool town. There is a record of a 'fullyinge mill' at Ivybridge in 1555, and there is reason to believe it could have been where 'The Chantry' property now stands in Beacon Road. There were tin workings at Addicombe in the Lukesland estate in Harford in the early-seventeenth century, and others on the Butterbrook stream (known to the tinners as 'Shillake') near the SWWA reservoir on the Harford Moor. At both sites the remains of the tinners' work can still be seen. The records of land possession reveal that there was a 'tynne Mylle' at Ivybridge in 1550, almost certainly on land now occupied by Stowford paper mills. The mill had belonged to one John Bury, who took part in the 'prayer book rebellion' in the West (1549). He was executed in about 1550, and his property and lands in Ivybridge, Ugborough and elsewhere were granted by King Edwards VI to William Gybbes of Fenton in Dartington 'for his services against the rebels in the West'. In 1553 William Gybbes was himself imprisoned in Exeter Castle and subsequently in the Tower of London because he objected to the intended marriage of Queen Mary to Philip of Spain. However, William Gybbes regained his freedom, and in 1555 sold the fulling mill and the tin mill to Thomas Prestwode, merchant of Exeter, after which date nothing more has come to light about the mills.

Except for the constant sales and resales of land, often in quite small parcels, and the disturbance caused by the movement of troops engaged in the Civil War, nothing much seems to have happened in Ivybridge during the seventeenth century. Travellers through Devonshire continued to complain about the appalling condition of the roads, and although Risdon (1630) found Ivybridge to be 'a place that admits a great thoroughfare', perhaps only those who were obliged to do so ventured to pass this way.

The estate which had taken the name 'Ivybridge' in the parish of Ermington in the thirteenth century had attained manor and barton status by 1576. It is not certain, however, where the mansion house stood. The ownership had descended from Alfred de Ponte to the Dymock family (c.1402) and from them to the Bonvilles in the same century. Early in the seventeenth century Thomas William of Stowford bought the manor, but within a few years it passed to the Drakes, a famous family of yeoman stock. The Drakes seemed to take little interest in Ivybridge, and the estate was sold to John Rogers of Wisdom and Blachford in Cornwood in 1691. The Rogers family kept Ivybridge as part of the Blachford estates throughout the eighteenth and nineteenth centuries, and saw their property change into the village which basically it is today.

Ivybridge in the Eighteenth Century

In the first half of the eighteenth century there appears to have been no attempt to add to the dwelling-houses which stood mainly along the west bank of the River Erme and formed the village of Ivybridge. During the first 43 years of the century the manor was held by John Rogers, the son of Sir John, who had bought the manor in 1692. John had been given Ivybridge and other of his father's properties on his marriage in 1698, in trust and with power to grant lease for lives. This power John exercised in rearranging the holding of existing leases when called upon to do so, but no further. It is not possible to be certain why this was so. It is well known that the cloth-making industry, on which Ivybridge was largely dependent, was in decline, as were other trades because of the wars with France. It may also be recognised that Ivybridge had passed into the hands of a family more at ease as merchants in the shipping business than as country gentlemen carrying the responsibilities of lords of the manor.

The second Sir John Rogers was succeeded by his son in January 1744. For the first ten years the third baronet continued to treat Ivybridge in much the same way as his father had done. In the 1750s the great post roads spreading out from Exeter were being subjected to improvement by adopting the turnpike system. The road between Exeter and South Brent which passed through Ashburton was turnpiked in 1755, so it could not be long before the continuation of this road to Ivybridge and on to Plymouth called for the same attention. In May 1758 Sir John, with other landowners in the Plymouth area, obtained the necessary Act of Parliament and proceeded to form the trust 'for repairing the Highroad between Brent bridge in the County of Devon and Gasking Gate in or near the Borough of Plymouth in the same County'. At the first meeting of the trustees, held at the George Inn at Plympton, Sir John Rogers was elected chairman. In the 12 months following the setting up of the trust quite a lot of work was done on the road. The total expenditure recorded for the two months May and June 1759 was £517.15s.5d., of which £92.19s.9d. was spent on the road at Ivybridge. There is a map of the road made by James Mogg and published in 1818 which marks 'Turnpike' at a spot where Filham Moor Lane turns into the main road, so it is likely that for a time a tollbar stood there before being moved to a site at the corner of Cole Lane further east in Harford parish.

Ivybridge did not respond quickly to the road improvements thrust upon it. Sir John had made some alterations to the interior of the inn house, the Royal Oak, probably in anticipation of the increased traffic the turnpike would encourage. This was in 1756, and it was not until the 1780s, when Sir John's nephew, Frederick Leman Rogers, the son of Sir John's brother Frederick, was the fifth baronet, that the village began a long period of expansion which was to continue throughout the nineteenth century.

It is difficult to discover exactly when Henry Rivers built the London Inn on the left bank of the River Erme. It was probably in the late 1770s. By the middle of the 1780s it had become the principal inn at Ivybridge. The old Royal Oak, kept by the widow Mrs Mary Allday with the assistance of her daughter Sarah, was in decline, so that in 1784 Mrs Mary Allday had some difficulty in paying her rents. The improved roads had made it easier for travellers by horse or carriage to visit Devonshire, and soon the London Inn gained the reputation of being one of the most comfortable inns in the West Country. Many artists came to Ivybridge to make paintings of the river and the ancient bridge because their topographical landscapes suited the cultural climate of the times, and engravings of their work sold well, as they still do in Ivybridge.

The year 1780 is probably when Sir Frederick Leman Rogers, who had become fifth baronet in 1777, engaged Mr Christopher Savery of Modbury as steward for the Rogers's manors of Blachford, Ivybridge and West Hooe. During the 40 years Mr Savery held this post there can be little doubt that his influence on the development of Ivybridge village was at least as great and most likely exceeded that of the two lords of the manor he served. How his influence was expressed may be deduced from the Steward's Accounts for work done which Mr Savery submitted each year to his employer.

The first major enterprise undertaken by Sir Frederick was to provide Ivybridge with a chapel of the Established Church. The history of the chapel is told separately: here it is sufficient to say that in February 1785 Mr Savery had his first meeting with Mr Bent, a local builder, who was commissioned to

The paper mill, established in 1787.

do the work, Sir Frederick giving a plot bridge leading towards Cornwood.

It was about this time that Ivybridge first felt the effects of the Industrial Revolution, albeit perhaps indirectly. Mr William Dunsterville of Plymouth, whose family was engaged in several industries, bought the estate of Stowford in Harford parish. In 1787 he established a paper mill on the lane adjoining the ancient Stowford corn mill. This affected the economy of Ivybridge and was close enough to the village to be always looked upon as part of it. Others, too, saw the industrial possibilities offered by the village, set on the main post road to London and with water power available from the River Erme. Before the end of the century another paper mill was built by Mr William Pim, next to the Ivybridge corn mill. A trade directory dated 1798 says there was also a block-mill, but no knowledge of this has come to light. The place-name 'Ivybridge' was, and still is, often used to denote areas beyond the true confines of the village.

The residential attractions of Ivybridge were also becoming known. The first gentleman's house to be built was Highland House. Colonel William Webber of Exmouth met Mr Savery on 21 February 1790 to discuss a proposition. A site agreed on was on the relatively high ground above the river which afterwards turned out to be rather badly chosen as regards its water supply. Negotiations were protracted and when completed the house and its amenities occupied about 12 acres. The property was leased from Sir Frederick for a term dependent on three young lives of the Webber family at the yearly ground rent of £18.17s.6d.

Mr Savery's account for 1793 records in December that a cattle market was started. This was at the west end of Fore Street below the orchard belonging to Colonel Webber of Highland House. It was intended to be a monthly market, but it is not known for how long it lasted, since the only other mention of it is in Mr Savery's account for January 1794.

Sir Frederick's journals reveal that from an early age he found pleasure in attending race meetings, although there is no suggestion that any of the Rogers were gamblers. In 1786, after he had lost his seat in Parliament, he had a small race-course made on Henlake Down, land which had been within the manor of Ivybridge since early times. Meetings were usually in May or June of each year and were held until Sir Frederick's death in 1797. Subscriptions were paid annually to Mr Rivers at his London Inn. Silver trophies were awarded to the principal winners. The little clubhouse built on the Down is marked on the first Ordnance Survey map of Devon, surveyed in 1803, and again on James Green's map in 1819, when he drew up plans for the realignment of the turnpike road between Exeter and Plymouth.

Shortly before Sir Frederick's sudden death in May 1797 he had been approached by Mr Christopher Lethbridge, one of a numerous local family, who proposed the building of a new inn to replace the old Royal Oak. This, since Mrs Allday's retirement, had given way completely to the London Inn, and according to the trade directory of 1798 was now a victualling house kept by Christopher Lethbridge. The chosen ground for the new inn was part of the demesne below the abandoned manor house and facing the turnpike road. Articles of agreement were ready for signing when Sir Frederick died. His son and heir was John, a young man of 17 years and still a scholar at Winchester School. It was probably on Mr Savery's advice that John honoured his father's agreement and the inn was built. It was named the Rogers Arms, but later became better known as the Ivybridge Hotel, serving the needs of the several coach services and the Royal Mail which passed through Ivybridge.

Ivybridge in the Nineteenth Century

The first 15 years of the nineteenth century are mainly concerned with the Napoleonic Wars. It has been estimated that 'one in every six male adults were engaged in the struggle by land and sea' (Prothero, 1912), and in the South West, close to the English Channel and its seaports, everyone would have been aware of the wars in one way or another. Sometimes French prisoners landed at Plymouth were marched through Ivybridge, no doubt to the benefit of alehouses in the village. In August 1800, a corporal of the Devon Militia commanding a guard at Ivybridge: '... disgraced the character of the Regiment by quitting his guard and permitting those under him to do the same by which the safety of the prisoners was endangered' (Walrond, 1897).

It seems likely that the corporal had been overcome by the hospitality of the villagers. There was also the fear of invasion, apparently not entirely dispelled by the victory at Trafalgar. A fire beacon on Butterdon Hill attended by a sergeant and three privates (all given extra pay and fuel allowance) in 1804, was still manned in 1809 when poor private George Atteo, aged 53, died at the beacon and was taken to Harford churchyard for burial. But perhaps what most interested the local people was the Admiralty telegraph station, set up in 1806 at Coyton (in Ermington parish) on the highest point of the rising ground behind Strashleigh Farm. This ingenious type of shutter telegraph, erected on a stout wooden frame above a small habitation and signals room, had a complement of one lieutenant RN, one midshipman and two assistants (with telescope), and passed messages (weather permitting) between London and Plymouth, the Ivybridge station (so called) being in communication eastward with the one at Marley (eight miles), and westward towards Plymouth with Hardwick Hill (5.4 miles). The system was discontinued in 1814 when it was thought the war with France was over (Wilson, 1976).

Peace between England and France in 1815 meant that attention could once more be directed to social and economic problems. One of the first decisions made in Devon was to have the turnpike roads brought up to date. The construction methods introduced by Telford and McAdam now allowed lower and wetter land to be used for coach roads, and in 1819 the county surveyor, James Green, produced a plan for the improvement of the Exeter to Plymouth road. Many sections of this road, some of great antiquity, winding steeply up and down the hills, would be replaced by straight roads keeping to lower and less hilly ground. Green proposed that the curving road from Torrhill to Ivybridge, east of the river, should be replaced by a new road which would turn off southward just west of the tollbar at Cole Lane (near where Rue St Pierre is now) and follow a straight course to a new crossing of the Erme at Costly Meadows, so to rejoin the old road opposite the Rogers Arms (Grosvenor House). The *Exeter Flying Post* of 6 December 1821 reported that the trustees of the Exeter-Plymouth Turnpike Trust had 'considered the propriety of such a measure' at their meeting the week before, but nothing more seems to have been heard of the proposal. Ivybridge people would not have taken kindly to the by-passing of their village centre (now Fore Street), nor would the proprietors of the London Inn. However, an amended plan went through a few years later with the building of a new bridge across the Erme within a stone's throw of the London Inn, the bridge that is in use today.

The house-by-house growth of the village at this time has not been fully researched, but it is likely to have been a fairly continous process spreading westward from the river. The first reliable evidence of development comes from the Tithes Survey in 1840. The Ermington parish Tithe Map shows that west of the Erme houses stood on both sides of what is now Fore Street as far as the town dairy; houses in Highland Street, Erme Road and Blachford Road opposite the church were already occupied in 1840; Western Road, then known as the Turnpike Road, was built only on the north side and as far as but not including the Imperial Inn property – this came later as the 'Albert' in about 1854. The Tithes Survey does not record if any trade or business was carried on at any of these premises, except to note an occasional 'shop' or where there was an inn, such as the 'King's Arms'. A corn mill and a paper mill, both powered by water from the Erme, occupied the land later known as Lee's Mills, and there was a tannery close by.

A woollen-mill, also using river water, was situated downstream where Waterside House stands. Just outside Ivybridge, at Filham, several shafts were being sunk to extract silver-lead, and other mining potentials in the Erme valley were advertised if not actually worked. On neighbouring Dartmoor, industry was springing up which would have brought people into Ivybridge. Granite was being quarried, replacing the ancient haphazard collection of surface granite, 'moorstone', which had hitherto been the source of supply. The extraction of clay from southern Dartmoor was attempted for a decade in the middle of the century, and the clay was probably carted down to Ivybridge from Harford Moorgate. The gentry were represented by Mr William Cotton at Highland House, built in 1792, a property he had bought from Mr John Lyne Templer, an Ugborough landowner, in 1839, and which now provided work and houses for a number of families. Overall, in 1840 the village probably contained about 100 houses, with a population of perhaps 500–600. In 1851 the population is said to have been 700 (Billings Directory, 1857), but this probably refers to the area of the Ecclesiastical District of Ivybridge, which extended somewhat beyond the village.

The coming of the railway in 1848 may be taken as an extension of an existing dimension in the growth of the village rather than as creating a new dimension. The railway certainly increased the importance of Ivybridge in the communications system linking Devon with the rest of the country, and it subsequently caused the discontinuance of the turnpikes. It brought in travellers and goods from the area south of Ivybridge, where there was no railway, although it had already been intended to link up this area with the Ivybridge turnpike in 1833, when the road to Ermington over Factory Bridge (now destroyed) and across the 'Runs' by Erme playing-fields was made suitable for coaches.

The urbanisation of Ivybridge, which continued throughout the nineteenth century can be seen as a microcosm of what had happened all over England since about 1760. New towns had sprung up where the Industrial Revolution had introduced new industrial methods requiring a concentration of work people, and families had left the depressed rural areas to look for work in the factories. During the years of peace after 1815 it became clear to the new class of liberal reformers who had come into English politics, that the old Tudor system of government at a parish level was no longer adequate. Beginning in 1834 with the reform of the Poor Laws, the responsibilities of the parish officers were progressively given over to local boards comprised of public-minded local gentlemen, each board being concerned with a particular aspect of local government in an area not always restricted to the traditional parish boundaries. In Ivybridge the significance of the 'four parishes' began to fade, and in civil matters the 'village' was considered as the Ecclesiastical District of Ivybridge which had been formed in 1836. It was not until December 1872 that a purely 'civil' area could be formed, when Whitehall consented to the District of Ivybridge adopting the local government of that year, and became the 'Ivybridge Local Board' for public health and village sanitary arrangements (these last were apparent to the villagers more by their absence than by their performance). This new board took care to define its area of influence in the four parishes by planting stone posts at chosen points on the boundary, each stone bearing in large letters the inscribed legend 'ILB'. They may be seen today if the road improvements and estate developments have left them alone. Another local Government Act in 1894 permitted the Ivybridge Local Board to raise its status and become a full civil parish under the title 'Ivybridge Urban District', taking in the land from Cornwood, Harford, Ermington and Ugborough, and having a population of about 1,800. Final severance from the four parishes came in September 1896, when the National School which had opened in Station Road in Cornwood parish in about 1850 under the Ermington School Board, was 'no longer required' by that board and was sold to the 'District of Ivybridge School Board' for the sum of £380.

So it was that in the course of 60 years, social reform by parliamentary statute, implemented by that invention of the Victorian era, the 'ad hoc' committee, had changed Ivybridge from a remote offshoot of several parishes into a village community aware of its civil entity and of its responsibility for its own well-being. Twentieth-century bureaucracy swept most of this away.

Milestone near Hookmoor Cross, Ugborough, on the Bittaford to Totnes Turnpike, 1759.

Roadside stone at 'Cross-in-Hand', Filham. The sides have the letters, in relief, 'P', 'E', 'M', 'B', but the stone is now very much reduced with age.

Ivybridge Becomes a Village

The Dissolution of the Monasteries in the 1530s and the redistribution of land which followed led to the Church losing much of its authority over the secular life of the people. The parish, however, was still the unit of local government, and in rural areas it was the only organised body available to carry on local services such as poor relief, and, what is relevant to Ivybridge, the repair of parish roads and bridges. But instead of acting under the authority of the Bishop at Exeter, the officers of a Devon parish were now bound by statutes passed by sovereign and parliament at Westminster.

Milestone at Monksmoor, Wrangaton Levels, near Bittaford, on the Plymouth Eastern Turnpike's new road, built in 1821.

The care of bridges had been a high priority service to the king since Saxon times. Under Henry VIII's 'Statute of Bridges',1531, it was enacted that if no other body would admit responsibility for a bridge, then the county, acting through its Justices at Quarter Sessions, would be liable not only for the maintenance of the bridge, but also for 300 feet of roadway from each end of the bridge. Later, it became the practice to place a stone inscribed with the letter 'C' at the appropriate distance to make the county bounds, and at Ivybridge, which not surprisingly became a county bridge, the stones can still be seen, although the one on the east bank of the river was moved to its present position early in twentieth century.

Apart from this particular care of bridges and the very inadequate statutory parish repair work, little attention was given to roads until well into the eighteenth century. In 1706 the first Turnpike Trust was formed for the more effective maintenance of a particular road, the cost to be offset by the charging of tolls. Some 50 years later the idea had penetrated to Plymouth, and in 1758 the road to Ivybridge and eastward to Ashburton was 'turnpiked', so making it, probably for the first time in its history, suitable for wheeled traffic. It is likely that it was at this period that the Ivy Bridge was widened to its present road width of 11 feet. A toll-gate with keeper's cottages and garden was set up on Exeter Road at the corner of Cole Lane, and this is still remembered as a small habitation which was destroyed when the road was widened in about 1931.

With the arrival of wheeled traffic along the road south of Dartmoor, Ivybridge was placed on the principal coach road between Plymouth and Exeter and London: hitherto travellers by coach had used the road through Tavistock and kept north of the moor to Okehampton. With this new importance there came commercial growth to Ivybridge. Within a few years of the opening of the turnpike, the 'London Inn', conveniently placed on the coach road at the bridge, was established by Henry Rivers, a Modbury innholder, and soon became one of the most highly spoken of inns in the South West. In 1800 the London Inn was described as 'an excellent good house… And there is a very romantic walk on the other side of the river above the bridge.' (Thomas Staniforth, 1800). Well-known artists would put up there when on professional commissions in the South West, and they would stand on the rocks in the river to sketch the torrent with the bridges above. Copies made from their finished work are now keenly sought-after collectors' items. In 1797 Sir Frederick Rogers of Blachford, owner of the land west of the river, agreed that Christopher Lethbridge should build a substantial inn just south of Ivybridge Barton Farm, and this became the 'Rogers Arms', later the 'Ivybridge Hotel' and Grosvenor House, an important inn for the coaches on the London to Plymouth Road.

The new commercial life at Ivybridge required a population to support it, not only to service the needs of travellers, horses and vehicles, but also to provide accommodation for those who could not afford the inns. Good communication towards London began to bring industry to Ivybridge, first a paper mill in about 1788 beside the River Erme at Stowford, where there was already a corn mill, then other industries, including another paper mill and a flour-mill on the west bank of the river below the bridge. There was probably no shortage of labour, for in the depressed state of the agricultural worker in Devon at that time, many families from the surrounding parishes would have come to look for better prospects in the new Ivybridge. Only a few houses were built along the turnpike east of the river; perhaps the landowners in the two parishes of Harford and Ugborough were still only interested in farming the land. West of the river all the land along the road was in Ermington parish and belonged to one owner, the Rogers family of Blachford. Their willingness to lease land for house building, and the choice of site for the Rogers Arms, made it inevitable that development would be mainly west of the river.

At the end of the century Ivybridge was described by one traveller as being 'a small group of houses delightfully situated on the banks of the river Erme'. (W.G. Maton, 1794–96), and by the turn of the century it was probably populous enough to be known as a village. It was not yet a centre of social organisation with the tradition of an old English village, nor yet the political unit of a parish. Ivybridge was to grow into a village because it fitted conveniently into the new pattern of road communications which was spreading throughout England, but politically most of the village was a part of Ermington, whilst its chapel of the established Church, dating from about 1789, was in Cornwood parish. Born in the late-eighteenth century, Ivybridge may be said to have come of age in the nineteenth, when it was big enough to become a parish, first as an ecclesiastical district with its own Parish Church in 1836, and later, in 1894, a civil parish known as Ivybridge Urban District (a status it was keen to keep until 1936), independent of the four ancient parishes from which it has sprung.

The Old Post Road Through Ivybridge

When Henry VIII ordered that in times of war and other emergencies 'a post shall be laid along the principal highways of the realm in order to provide a rapid means of communication' between places of strategic importance and the court in London, Plymouth was a place of great importance in the realm, a seaport trading with most parts of the Old World, and, since the discovery of the Americas, with the New World, too, whilst as a naval port it was the guardian of the Western Channel and of the western seas.

King Henry's post was intended only for communications of state. The messenger on horseback, if riding the whole journey – a 'through post' – changed horses at each post at a distance within the easy capability of a horse, since speed was the essence of the system. Some letters might be committed to the 'standing post', whereby a postboy would carry them for one post and give them to another postboy. Naturally enough, the house where the post was set up was often an inn, accustomed to stabling horses and providing sustenance to travellers. Between Plymouth and Exeter, where the London road would be joined, there were three possible routes: west of Dartmoor by way of Horrabridge and Okehampton; south of the moor through Ivybridge to Avonwick, Harberton and Totnes to Newton Bushell and Chudleigh; or the shortest route by several miles, through Ivybridge to Ashburton and Chudleigh. It was this third choice which became the great post road west of Exeter.

The road from Plympton to Ivybridge and on to Exeter was already ancient and of some importance. In the days of the monasteries it had been the means of communication between the priory of Plympton and the superior diocesan church at Exeter. It was certainly important enough in 1411 for Bishop Stafford to grant indulgence to anyone who would help in the repair of the road near Challonsleigh leading from Plympton to Ivybridge; 25 years later Bishop Lacy went further and offered 40 days' indulgence to all who contributed money or labour towards the repair and maintenance of the whole length of road between Plympton and Ivybridge. Travellers to and from the town of Plymouth would have to go by way of Plymbridge or make their way across the estuary, depending on the tides. In the sixteenth century there were villages along the road to Exeter well spaced for the siting of posthouses: Plymouth to Ivybridge was about 11 miles, Ivybridge to Ashburton 13½, Ashburton to Chudleigh 9½, and Chudleigh to Exeter about 10 miles. The road was not an easy ride, as Celia Fiennes was to discover over a century later, being very hilly and in places exceedingly narrow.

During Queen Elizabeth's reign the post service was opened to private persons. Their letters were more likely to be carried by the 'standing post' on fixed post days. Travellers could also 'ride post' by hiring horses at each post, except on post days. The service was controlled by a set of rules. The traveller must be accompanied by a guide, who was allowed to carry up to 40lbs of luggage and return with the horses at the next post. A horn had to be carried and blown three times every mile, or when meeting company or passing through a town. Official letters and packets going by post were given special care. Everyone riding 'by commission' paid 1½d. a mile, others paid 2d. a mile. The charge for the guide was 4d. for each post. On postal service the boys were expected to ride seven miles in one hour in summer and five miles in winter, if the road permitted, speeds which were found hard to maintain. In 1597 it was found that a letter between Exeter and London, reckoned to be a distance of 173 miles, travelled at an average speed of no more than three miles an hour. Whatever the difficulties, in Elizabeth's time the road from London to Plymouth was one of five great post roads in Britain.

One private user of the road from Plymouth to London in the late-sixteenth century was the merchant banking house of Corsini. Originating in Tuscany, the Corsinis had spread their business to many parts of Europe. In London they were established in Gracechurch Street, where one of the family lived, and appointed an agent at Plymouth. The agent wrote frequently to his employers in London, mostly in the form of 'situation reports' on ships and their cargoes arriving at Plymouth, sometimes on the prospects of fleets fishing for pilchards, or for cod off the coast of Newfoundland, presumably ventures in which the house had a financial interest. Photocopies of letters written in 1579 and 1594 are held at West Devon Record Office. The sixteenth-century Italian is difficult to read and even harder to translate. The Corsinis had their own postal organisation and postmaster, and probably always employed their own messengers.

James I carried on the system but rearranged the charges. Those riding on special commissions paid 2½d. a mile, whilst others paid the charge set by the posthouse keeper. The luggage to be carried was reduced to 30lbs.

In the time of Charles I the postal service was extended to towns off the main post roads. The posthouse keepers on the London to Plymouth road agreed amongst themselves to despatch letters within three days of receiving them, and would serve places within 20 miles of the main post road. Ashburton sent out to Totnes and Dartmouth: later evidence suggests that Ivybridge took care of Modbury and Salcombe. Postal charges were usually payable at the last place of delivery, unless the sender had prepaid or had the privilege of 'franking' his letters free of charge. A single-sheet letter, folded and sealed, with the address written on the back, cost 2d. for the first 80 miles, 4d. if carried 80–140 miles, 6d. for longer distances. A letter from Plymouth to London should take just over two days, so that a reply could be expected after five days. In 1666, after the Restoration, there were complaints from different parts of the country that the post was slow; it was said that a letter from Plymouth took 56 hours to reach London, a journey of perhaps 217 miles, an average of 3.8 miles in one hour. About one-third of the distance was in Devon, where the roads were notoriously bad.

The road to Exeter left the town of Plymouth near the modern Ebrington Street, climbed Lipson hill and descended to the Plym. The crossing at Crabtree depended on the tides, but once over, the road made its way to the village of Ridgeway and thence to Ivybridge. From Exeter the post was relayed to Honiton, from where it took the road to Chard and Yeovil, Sherborne, Shaftesbury and Andover to Salisbury, Basingstoke and Staines, crossing the Thames before reaching London. There was an alternative route to London from Exeter which, after Honiton, went through Axminster and the Dorset towns to Blandford before reaching Salisbury, a popular road for coaches in later years.

In other parts of the country stage wagons and hackney carriages were in use before 1660, mainly patronised, it is said, by the lower classes, but in Devon the hills, the narrow roads and bridges, made it very difficult for vehicles. It has been said many times that wheeled vehicles were almost unknown in Devon before the early-seventeenth century, a claim which documentary evidence suggests bears a degree of exaggeration. In 1669, however, when Cosmos III, Grand Duke of Tuscany, travelled by coach from Plymouth to Exeter, he chose to go by way of Horrabridge and Dartmoor to Okehampton, 'going by the direct route till they passed Crediton'. It is likely that the narrow bridge at Ivybridge, and perhaps others, forbade the journey being kept south of Dartmoor.

The earliest known reference to an inn house at Ivybridge appears in an indenture dated 1672 which says that Alexander Pearse then held a ten years' lease on a house at Ivybridge known as an inn called the 'Three Tonns'. It is possible to place this house with fair accuracy on the north side of Fore Street, opposite the entrance to the old corn mill site. There is no way of knowing to what extent Alexander Pearse was involved in the post service.

Before the end of the seventeenth century the road from London to Plymouth had become the 'Western road', one of six great post roads in Britain. There, were 'cross-posts' between towns on different main post roads, and 'by posts' that dealt with letters not going to London but used the main post roads or simply travelled on minor roads between despatch and delivery. The road between Plymouth and Ashburton, and perhaps east of that town, was under the control of a postmaster at Ashburton. His was a position of considerable responsibility: to see that the posts ran well, but he was also responsible for the money due to be collected on the delivery of letters. The London newspapers were also distributed by him to those who had ordered them

It was the postmaster Mr Sowter, in 1734, who was directed by the Postmaster General to order his postboys to divert from the road through Ridgeway and go instead through old Plympton, where George Treby, Esquire, lived, he having made application to 'their honours for this convenience to himself'. Mr Sowter was to appoint Mr Henry Cooper to have care of the letter entrusted and to collect the money due for postage. Since George Treby was sometime MP for Plympton, one can understand why 'their honours' in London were willing, on occasion, to bend the rules.

This favour shown to one of the gentry, 24 years later, drew Sir John Rogers, 3rd Baronet, into an embarrassing lawsuit. In 1758 the Plymouth Road Act introduced the road between Plymouth and South Brent into the turnpike system, the persons who drafted the Bill feeling competent to declare the road to be:

> *... in a very ruinous Condition and from the Nature of the Soil and Narrowness of the Passages in several Parts there-of is become very ruinous and dangerous for Travellers and in the Winter and rainy Seasons impassable for Wheel Carriages.*

This was probably as fair an assessment of road conditions in this part of Devon as could be given in the middle of the eighteenth century. At the second meeting of the trust which was then formed, held at the George at Ridgeway, Sir John was elected chairman. It had been decided to retain the historic line of the old post road by keeping Ridgeway on the turnpike, taking advantage of the recently improved crossing of the Plym by the 'new bridge' at Marsh Mills which had been opened in the same year, 1758. But a number of the gentry who had interests in old Plympton, some of whom were probably Sir John's friends, petitioned to keep their 1734 concession, and they proposed a new route from the Plym to old Plympton, regardless of this requiring at least one more bridge and a lot of extra expense. The case went to court and was heard by Lord Chief Justice Mansfield who, a friend told Sir John, 'with great sagacity demolished their opponents' case'.

In 1755 a daily post (except Saturdays) between London and Plymouth had been set up. Although stagecoaches were by then well established, it was not until August 1784 that the first mail coach left Bristol for London. Thereafter the service spread, and in 1785 Plymouth received its first delivery of mail from London by coach. At first the mail coaches left London after midnight, but this was later changed to 8p.m. It became one of the sights of London to see them drive away from the General Post Office near St Paul's. In 1793 the post set out from Exeter for London every morning (except on Saturdays) at 5 o'clock from Plymouth and other places; south-west of Exeter the departure was at midnight. In 1785 the mail coaches were freed from tolls on the turnpikes – the Plymouth Turnpike Trust had never charged tolls on horses carrying mail. To facilitate administration, in 1794 the key posthouses from which letters were despatched to London were given a 'mileage stamp' bearing the name of the place of despatch and its distance from London which was impressed on all letters going there. Ivybridge had the mileage '207'.

In 1804 the way out of Plymouth was greatly eased by the opening of the Embankment Road on land reclaimed from the Plym estuary, thus avoiding Lipson Hill. Then in the 1820s a second turnpike phase in Devon, adopting James L. McAdam's principles of road construction, encouraged the Plymouth Turnpike Trust (which had become the Plymouth Eastern Turnpike) to carry out some of the improvements James Green had proposed for the road at Ivybridge. Green's plan, covering the whole road from Exeter to Plymouth, was to replace the

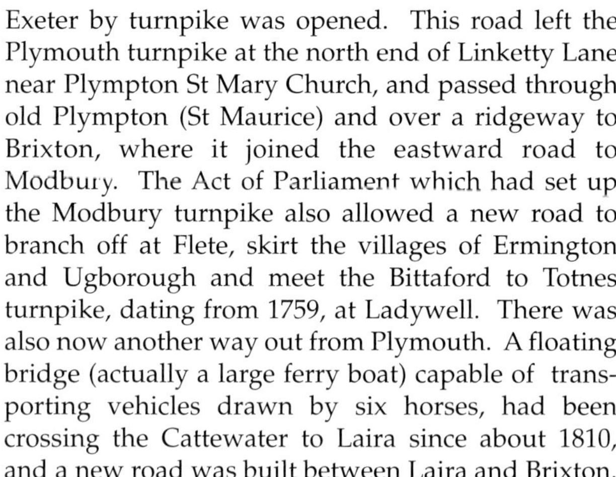

hilly, awkward sections of the road with straight, less hilly parts. Apparently the turnpike trusts had the power to accept or reject his proposals, since they were to pay for any work done. Green's plan to bypass the main part of Ivybridge village and the U-turn over the old bridge was rejected, probably in the interests of the traders, but a compromise was reached by building a new bridge over the Erme with direct connection between Fore Street and the Exeter road. At Bittaford the steep hill leading to Wrangaton and Glaze bridge were avoided by a new straight and level road to South Brent, with a bridge that cut out the narrow old bridge at Bittaford. On the west side of Ivybridge a new straight road to Lee Mill bridge replaced the road through the village of Woodland and round by Cadleigh Cross.

With its entry into the nineteenth century Ivybridge had welcomed the newly erected inn, the Rogers Arms. This house, like the old Royal Oak, whose functions it took over, was a property of the manor, leased to the innkeeper. Well placed on the turnpike road, the Rogers Arms remained the principal coaching inn at Ivybridge for the next 50 years, and for a time at least was probably the Post Office. On the Exeter side of the River Erme Henry Rivers's London Inn could still offer highly commended hospitality. Although not named, in August 1800 Thomas Staniforth, a Liverpool gentleman, had found it '... an Excellent good house... cool and pleasant and with a very romantic walk on the other side of the river above the bridge'. Mr and Mrs Staniforth were on their way to Cornwall in the 'travelling carriage with [a named servant] on post horses'. Mr Staniforth says that it took them about one and a half hours, in the evening, to reach Plymouth Dock from Ivybridge.

The war with France during the first 15 years of the nineteenth century would have helped to make the roads to Plymouth very busy. The threat of invasion, relieved to some extent after Trafalgar, kept the villages of the South Hams on the alert. Troops of the militia passing through Ivybridge, sometimes with French prisoners of war, left their mark on Ivybridge, as the records show; a fire beacon manned by soldiers was kept ready on Butterdon Hill on Dartmoor. There would also be the traffic of men joining or leaving their ships at Plymouth. Probably the most memorable event came in 1815, when people within easy reach of Plymouth flocked to catch a glimpse of Napoleon on the deck of HMS *Bellerophon*, anchored in the Sound.

With the peace came a recession, one contributing factor being the rapid reduction in the commissioning of ships in the Royal Navy. The availability of labour which occurs at such a time may be partly responsible for the intense activity in road building in Devon in the 1820s during the second turnpike phase.

In 1824 an alternative route from Plymouth to Exeter by turnpike was opened. This road left the Plymouth turnpike at the north end of Linketty Lane near Plympton St Mary Church, and passed through old Plympton (St Maurice) and over a ridgeway to Brixton, where it joined the eastward road to Modbury. The Act of Parliament which had set up the Modbury turnpike also allowed a new road to branch off at Flete, skirt the villages of Ermington and Ugborough and meet the Bittaford to Totnes turnpike, dating from 1759, at Ladywell. There was also now another way out from Plymouth. A floating bridge (actually a large ferry boat) capable of transporting vehicles drawn by six horses, had been crossing the Cattewater to Laira since about 1810, and a new road was built between Laira and Brixton.

In 1827 a five-arch iron bridge across the Cattewater from Prince Rock to Laira replaced the floating bridge, so bringing into use a good coach road with easy gradients to Totnes. Under the same turnpike trust as the Bittaford road, the turnpike went on to Newton Bushell and then to Chudleigh, where it joined the Ashburton road to Exeter. A measurement of the two roads between Plymouth and Exeter made in 1827 found that the road through Totnes was $4\frac{1}{2}$ miles longer than the Ashburton road. In 1833 or 1834 the Ermington Parish Council proposed that there should be a road fit for coaches from the village of Ermington to Ivybridge. Some widening of the road at Ermington was carried out and a new length of road was built between Thornham and Keaton, where a stone bridge was provided across the Erme. In Ugborough parish a new road was made across Filham Moor, then unenclosed pasture land, to another new stone bridge across the river into the village of Ivybridge. It seems that this road between the two villages retained only parish road status, but at the Caton Lane junction near Keaton Bridge there is a small cottage which, before modernisation, had many of the characteristics of a toll-house.

Competition to both turnpikes and to the coach services that used them came in 1846 with the South Devon Railway opening its line as far as Laira, within three miles of Plymouth, on 8 May. Plympton, Ivybridge and South Brent were awarded a station almost immediately, the public showing no hesitation at all in changing their travelling habits from horse to steam. The line was extended to near Millbay in the following April. When cheap excursions to London were put on it was said the town of Plymouth almost emptied, the shopkeepers standing at their doors, (Robert Henley Rogers in a letter to his brother, 14 June 1851).

At Ivybridge the lease on the 'Ivybridge Hotel', the name by which the Rogers Arms was now known, still held by a member of the Rivers family, was soon to expire. All parties realised that the hotel's days as a coaching inn would soon expire also. After some indecision it was agreed not to

Agriculture

Cutting grass for hay.

Building a hay rick.

Dinnaton farm in the early part of the twentieth century, now a country club and health farm.

Haymaking at Ivybridge.

Cutting corn with a binder pulled by three horses.

Harrowing at Cantrel.

Right: *Gathering mangles for winter feed.*

continue the hotel after 1851, but leave such business as survived to the London Inn on the far side of the river, and to John Seldon's King's Arms in Fore Street, a house that had proved to be very popular and had some accommodation for vehicles, of which there would still be plenty in daily use. In February 1855 a night mail train service between Paddington and Plymouth in both directions was started. Perhaps it was then that the Post Office transferred all its Ivybridge business to a postmaster who established his own premises in Fore Street.

Most turnpike trusts carried on with diminishing revenues until the early 1870s and then petitioned for dissolution. Some, particularly in the Exeter area, continued in the 1880s. The Plymouth Eastern dissolved in about 1873 and sold off its toll-houses at Ivybridge and Bittaford as private dwellings. For a while the responsibility for the roads returned to the parishes or whoever was the Highways Authority at the time, until a later statute enacted that roads that had ceased to be turnpikes after 31 December 1870 became Class I roads under the newly constituted County Councils.

The information on the history of the postal services has been taken from Howard Robinson's *History of the British Post Office*, 1970. It has been included in some detail in the hope that, knowing something of the overall history, the reader may succeed in forming in his or her own mind a picture of what may have gone on in Ivybridge in the days when the village was a stage in the Plymouth to London post road. Dr M. Brayshay says that the first London to Plymouth post was started in 1579 and was re-established in 1595, not unlike the years the Corsini agent's letters were written. Writing in about 1630, Risdon found Ivybridge to be 'a place that admits a great thoroughfare', but no record of the part played by Ivybridge in the post system appears before the fifth decade of the eighteenth century. To what degree the village owed its growth, perhaps its existence, to its position on the post road is debatable, but it must be very high, reaching its zenith in the early years of the nineteenth century. Western Road and the scattered milestones along the two roads leading to Exeter are the memorials to a long and worthy period in the history of the village.

Natural History – Badgers

Celia Ralph, 1982

It is unlikely that many of us will see a badger, unless it is in captivity or lying dead by the roadside, although they are fairly common in this country, and widely distributed.

Throughout history the badger has been persecuted whether by badger baiting (the verb 'to badger' derived from this practice), badger digging for sport, or by the Ministry of Agriculture's 'badger gassing' to try to prevent the spread of bovine tuberculosis.

The badger is our largest native carnivore, about 28 inches in length plus eight inches of tail, 12 inches high and weighing some 22–30 lbs. They are most abundant in deciduous woodland bordered by pasture land, especially where there are sandy banks in which they can dig their setts easily. These setts may be extensive, a vast labyrinth of tunnels and chambers with many entrances where the badger family will live, sometimes with foxes and rabbits. The boar and sows keep the sett very clean, bringing in fresh bedding of dry leaves, bracken and grass on dry nights, and bringing it out to air on sunny days. Close by the sett they dig small pits to use as latrines.

Nocturnal animals, they usually emerge from their sleep at sunset and begin to search for food, travelling along their well-worn paths, covering as much as six miles each night.

Very keen of scent and hearing, they eat roots, fruit, slugs and snails, wasps, insects, snakes, young rabbits and berries. Their main diet is worms, which they mostly find in pasture land, where they come into contact with the cattle. They also eat carrion: they will eat dead hedgehogs, leaving the skin and prickles in a complete shape like the skin of an avocado pear. Where we lived previously in a wooded area, we kept chickens, and when one died we would bury it; after several weeks, when the carcass was 'ripe', it would be dug up and eaten by a badger, leaving the distinct marks of its clawed feet.

All told, the badger brock, or bawson grey, is one of our most attractive animals. Since 1975 setts have been gassed by the Ministry of Agriculture, and it is estimated that in the West Country 10,000 badgers have been killed. Now badger gassing is to be stopped, as it has been judged to be inhumane, but presumably they will be controlled in some other way. It would be a disaster if the badger was lost in this area.

Filham Between the Wars

Alec Rogers

At Lady Day in March 1928 my family moved to Filham Farm from Holberton and I have lived there since that time.

Mr and Mrs Algar lived at Filham House and I am greatly indebted to Mr George Lomas of Mill Meadow for information on the life and workings of a small country estate from 1925 to 1940.

Mr Lomas began work at Filham House in 1926 for a salary of £52 per year. Living at that time with his parents at Flete, his father being head groom for Lord Mildmay, meant getting up at 4a.m. to have the Algars' hunters ready for a day with the Dartmoor

Agriculture

Moorland scene near Ivybridge.

A tranquil scene at Ermington.

Charles Colton of Brooker's Farm, Lutton, near Cornwood. He died in 1982.

The hunt at Cornwood.

Mrs Algar at Ermington.

South Dartmoor hunt celebrate a wedding.

Left: *The ancient beehive hut, 'the most perfect in Devon'.*

Gathering watercress from the Erme at Ermington.

Jack Tarr, a policeman, helping out at David's Cross sowing corn.

Hounds. Breakfast was brought out to the stable on a silver tray. Later, when five hunters were kept and George was married, his day began at 7a.m. and finished at 5.30p.m. – there was no overtime.

In the house, a cook and two parlour maids waited on Mr and Mrs Algar, but the cook demanded a kitchen maid, so an extra room was built to accommodate her. A chauffeur drove Mr Algar to business each morning – he was head of a Cattedown-based firm of artificial manure manufacturers.

The gardens were looked after by a head gardener and two under gardeners and the whole place had a 'picture book' appearance.

Each working day at 4.30p.m., all ten of the staff assembled in the kitchen for tea, slabs of cake, bread and butter, etc. Also any other men such as

An old glass-plate photograph of the Erme at Fleet.

painters or carpenters working there were included in the meal.

In the summer the two grooms worked around the estate mending fences, or in Wadland Wood cutting up fallen trees with a saw which was kept in a box on which was written 'YOU NEVER SAW A SAW SAW LIKE THIS SAW SAWS'. Mr Algar was a keen carpenter and was proud of a large kennel he had made. Unfortunately the door of his workshop was narrow and when two of the staff attempted to carry the kennel outside it was too large for the doorway. A window had to be removed and Mr Sam Daniels, Ivybridge carpenter, was called in to replace the window after the kennel had passed safely through.

After the death of Mr Algar, the whole estate, including some 60 acres of farmland, was withdrawn at the sale, no bid being offered. Afterwards it was sold for about £13,000. In this period of our history preceding the Second World War, life on the farms and over the whole hamlet ran its quiet, seasonal course.

Horses still provided the power and on a day of light rain Mr Henry Luscombe could be seen at plough with two horses who moved steadily to and fro without any guiding reins in the ploughman's hands, so well did these marvellous animals respond to vocal commands only.

At twilight on a winter's day, a thin trail of smoke and the sound of the lumbering engine would herald the arrival of the 'thresher', hauled by an old traction machine. Leaking steam from every joint, I have known two men and a horse and cart with a 50 gallon barrel occupied all day drawing water from a stream, perhaps half a mile distant, to keep the engine 'in steam'; I often wish that I could attend one of those 'threshing days' now. At that time I was the youngest of the gang of local farmers and farm workers who would help each other over the threshing of the corn ricks. The youngest got the vilest job, and many days I've spent on the rocking deck of the threshing machine, enveloped at times in smoke and dust,

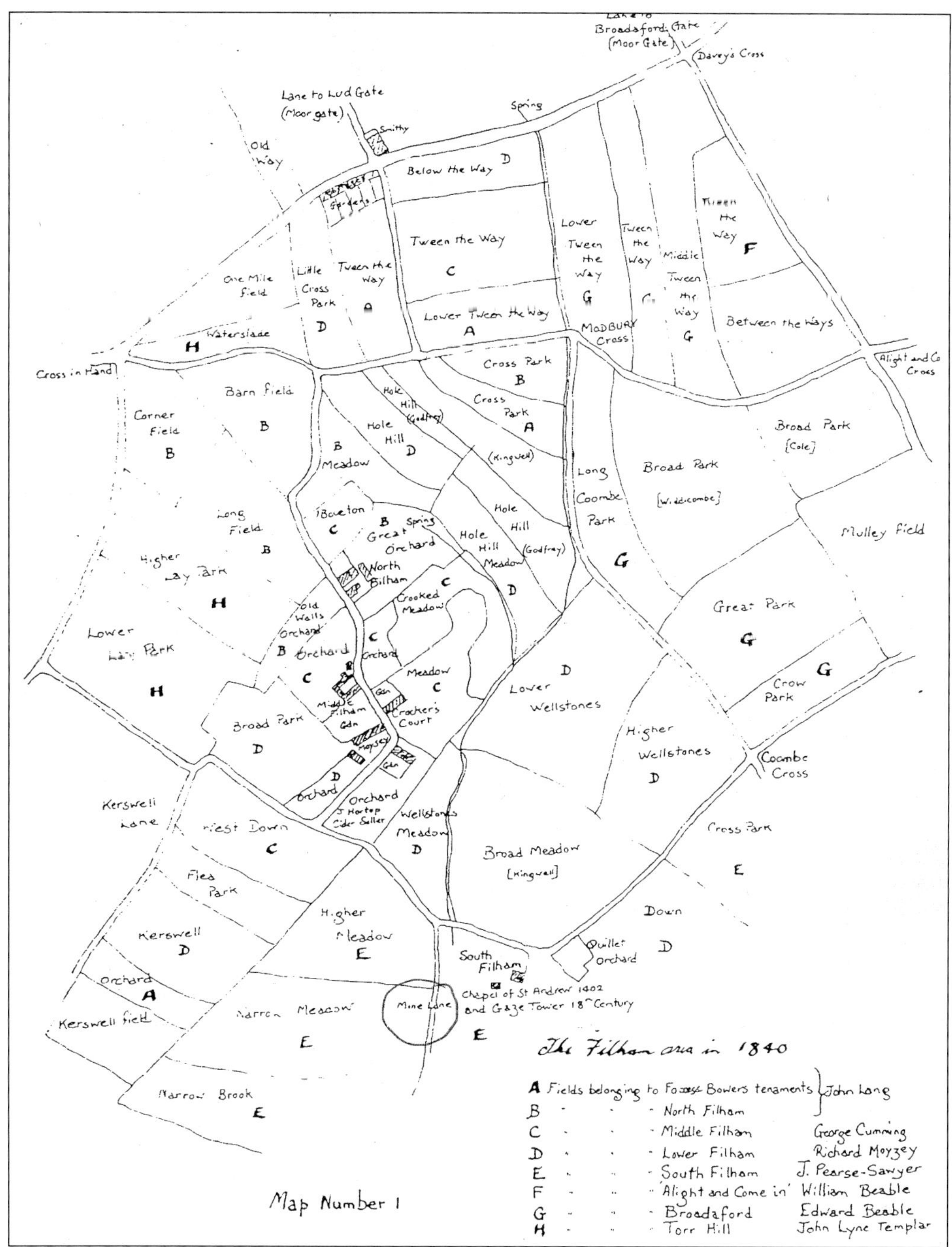

The Filham area in 1840.

cutting with a sharp knife every sheaf that about three men on the corn rick would throw at me from all directions. And always, very close to us, myself and the man who fed the machine, behind an aperture of about 1 ft, the drum screamed around at a fearful rate, ready to draw in anything, from the sheaves of corn to parts of anyone unfortunate enough to get caught by arm, or as I have known, a leg.

On some farms, cider flowed at threshing time and I remember one Charles Manning, well under the influence of several pints and building the straw rick, disappearing suddenly in a flurry of straw across the lane into the neighbouring field.

The year 1930 marked the beginning of the great depression. Indelibly printed on my memory was the sad sight that daily could be seen at Cross-in-Hand. At about 11a.m. perhaps 30 men in various stages of dejection would pass down the main road on their way to Plympton workhouse from South Brent, where they had spent the previous night. Around 3 o'clock in the afternoon, a similar number would be making their way to South Brent workhouse from Plympton. Farm prices were low. Competition from abroad was keen. Russian-rolled barley cost only £6 per ton, delivered to our farm. Agricultural workers' basic wage was 30s. per week, on which our neighbour Mr Tooley's man supported a wife and small son at 'Wellstones' cottage, now sadly renamed 'Spring Cottage'.

These were desperate times, but we were thankful that there was no unemployment here at Filham.

Filham Moor

C.F. Hankin

Before the 1830s Filham Moor was an area of about 63 acres of open pasture situated on the left side of the River Erme half a mile to a mile below the old Ivy Bridge. Historically, the land is in Ugborough parish, but at the end of the nineteenth century it was transferred to the civil parish of Ivybridge.

The subsoil and the flat nature of the area suggest that at the melting of the last ice age the water released from north Dartmoor and beyond spread southwards over Filham Moor, ultimately receding to what is now the River Erme. However, water still continued to flow down from the moor above Stowford on its way to the Erme throughout the year, so warding off the frost and keeping the land of Filham Moor good pasture in all seasons and a valuable asset to whoever owned it.

Although Filham Moor does not appear to have been within the manor of Ivybridge, in the fifteenth century the rights to pasture there were held by the lord of the manor of Ivybridge. In the eighteenth century ownership is recorded as passing through various hands. In 1825 Richard Derry of Marsh House, near Exeter, bought Filham Moor, and it was during the next 15 years, probably about 1835, that the land was enclosed into a pattern of fields, mostly of about 4½ acres, separated by straight drystone walls for which some of the material obviously came from the bed of the river. Mr Derry let out the fields to various tenants. Possibly at the same time as the land was enclosed, a system of sub-surface stone land drains was put in to dry out the land. This was discovered in 1973/74 by a group of students from Plymouth Polytechnic Geo-Society, who analysed the stone walls and the drains they found there. Their estimation was that the drainage system pre-dated the walls, but their dating of both was not decisive.

The Filham Moor enclosure did not reach to the river, but only as far as the Ivybridge to Ermington road: this was built in 1834. The land nearer the river, known as 'the Runs' and the 'Yeo' lands, has its own history.

Cheese and Wine at Ivybridge

Frederick Rogers was the first son of Sir John Rogers of Blachford, the second baronet, to marry. Born in 1716, he was the fifth son to come of age, but in 1742, the year of his marriage, his only surviving brother was John, the eldest of the sons and heir apparent to the baronetcy. When he was 16 Frederick had entered the Navy. After four years in the service and having passed all his examinations he was recommended to be made a lieutenant, his patron or 'interest' for this promotion being his father's friend of parliamentary days, Sir Robert Walpole, who had since become prime minister. In May 1741, at the age of 24, Frederick was given command of the sloop *Otter*, and a year later was appointed captain of *Bridgwater*, a ship of 24 guns.

Frederick was married at Stonehouse Chapel on 22 April 1742. His bride, Miss Grace Cooper, was the daughter of Nathaniel Cooper, an associate of Sir John in the shipping business and in 1742 Agent at the Victualling Office at Plymouth. Mr Cooper's mother was the daughter of Thomas Leman, the Lemans being a wealthy Norfolk family, one of whom had been Lord Mayor of London; a pedigree, probably searched for the benefit of a later Rogers, shows that Thomas's wife, Ann Catelyn of Mayfield Castle, Suffolk, was descended through the Nevilles from 'old John of Gaunt', son of Edward III, so that all later Rogers resulting from the union of Frederick and Grace could, if they wished, claim to be very distantly related to the English royal family. To comply with the terms of his mother's will, Mr Nathaniel Cooper had adopted the name Leman, becoming known as Nathaniel Cooper Leman, but his daughter kept the name Miss Grace Cooper until she married.

Soon after the wedding Frederick must have been ordered to take his ship the *Bridgwater* to sea, for it was on her way home to Plymouth in December 1742 that she nearly met with disaster. John Elford, who had some sort of business relationship with the Rogers, wrote to John, who was himself on honeymoon at the time, telling how, when the *Bridgwater* was three or four days' sailing from Plymouth:

> *... a Spanish privateer took her for a merchantman and bore down upon her and would have boarded her before they discovered what she was had it not been for the man at the helm who ran down and begs the Capt. to alter course by which means they prevented her boarding them and got time to prepare for her reception they being before quite unprepared.*

The Spanish vessel was then taken by the *Bridgwater* and turned out to be a ship of 18–20 guns carrying a lot of money. Frederick brought her safely into Plymouth, but Elford tells John Rogers he 'fears the lucrative appointment as Agent for the disposal of the prise will not be given to them, but will go to "the Old Serpent or Wishee Washee"', evidently Plymouth gentlemen whom John would have no difficulty in recognising. Equally excited by the event, Frederick's sister, Mrs Mary Tolcher, also wrote to their brother John to tell him how, when the prize was brought into Plymouth, 'the bells were set ringing', and that the only casualty had been one of their own men 'shot by their Lieutenant In mistake for a Spaniard' so that the lieutenant was now very melancholy, but fortunately no one had been killed! Mr Tolcher adds a note to his wife's letter, but is not quite so impressed by his brother-in-law's achievement. He says it was only 'the intelligence of the helmsman' that had saved the *Bridgewater*.

Meanwhile, whilst Frederick was seeking glory and riches on the high sea, his brother John was in London getting married. He was now 39, and it appears that the sudden termination of his attachment to the lady of Lindridge Park, since when ten years had gone by, had not been his only disappointment. On 2 October 1742, at the church of St Benet's in Paul's Wharf, near St Paul's Cathedral, John Rogers married Miss Hannah Trefusis. Hannah's father, Thomas Trefusis of Penryn, held the rank of captain in the Navy and was a Commissioner for Victualling at the Navy Office. She was 23, and, provided the marriage was with her father's consent, she would receive £5,000 by the will of her late uncle, Mr Samuel Addis, her mother's brother. This condition evidently being satisfied by her marriage to John Rogers, and with a further £5,000 added to her dowry, Hannah was a rich woman in her own right. For his part, Sir John put in trust for the benefit of his son the manors of Ivybridge and Blachford (but not Wisdome), and some other properties in Devon. Sir John, now aged 66 and anxious to see his eldest son settled in marriage, could not risk a second rebuff through lack of means.

On 2 November Mr Elford, true to form, sent off a letter of congratulation to the newlyweds, and described the:

> *... Rejoicings there were at Plymouth on the day before on the occasion of your Happy Marriage. The bells of both churches (St Andrew's and Charles) were rung from five in the morning till late at night; a great bonfire was lit on the quay after opposition from the mayor had been overcome; fireworks, the best ever seen in Plymouth, were let off from a stage on the water in the harbour, and boys were set huzzaing 'Squire Rogers for ever'.*

The bells at Cornwood had been set ringing by Harry Elford, who lived at Hele, and (Mr Elford has been told) so were the bells at Ermington, Holbeton, Yealmpton, Brixton, Newton, Wembury and Plymstock 'and no doubt elsewhere'. Elford ends by telling John Rogers that 'the people are now praying heartily you may have a son'. John Rogers knew Elford well enough to judge how much of all this could be swallowed.

John and Hannah did not hurry back to Plymouth. It was February 1743 when John informed Elford of their intended return. He and Hannah were staying with John's mother's relations, the Henleys, at Sherborne in Dorset, and apparently Elford was asked to advise on the road they should take from Exeter. In his reply Elford says, after consultation, he thinks Totnes or Ashburton the best, shorter by at least eight miles than Okehampton. He will bring a party of friends to meet Mr and Mrs Rogers at Ivybridge, if they come that way (or at Horrabridge on the other road), and he is pleased to accept Mr Rogers's offer of 'a treat or entertainment at that place, so unexpected'. As to the expense:

> *... it will be not worth minding for the Company can expect nothing but a Glass or two of Wine, and perhaps a bit of Bread and Cheese. Some indeed may choose to drink Beer or Cider, or a glass of Punch, so that a Bowl of Punch and a dozen bottles of Wine should be sufficient and cost Mr. Rogers not exceeding Twenty shillings.*

Elford does not say where this happy reunion of friends would take place, but it would almost certainly have been at the Royal Oak, the old inn and posthouse at Ivybridge kept in 1743 by Thomas Hawkins.

Elford also gives John Rogers some suggestions for the route they will take from Ivybridge to Plymouth: 'if they come that way', he writes: 'as it will be near the full of the moon the Tydes will serve as we imagine but if not 'twill be no great difficulty to come up Lypson hill as you will be so near home.' This, we imagine, was clearer to John Rogers than it is to us. In 1743 there was not yet a bridge across the Plym at Marsh Mills; there was only the raised causeway, known as Long Bridge, built in 1618/19 as an improvement on the ancient ebb-tide crossing to Crabtree. To avoid the steep ascent of Lipson Hill as Elford hoped to do, they would have to cross lower down than Crabtree, travelling either to Cattedown, or if the water were calm, perhaps round to Sutton harbour.

Before his marriage John had been living at Hooe, an estate bought in the 1720s with money left by his grandmother, wife of the first Sir John. In the summer of 1742, when he felt his marriage to Miss Trefusis was reasonably assured, he set about acquiring a house in Plymouth. He looked at several properties before deciding on a late-1690s house near the Old Town. The house was in bad repair and damp to a degree that Mrs Tolcher could only describe as 'wet'. Furthermore, it had stabling for only three horses. With their usual good humour, Mr and Mrs Tolcher took charge of all the work of restoration and measured the rooms for paper and tapestries, whilst John went back to London to be with his in-laws until the wedding. Some furniture was shipped round from London. In one drawer two mice were found to have died (Mr Tolcher said because John had not provided water for their journey), but not before they had eaten through the bed tester. Mr Elford knew a man who had some stables to let in the Old Town. Whatever Hannah thought of her new home, within a year of their moving in she and John were to find their circumstances dramatically changed. On 21 January 1744 Sir John Rogers died, aged 67, and he was buried at Cornwood on 27 January, registered 1743 in the old-style calendar.

Sir John had made his will in June 1742. He left £2,000 to his youngest daughter and legacies to his married daughters. John inherited the real estate and Frederick had been provided for on his marriage. There were, however, certain settlements, some made in 1740, which Dame Mary now found objectionable, on the grounds that they were contrary to the terms of her marriage settlement made by her father-in-law, the first Sir John, in 1698. There can be little doubt that she thought her son John was proving inadequate in dealing with the family affairs, particularly so far as they affected her, and for a time she refused to leave Blachford. Matters came to a head when she disputed her son's right to a half share in the Rogers's ship *Plymouth*, and in February 1746 John was obliged to bring a Bill of Complaint against his mother based on her refusal to give up her late husband's chattels at Blachford,

In the deposition for her defence Dame Mary describes how John had been sent away to school at Fulham and elsewhere, and afterwards to Oxford. She says that some time after university he had travelled abroad to France and other places to complete his education into becoming a country gentleman, but had been given no training in business and did not help his father in the family business as merchants in any way. John's friends told a different story. Mr Tolcher said that since 1729 John had been very active in Plymouth, helping his father in trade as Sir John himself had made known, and John had been given a half-share in the *Plymouth*. The former ship's master Mr Pearse also understood John to be with his father in trading with the ship, and he had always found him very assiduous and helpful. Mr Pentecost Barker, a notorious Plymouth gossip and diarist, agreed with what both Mr Tolcher and Mr Pearse had said.

Local Recipes for Soft Fruit

Now that the soft fruit season is here, try your hand at making your own jam.

Raspberry Jam

4lbs raspberries
4lbs sugar

Place raspberries, in a pan over a low heat. Cook gently and then simmer for 20 minutes until fruit is tender and contents reduced. Add sugar, boil 5 minutes or until fruit stiffens when dropped on a cold saucer. Pot and seal immediately. Seal with waxed paper while still hot (to melt wax) and place cellophane in position at once.

Strawberry Jam

4lbs strawberries
4lbs sugar
Juice of 4 lemons (or 1tsp tartaric acid)

Hull strawberries and put in pan with lemon juice or tartaric acid. Simmer until tender and reduced somewhat (about 35–40 minutes' hard boiling). Add sugar. Bring to boil and boil hard for 10–15 minutes or until sets on cold saucer. Pot and seal immediately.

Be different. Try this dessert for a special treat:

Raspberry Japonais

4 egg whites
3 drops vanilla essence
½lb raspberries (fresh or frozen)
2–4ozs chopped skinned hazel nuts (or any ground nuts, eg almonds)
9 ozs caster sugar
½tsp vinegar
½pt double cream
icing sugar

Butter and flour the sides of two sandwich tins, cover the bottoms with Bakewell paper.
Set oven at 350–370°F (Gas 4, 180°C)
Whisk egg whites stiff, add sugar 1 tbsp at a time, continue whisking until it peaks.
Add vanilla and sugar
Fold in nuts.
Divide mixture into tins, smooth with knife and cook for 30–40 minutes.
Cool
At least three hours before serving add the filling:
Whisk cream, sweeten, add vanilla.
Fill with layers of cream and raspberries.
Sieve icing sugar over the top and pipe with cream.

Raspberry Soufflé

3 eggs
3ozs caster sugar
1/2oz gelatine
1/2pt cream or evaporated milk
1/2pt raspberry puree ,made from 1lb raspberries

Prepare souffle dish with greaseproof paper.
Whisk 1 whole egg and 2 yolks with caster sugar over

a pan of hot water until fluffy.
Dissolve gelatine in water and allow to cool.
Whisk evaporated milk or cream.
Add cream, purée and gelatine to egg mixture.
Whisk remaining whites and fold into this mixture.
Turn into prepared dish and chill.
Decorate sides with crushed biscuit crumbs or nuts.
Pipe top with cream.

Natural History – Mimicry

Picking raspberries last week I noticed a pair of unusual insects on one of the leaves, rather wasp-like with black bodies bearing yellow stripes and more or less transparent wings. Closer examination showed them to be moths, in fact, and a look in Richard South's classic book indicated clearwing moths, probably currant clearwings, sometimes a serious pest of currant bushes where the caterpillars bore into the stem.

The resemblance to a wasp-like insect is not accidental. A coloration and shape resembling an 'unpleasant' insect has evolved as a protective device, a phenomenon known as mimicry. Birds, which are the main predators of flying insects, learn that wasps are distasteful (they sting) and so leave insects of the appropriate appearance alone. A mimic adopting the colours of the 'model' is protected because a bird will treat it as distasteful and hence tend to leave it alone.

Although butterflies mimicking distasteful butterflies are common in the tropics, butterfly and moth mimics are not all that common in Britain. We do have, however, a number of other types of insect mimics. Perhaps some of the commonest are hoverflies, often seen at this time of year, harmless flies which perform such useful tasks as having larvae that feed on aphids (greenflies). Many hoverflies are striped like wasps and are presumably protected by mimicry. Our largest hoverflies (*Volucella*), rather less commonly seen, are large insects with a 3cm wingspan and resembling bumblebees or hornets. They are handsome insects but somewhat frightening to the uninitiated. They can usually be distinguished by their large head and conspicuous eyes, lack of a waist, and having only one pair of wings (wasps and hornets have two pairs). Another hornet mimic is the striking but rather uncommon greater horntail, a wood-boring wasp relative of pine woods with a wingspan of nearly 6cm and a length in the female of 4½cm.

Not all mimicry is of the type just described (technically called Batesian mimicry). There is also the resemblance between species of similarly distasteful characteristics – common cinnabar moth caterpillars (often found on ragwort) are apparently distasteful – they use the same black/yellow warning colours as wasps and certain other distasteful animals.

The King's Gutter

C.F. Hankin

The Ordnance Survey map of Ivybridge (SX65) shows a leat or water-course called 'King's Gutter', above the west bank of the River Erme, running from the area around King's Barn (SX 630594) in Harford parish, downstream to the fields above the farms of Langham and Dinnaton on the south-west side of Henlake Down (SX627569) in Cornwood parish. The leat appears on Harford Tithe Map dated 1838, where it is seen at King's Meadow taking water off the streams which flow down from the southern slopes of Stalldown on Dartmoor and which, with other spring waters, pass through the ancient estate known as 'King's' before joining the River Erme below Harford bridge. At King's Barn the altitude is approximately 575ft OD, and after running its course of about 3½ miles to Langham the leat is shown on the OS map at approximately 450ft OD, a fall of 125 feet.

King's Gutter is now dry. Its best preserved section, cut to a mean width of about 3½ feet, may be clearly traced along its course in Erme Wood. It

Woodland scene, Ivybridge.

Some Ivybridge Families

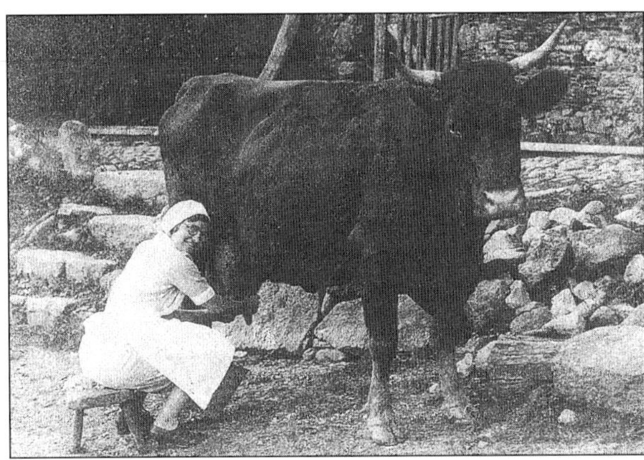

Top: *The Cane family at Hunsdon Farm, Ivybridge. Dorothy* (above) *was a champion butter maker.*

Mrs William Daw, mother of Mary-Jane Cane of Hunsdon Farm.

In the last two decades of the nineteenth century, and probably earlier, the Smallbridges were prominent residents of Ivybridge. Richard Smallbridge, who lived at Yew Tree House in Fore Street, died in 1810, aged 86. A Charles Smallbridge was a grocer, draper and wine merchant at No. 54 Fore Street, whilst George Smallbridge was a saddler and ironmonger at No. 53. Another Charles Smallbridge, a photographer, died in 1938 at the age of 79. It is not known which members of the family are shown here.

The Drew family outside Rose Cottage, 1957. Left to right, back: *Barbara, Dick, Douglas;* front: *Ruth, Barney, Rosemary, ?.*

Some Ivybridge Families

The Spurnel family, 1900.

The Partington Family at 'Nirvana'.

Some Ivybridge Families

Frank, Hilda and Isabella Partington, who lived at No. 12 Keaton Road in 1891,

Members of the Gregory family.

Frances Partington, who in 1881 and 1891 was shown in the records as living at the same adddress as her children.

Lizzie Partington, who worked for the Allens.

Frances Partington junr, who married Frank Johns (see below).

Far left: *John (Jack) Partington, who married Renee, a school-teacher.*

Left: *Frank Johns, surveyor, married Frances Partington* (see above).

Some Ivybridge Families

The Dowdell family. Left to right, back row: *eldest son Alfred, mother Maud (née Symons, formerly of No. 32 Fore Street), father William, Walter;* front row: *William, Grace, Cyril. Alf was known as 'Titbits' at school, and Cyril as 'Hoot-Doots'. The family emigrated to Canada in 1924.*

Right: *At Challaborough, c.1928.* Left to right: *Peggy Harvey, Norah Bowden, Bill Bowden, Dosic Harvey, Jimmy Harvey, ?.*

Some Ivybridge Families

The wedding of Sydney Francis Folley to Betty Irene Pawley, 3 August 1940. Left to right: Jessie Folley, Albert Folley, Sydney, Betty, Doris Pawley, Rosa Pawley, Henry Pawley. Rosa worked at Sparkwell Vicarage in 1923/24 when she was about 15.

Sidney Francis Folley, c.1936. His grandfather, Henry Folley, was a groom at Highlands.

Sidney Francis Folley, Charles Pawley and Albert Henry Folley, c.1940.

Some Ivybridge Families

This group of mums and children, photographed in the 1940s, includes Angela Cox, Marge Avery, Cristen Northmore and Marge Vincent.

The christening of the Chadwick twins aboard HMS Caprice.

survives, also as a dry ditch, along the outer side of the perimeter wall of Longtimbers estate adjoining Henlake Down. The dry bed of the gutter in Erme Wood has been converted to a public footpath, access to it being clearly signposted at about 300 yards up the road leading to Pithill above the Ivybridge Viaduct. The upper parts of the leat are in private lands.

The gutter was cut in 1818. Its purpose was to water the meadows at Langham Farm, after which any surplus water would pass through land belonging to Woodland and then irrigate a meadow at Ivybridge. From 1815 all the land through which the gutter was cut had been the property of Sir John Rogers of Blachford, and he also held the manor and lands of Ivybridge. At that time Sir John, who never married, had interests away in London, his estates in Devon being left in the care of his steward, Mr Christopher Savery, a man then approaching his seventies. It was probably Savery's idea to bring the King's Water to Langham. Expert advice came from a Mr Robert Handle, who appears to have been a specialist in cutting leats. In 1813 he and Mr Savery had together planned and cut the leat which took water from the River Erme at a weir in Henlake Down Woods (under the old viaduct) to supply the new houses in Ivybridge.

Work on King's Gutter probably started in December 1817, and continued through the following year. As work progressed it was discovered that the level of water at Langham would permit the gutter to be extended to the Dinnaton fields. Some time after 1818 Christopher Savery's son, Mr Servington Savery, took over the estate management from his father, but he does not seem to have been fully briefed as to what his father had accomplished on the estates during his stewardship.

In 1847 a dispute over the use of water at Langham and Woodland, which to some extent was caused by the presence of King's Water, gave rise to a long correspondence, first between Sir John Rogers and Mr Servington Savery, and later between Sir Frederick Rogers' who succeeded to the title and estates on the death of his brother on 10 December 1847, and Mr John S. Savery, brother of Mr Servington Savery. The principal parties in the dispute, which went on unresolved for more than five years, were the Rogers of Blachford and Mr Thomas Pode of Fardel, whose tenant at Woodland had been interfering with the flow of water at Langham in 1846. The Saverys's letters are a somewhat unsuccessful attempt to explain the facts of the dispute to the Rogers, and to tell their employers what little they, the stewards, knew of the history of the King's Water.

In November 1847, a month before Sir John Rogers died, Mr Servington Savery, fearing there would have to be litigation, presented a statement in which he set out the history of the dispute as he saw it. He informs Sir John that 'King's Water was brought in about 30 years ago'. Just 14 months later, in a letter dated 20 January 1849 to Sir Frederick Rogers, Mr John Savery says 'he believes the King's Water was brought in by my father for the irrigation of Dunnaton, thence to Langham Meadow and on to the Ivybridge Great Meadow'. Another letter, dated 25 May 1850, informs Sir Frederick that 'as to King's Water find it was taken in about 30 years ago'.

We are left to wonder how it was that after such a short time the Saverys and indeed the Rogers themselves had such a vague knowledge of the gutter's origin. The numerous meetings between Mr Christopher Savery and Mr Handle, at which the work of cutting the channel was inspected and discussed, are explicitly recorded by Mr Savery in his Stewards Bill of Costs for the year 1818. It would seem that after Sir John had examined the list of items and agreed the payment to Mr Savery, the accounts were filed away at Blachford and forgotten.

In bringing water round the south side of Henlake Down, King's Water overran and mixed with the natural streams which flowed from Henlake Down to the Rogers's lands at Langham and to Mr Pode's fields at Woodland. It was the mixing of the waters which prompted Mr Heathrel, the tenant at Woodland, to interfere with the flow of water below Langham. Letters written by the Saverys indicate that the use of King's Water was partly seasonal, apparently on the 'water meadow' principle for producing lush spring pasture. It was said that in some years it did not run at all. The water was said to be inferior to that from the Langham springs, and in his letter of 20 January 1849 Mr Savery expresses doubt as to 'whether the King's Water has ever repaid the expense of bringing it so many miles or whether it even pays for keeping the Gutter open'.

At the same time as the dispute with Mr Pode's tenant at Woodland was running on, King's Water was creating problems for other users of the Erme River. Stowford paper mill on the Harford side of the Erme had been using the river water for power and paper-making for 60 years, since 1787. In 1837 new machinery had been installed, and as the business prospered, so more water was required. Mr William Ackland bought the mill in 1839, and in the succeeding years, during periods of drought, it was known that it was his men who had trespassed upon the Rogers's land and turned off King's Water. This had happened in May and June 1849, the year Mr John Allen bought the paper mill, when Mr Savery discovered the gutter 'turned off somewhere near Wilkiesmore, the banks being wilfully dug down and large rocks thrown into the channel'. It happened again in 1851, and Mr Savery was sure it was Mr Allens's people who were responsible. Apparently there were times when the paper mill needed all the water the river could provide.

In spite of having recurring trouble with the

neighbours, King's Water continued to flow until some time in the present century. Then, about the time of the First World War, a tenant in the Wilkiesmore area was given permissions to fill in the gutter across his land. By this time, however, the practice of 'drowning' the meadows during the winter months had fallen, or was falling, into disuse, and for that, as well as perhaps other reasons, the water was no longer wanted at Langham or at Ivybridge.

Letters Concerning the King's Gutter

Mr Servington Savery's Statement as to Water Courses on Langham, 26 November 26 1847:

S. Savery, Solicitor, Modbury.

In the Matter of Disputes between Sir John Leman; Rogers Bart and William Meathrel and Mr Thomas Pode.

I met yesterday by appointment Mr Whiteford on behalf of Meathrel and Pode and such Meeting was attended by Mr Stephen Pode Vr. Meathrel and Philip Horton and William Dodderidge.

The matter in dispute between Meathrel and Sir John Rogers as to Stibb Water Mr Meathrel stated to be settled between himself and Mr John Servington Savery according to his proposition of taking the Water by alternate fortnights which Meathrel has accepted. As neither Dodderidge, Philip Horton or myself were aware of this agreement although having been informed of the proposition to that effect made by the said John Servington Savery, I said nothing beyond that I was not aware of the agreement having been entered into. The Water according to this arrangement was turned into Langham Meadow from Stibb on Monday last.

The complaint of Mr Meathrel and adopted by Mr Pode was 1st. That no Water flowing from Stibb returned to Mr Pode's Estate at Woodland as in consequence of an underground deep Drain being cut or sunk last year near the bottom of Langham Meadow all the Stibb Water as well as the King's and Langham Water sunk away into this Drain and was carried off to Barratt's Woodland not allowing any Water to return to the Original course into Pode's Woodland. Also that a very excellent Spring of Water rising in Pode's Field and used for irrigating Barratt's Field underneath fell into the same Gutter and was carried off from Pode's Woodland.

The Stibb Water I visited about two years ago and proposed that a Gutter should be cut below the original leading Gutter (which took then the King's Water, Langham Water and Stibb Water, which was very frequently carried together into Sir John's Woodland) for the purpose of keeping the Stibb Water alone and preventing the two streams from uniting. This I considered would have avoided the possibility of future disputes. On my visit I found the old Gutter intended for receipt of the King's and Langham Water was not used but in some places filled in. The new Gutter cut for the Stibb Water was full with the Stibb Stream, and both the King's and Langham Water and Stibb Water were carried over the Langham Water, but no part of such Water went over the new underground Drain made last year, into which all the Water sunk and the full Stream flowed from thence on to the road and through Sir John's new Woodland Court to his Lands below and no part of it fell into the original Channel to Mr Pode's Woodland (Mr Dodderidge complains that he has now no power to irrigate the Langham Meadow as heretofore on account of the whole Stream sinking into the new underground Drain).

By Sir John's Conveyance or Deed of Exchange with old Meathrel all the Stibb Water was after irrigating Langham Meadow to fall down to its original course into Meathrel's Moor and of course to Pode's Woodland. To this Mr Meathrel and Mr Pode are already entitled, and as all this Water is now sunk into the new underground Drain and carried in conjunction with the King's and Langham Water to Sir John's Woodland, I scarcely know what arrangement can be made to obviate the difficulty.

Mr Pode in consideration that all the Water from Langham and Stibb which he claims is carried off by this new underground Drain proposes that a division of all the Water flowing in the Channel into Sir John's Woodland should be made in the Woodland Road which would obviate every difficulty and guard the Stibb Water, this would be fair enough. I contended, and I believe agreeable to the evidence in the case, that since the King's Water was brought in about 30 years ago, all the Langham Water had been consolidated therewith and carried into Sir John's Woodland, and that the lapse of time prevented this Course being disturbed. That a small Stream of water rising in Pode's Fields, and used by Barratt in irrigating his Field below had also fallen into and been consolidated with the King's and Langham Water and flowed into Sir John's Woodland for nearly 30 years and could not now be disturbed. If we are correct in these points, the only claim of Mr Pode can be as to the Stibb Water, and if the Agreement stated by Mr Meathrel to be made agreeable to Mr J.S. Savery's proposals for using the Water by alternate fortnights be correct, I consider Mr Pode can claim a division of this Water only for the fortnight which Sir John enjoys it, and not for the fortnight when it is carried by Meathrel over his own Lands on the opposite side of the valley to the exclusion of Langham Meadow altogether. Mr Meathrel's statements are most outrageous, and I am fully convinced founded generally on falsehood. He declared first, that the matter as to the Stibb Water between himself and Sir John is settled by agreement with Mr J.S. Savery. Secondly, that up to three years ago when Sir John cut a new channel and carried an additional Stream from Dunnaton to Langham the whole of the Dunnaton and Langham Water fell into the original Course to Pode's Woodland, and was not carried on to Sir John's Woodland. But when it was taken across the King's Water Stream I could not discover, and Mr Dodderidge and Mr Horton declare that since the former's occupation Mr Meathrel and Mr Pode have never had this Water. Mr Meathrel also declares that he has also often by himself and Servants turned off the whole of King's Langham and Stibb Water from the Woodland road to Pode's Woodland, and that Mr J.S. Savery once ordered him to do so, and that Mr J.S. Savery admitted this to him in his and my presence at my office in Modbury. All I can say I have no recollection of it, nor do I believe it, or indeed one word Mr Meathrel states. The Stibb Water is clearly to be returned in its Course to Pode's Woodland and a doubt arises with me, whether it might not be a prudent course to obviate the difficulty of this Water falling into the new underground drain, to carry the Stibb Stream only below this new Drain and irrigate that part of the Langham Meadow below, and allow such Water to fall into its original course into Meathrel's Moor and on to Pode's Woodland, and to irrigate the upper part of Langham Meadow with the King's and Langham Water which will fall into the under Drain and flow on to Sir John's Woodland. This course or a division of the Water in the Woodland road during the fortnight's use of the Stibb Water in the Langham Meadow, or during its use above the new under Drain seems to me the best means of preventing Litigation.

I have suggested to Mr Pode and Mr Whiteford the fact of their Tenant Mr Meathrel taking off the Stibb Water from the original Course to irrigate his own Lands to a great extent, and thereby preventing such Water ever returning to Pode's Woodland being allowed, and they have promised to take this into Consideration, as I imagine they have not a much better opinion of Mr Meathrel than I have. If, as heretofore, all the Stibb Water is allowed to flow constantly into Langham Meadow I consider there is not much objection to a division of the Water in the Woodland road as proposed by Mr Pode, which would obviate every dispute, but Claim of half the Water constantly when all the Stibb Water is diverted for every alternate fortnight into Meathrel's Land on the opposite side of the Vale seems to me an unfair and unreasonable demand, and I think Mr Pode might waive the half for such fortnight, if he allows his Tenant Mr Meathrel to divert it. As to the rights or use of the Langham Water flowing from Dunnaton as claimed by Meathrel, as also of the small Stream rising in Pode's Field and now used by Barratt, I have no means of forming an opinion except from the evidence of Dodderidge and P. Horton, who both declare that these Streams have fallen into the King's Water Channel for upwards of 23 years and been consolidated therewith, and carried on to Sir John's Woodland, and I cannot see, or understand, how such Streams can have been enjoyed by Meathrel as there appears to be no Channel to Convey such Streams either under or over the King's Water Channel now about 30 years in existence. I can imagine that when the Stibb Water was allowed to join and flow on with the King's and Langham Water into Sir John's Woodland Mr Meathrel might have objected to it, and might have turned it off altogether in the road, and this has been hitherto his complaint to me, but I never heard of this claim of the Langham Water, or the Small Stream rising in Pode's Field until this interview. Mr J.S. Savery can, of course, explain this matter better than I can, having had the entire management of this department.

The evidence of the Coultons, Sercombe and others (seven in number) is very clear as to Sir John's right to the Stibb Water in Langham Meadow, but by Sir John's Deed of Exchange with old Meathrel he is bound to return it to the Buddie Hole into Meathrel's Moor to Pode's Woodland, and cannot carry it on with the King's and Langham Water into Sir John's Woodland.

Mr Pode seems disposed to settle the matter, being quite aware that Mr Meathrel's object is to bring him into litigation with Sir John, and the only Question is: How it can be done so as to secure Sir John's rights without interfering with Mr Pode's?

As the case stands at present it is quite clear, that when Meathrel diverts the Stibb Water over his Fields, Mr Pode receives no benefit from it, and then when the Stibb Water is used by Dodderidge for irrigating above the new Underground Gutter made in Langham Meadow last year, the whole Stream sinks away into such underground Gutter and is thence carried into Sir John's Woodland, and Mr Pode has no benefit from it also in this instance. If the part of Langham Meadow above the underground Gutter be deprived of the Stibb Water, Dodderidge must rely entirely upon the King's and Langham Water, and he considers the loss to him by this new underground Gutter is at least £5 per year, being also deprived of a very beneficial Spring which he always used, and which has now quite disappeared and fallen into the same drain.

Servington Savery
November 26 1847
Plymouth

My Dear Sir
After you left yesterday I succeeded in coming to a clear understanding with Meathrel as to the real question at issue between Sir John Rogers and Mr Pode.

The question has nothing to do with Stibb Water which is regulated by the Deed, but tho' now somewhat altered in form, really dates from the time of Sir John's bringing in the Water from King's.

Before this Water was brought in, a quantity of Water rising in Dennaton and Langham used to flow down to Woodland, but after the Gutter for King's Water was cut, all these latter Streams were intercepted and if Meathrel had not interfered would have been carried on to the Ivybridge Meadows.

Meathrel however has made a constant practice as he is prepared to prove, of going to the Gutter in the Lane near Barratt's and there turning the Water (the mixed Streams of King's Water with the Water from Langham and Dennaton) down the Lane so that it flowed to Woodland and as he could make no division of the Water he has taken a quantity of the mingled Stream equal to what Belonged to him. This was the occasion of his Annual Strife with Old Cameron which I well remember, and this is what he meant yesterday by. saying he was entitled to take the King's Water, not meaning that Stream in its unmingled State, but as he found it mixed with Water belonging to him – Meathrel also says that, for some time after the King's Water Gutter was cut there was great regulatory to bringing the Stream in and that for some years the Gutter was not opened. At such times the whole of the Water brought on to Barratt's was Water rising on Dennaton and Langham, and it was on one of these occasions that he referred speaking of your Brother's admission to him that he was entitled, to take the Water, and employing the expression which you may remember his quoting yesterday 'If we don't bring in any Water, of course we are not entitled to any'. You will understand therefore that we lay no sort of claim to the Water brought in from King's whilst it forms a separate and distinct Stream, but after it is nixed with the Water from Langham and Dennaton we claim as much of the joint Stream as these additions amount to. If thought necessary the proportions can be easily ascertained by stopping the Water coming in from King's and seeing what the remainder coming down to Barratt's amounts to.

This statement I think removes all Contradictions between Meathrel and Dodderidge and explains all that was said yesterday, tho' Meathrel's confused mode of explanation rendered it difficult to understand him. The immediate cause of my now interfering, is the covering up of the place in the road outside Barratt's Gate where Meathrel used to take the Water. As long as he could supply himself he used to limit himself to complaining, which he certainly did to me both in Mr John S. Pode's time and since, very constantly, but he now sees the means of supplying himself taken from him and he calls on his Landlord for redress. Practically therefore the encroachment on our rights dates from the Covering the Gutter in the Lane tho' the original Cutting the Gutter for bringing in the Water from King's was the first invasion and if we can show that since the Gutter was cut we have constantly and Uniformly taken the Water at Barratt's Gate, you will I think admit that our right has been kept up, and that our proposal to divide the Water there (by a constant division) is a fair one. The proportion which the Stream from King's bears to the other Water brought on with it may at first sight appear to he the correct principle of division, but you must remember that a great deal of King's Water would be lost before it came on to Barratt's, and that you also take off a small Stream from Woodland. Considering also the inferior quality of King's Water an equal division seems but fair.

Scouts beating the bounds in 1996.

Beating the Bounds

We all go through many traditions in our lives, such as the Christmas dinner or the giving out of chocolate eggs at Easter. But not all traditions are celebrated by everyone.

The town of Ivybridge has its own tradition, just like many others. This tradition came about centuries ago when the Mayor of Ivybridge was asked to pay a fee for the continued use of the small stone bridge that crosses the River Erme near the mill. This fee consisted of one fat duck from the river, some new paper from the mill and a single red rose. This was to be renewed every year.

This tradition has gone on for a long time and, as a result, has obviously been subject to some degree of change. The bridge ceremony is still celebrated, and there is also the Beating of the Bounds, when the Chair of Ivybridge and the Chair of Ermington walk round the edge of Ivybridge (the boundary) and beat it with sticks. This is indeed a very strange tradition.

Unfortunately some of the boundary markers around Ivybridge have been lost. As far as the Town Council knew no one had walked around the boundary and taken the exact distance and the time it takes to walk it. But that was about to change...

Gary Rendle (SPL)

On a wet 13 June, 3rd Ivybridge Scout Group took on the task of finding and beating one of the bounds in Longtimber Woods. We beat the bound with a stick which had a rattle on the end of it. We didn't have to look far because it was near the path that goes through the woods, and then we headed back to the bridge for a ceremony. A bound is a boundary stone that marks the edge of the town. Ten stones are dotted around the perimeter of Ivybridge. Ivybridge

Top and above: *Beating the bounds on the bridge.*

has grown so much since the stones were laid that some of them may have been built over. At the bridge the manager of the paper mill gave the deputy mayor some paper. I'm not totally sure why that happened. There was also a representative from each primary school in Ivybridge. They had their photograph taken with the mayor. Then we went to Ivor Martin's house and we signed a book to show that we went. On this day it is tradition to decorate your gate. This is an annual event which happens every year and is a tradition within the town.

Alec Maddison

Beating the bounds, July 1996, using the boundary stones as marked on 1952 OS map.

Distance 5.7 miles. Time 2 hours 15 minutes

From the Old Ivy Bridge GR636 563 go up Station Road to railway viaduct GR636 569. Take path under viaduct into woods, go on past old swimming pool to footpath sign.
1st Boundary Stone: found towards river GR636 575

Take footpath leading up slope away from river, carry on until stile is reached GR637 572. Cross road to gateway on to Henlake Down. Take footpath on right and follow boundary wall until gate is found GR629 573.
2nd Boundary Stone: in corner (now missing)

Follow wall and path down hill until next gate is reached GR628 571
Go through gate and down track past houses and over railway out onto Langham Levels. Bear left along Langham Levels towards Cleeve Drive.
3rd Boundary Stone: on right at Kennel Lane GR626 567

Go down Kennel Lane to Woodlands Road GR624 562.
4th Boundary Stone: on other side of road by wall (probably buried).

Walk along Woodlands Road and turn right into Cleeve Drive and on to roundabout. Go over A38 and turn left down Ermington Road until you reach bridge over River Erme. Go under road bridge by

footpath along side of river and carry on to bend in river behind tennis courts GR632 555.
5th Boundary Stone: At bend of river (now missing)

Go round the tennis courts and head towards the main entrance on the Ermington Road.
6th Boundary Stone: in a wall GR633 554 (wall and stone now missing)

The official boundary then ran across adjacent fields towards Godwell Lane. As you are unable to follow that route, walk towards Ermington until Newlands cross is reached GR638 552. Turn left up Godwell Lane.
7th Boundary Stone: just before entrance drive to Filham Park GR641 555 (now missing)

Carry on up Godwell Lane past Torrhill Cottages and farm and left bend in road.
8th Boundary Stone: on right GR646 558

Proceed to Cross in Hand GR647 562. Turn left down Exeter Road, keeping to left side footpath until you pass Rue St Pierre.
9th Boundary Stone: found in grass

Shortly afterwards
10th Boundary Stone: in wall approximately 100 yards further along.
From here the boundary passed through houses on the other side of the road and through school grounds to join up with 1st Boundary stone found in woods. As you are unable to follow that route carry on down Exeter Road past Bridge Inn and back to Old Ivy Bridge.

Buildings in Ivybridge of Architectural or Historic Interest

Ivybridge Viaduct/Aqueduct
Late C18 or early C19 built to serve John Berry's Woollen Mill, latter known as the Lower Mill after 1849 when it became a Paper Mill; in c.1927 the aqueduct served an Electricity Generating Plant in part of the old mill building, and finally went out of use in c.1940. Supply from River use in c.1940. Supply from River Erme to north-east with widening open leat and raised channel leading to 12-arch aqueduct serving an over-shot wheelhouse forming part of the mill (wheel and mill taken down). Overflow channel to river alongside aqueduct on east side served by three sluices. Coursed squared granite rubble with red brick, round arched openings with later brick reopening and block way of two arches; Red brick walls of water channel rebuilt 1896 (cast-iron date over arch) with dentil coping; older brick channel wall at north-east and with recessed panels and plain coping partly cement rendered. Narrow arched opening to southern sluice retains original parts of the overflow channel. Remains of mill wheelhouse of

Lower Mill, Ivybridge, which produced 'half stuff', part-finished paper which was then transported to the upper mill where the process was completed.

An old wheel from the mill.

Moving a section of the old mill wheel.

The old mill workings.

slate random rubble with squared granite dressings rendered interior with stopped wheel pit; plain red brick channel walls; small, blocked arched opening on east side. Tail-race from wheelhouse now fitted-in.

Ivybridge, Western Road
Westover Farmhouse House

Early C17, remodelled in early and later C19. Roughcast stone rubble slate roof with gabled ends and late C19 crested ridge tiles. Rendered stacks at gable end and at rear.

Two-room-plan house, originally with through passage and kitchen to left with gable end stack and parlour to right with rear lateral stack and a stair turret at rear of the kitchen. It may have had a third (inner) room to right. In circa early C19 the first storey and roof were raised and the passage widened into a stair hall. Probably no later in the C19 a two-storey out shut was built at the rear of the parlour; it contains the kitchen and has a rear lateral stack.

Two storey. Symmetrical three-window range. C19 16-pane sashes, ground floor larger first floor centre narrower 12-pane sash. Central early C19 panelled door and large late C19 or early C20 glazed porch. Large projecting stack at left gable end with set offs. Former stair turret at rear right and two-storey out shut at rear left with lateral stack and late C19 cantilevered room in the angle to right.

Interior: much of the C19 joinery survives, including panelled doors and staircase with turned newel, steep balusters and open string with shaped tread ends. Parlour to right has early C19 panelled door flanked by round-headed riches moulded architraves, and rear lateral fireplace blocked by C20 fireplace. Left-hand room, the kitchen, has open fireplace with oven and ovolo moulded timber lintel reset at lower level. Roof space not inspected, but it is unlikely to contain pre-C19 trusses.

Glazed door to left of centre. Date stone c.830. Large rendered chimney stack on rear wall and stacks at gable ends. Rear wing has two ovolo moulded three-light wooden mullion windows with leaded panes.

Including C19 cart-shed with loft, adjoining rear wing at right angles, and forming U-shaped plan around small yard.

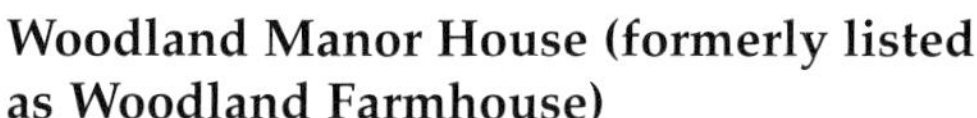

Woodland Manor House (formerly listed as Woodland Farmhouse)
Farmhouse which is the surviving part of a former manor house. Circa C16 and C17. Stone rubble, partly rendered. Hipped scantle slate roof, partly replaced with asbestos slates. Two tall storeys. Long five to six window range. Mainly C18 sashes with glazing bars in reduced openings. Ground floor with a two-light hollow-chamfered stone mullion window and another window with chamfered wooden lintel and part of moulded wooden frame. String course at floor level. C20 two storey rendered porch to left of centre. Large stone chimney stack over front wall to right. Another external chimney stack at rear.

Interior: very high ceilings with stopped chamfer beams. Former hall has fireplace with massive chamfered granite lintel. It appears that this is a wing and all that remains of a larger house. Woodland Manor was the seat of the Woodlands, of whom Sir Walter de Woodland was a servant to the Black Prince.

Stables adjoining west of Woodland Manor House
Stables with hay loft above. Circa C18/19. Stone rubble with granite quoins. Slurried slate half-hipped roof. Slate canopy over loft door at centre, with reused granite jambs. Ground floor window also has reused granite hollow-chamfered frame. Two rows of pigeon holes below the eaves.

Ermington
Barn west of Woodland Manor
Barn with cow house below. Circa C18/19. Stone rubble with granite quoins. Slurried scantle slate half-hipped roof. Central external stone stairs to barn on first floor. Doors to cow house either side with granite lintels. Lean-to extension at north end with pigeon holes. Included for group value.

Shippen and cart shed south-west of Woodland Manor
Shippen with cart shed and loft. C18/19. Stone rubble with granite quoins and lintels. Slurried scantle slate roof with half-hipped ends. Central cart entrance with slightly cambered arch of granite ashlars visors, flanked by external stone stairs to loft doors. Stable doors to left and right. Ventilation slits in rear wall and pigeon holes in east end.

Ermington, Click land
Farmhouse. Early C19. Stone rubble. Asbestos slate hipped roof. Two storeys. Three bays. Sash windows with glazing bars. Central plastered doorway with entablature and panelled door. Small single storey, one bay flanking wings with slightly advanced centres with round-headed windows with intersecting glazing bars. Rendered side chimney stacks.

Cornwood, Hele Cross
South (or Lower) Hele including range of farm buildings adjoining north (south (or lower) Hele only previously listed)
Farmhouse and farm buildings. Circa C16/17 with later alterations. Rendered stone with granite dressings. Slate hipped roof. Two storeys. Three window range. C19/20 casements in enlarged openings. Two of ground floor windows have original lintels of what were stone mullion windows. C20 gabled porch at centre with panelled and glazed door. Stone chimneystack at higher end. Wing at rear of higher end with half-hipped roof and forming L-shaped plan. Out shuts and chimneystack on rear wall. Byre at lower end with some stone mullion windows with hood moulds, possibly revised. Interior of north wing a chamfered ceiling beam with pyramid stops possibly reused. Including range of farm buildings adjoining at rear (north). Built around three sides of a farmyard with the house on the south side. Circa C15. Granite with corrugated iron roofs. Barns and cattle sheds. Through the east range a segmental arched cart way.

Hele was the seat of the Heles, an important South Devon family and considerable landowners in C16 and C17.

Cornwood, Ivybridge Road
Langham Farmhouse
Circa early C17. Granite rubble with colour-washed plaster front. Slate roof with gabled ends. Two storeys. Three window range. Two and three and four-light hollow-chamfered stone mullion windows. Ground floor left-hand four-light window. Central doorway to cross passage with C19/20 hipped roof porch. Large granite chimneystack to left of centre backing onto cross passage. Another granite stack at the gabled higher end to right. The lower end has been demolished.

Cornwood, Moor Cross
Moor Cross Bridge
Road bridge over River Yealm. Circa early C19. Granite rubble. Small bridge with single wide elliptical arch. Parapet with granite coping.

Harford, Ivybridge Road
Lukesland
Large country house in landscaped garden. Built 1862 extended in c.1880. Tudor style. Uncoursed pink granite with grey granite quoins and dressings. Steeply pitched slate roof with shaped gables. Asymmetrical. Two storeys and attic. West front four bays, left and right slightly advanced and with shaped gables with large finials. Right hand first floor oriel, left hand with stone porch with four-centred arch. Central two-storeyed splayed bay. All stone mullioned and transomed windows with four-centred or ogee-headed lights. Set back to left (north)

A watercolour painting of the bridge over the Erme.

a three-storey tower with embattled parapet and polygonal stair turret. Shaped gables to north and south sides. Built on three sides of a courtyard with service wings at the rear and a large traceried window at the back of the main building. Interior: moulded plaster vaulted ceiling in the hall. Probably also has other good interior features.

Ivybridge, Blachford Road
The Bridge
Road bridge over River Erme. Circa C17 widened in C18 or C19. Single span slightly pointed high round arch. Granite rubble with dressed granite voussoirs. Curved parapets splayed out over the abutments. Chamfered granite parapet coping. Originally a narrow packhorse bridge which has been widened on the upstream side probably in C18 or C19. Granite bollards at either end of south side, one inscribed Ermington, the other inscribed Ugborough. There was a bridge on this site in the Middle Ages.

Ivybridge, Blachford Road
Erme House
Early C19. Stone with slate hung front and rendered side. Slate roof with hipped corner. Three storeys. Three bays. Sash windows without glazing bars. Ground floor: C19 splayed bay windows. Central door case with fluted pilasters, open pediment.

Panelled reveals, semi-circular fanlight with glazing bars. Situated on corner of terrace of houses.

Ivybridge, Erme Road
Ermeside House
Early C19. Stuccoed front with slate hung end wall. Slate roof with gabled ends. Two storeys. Three bays. Sash windows with glazing bars and small brackets to the cills. Central plastered door case with open pediment panelled reveals, semi-circular fanlight with glazing bars and panelled door. Brick chimneystacks at gable ends.

Ivybridge, Exeter Road
Milestone immediately north-east of Torr Hill (House)
Milestone. C19. Cast iron. Triangular in section with semi-pyramidal top like an obelisk. Situated against wall with 11 miles to Plymo (Plymouth) and 11 miles from Plymo on either face.

Ivybridge, Fore Street
Methodist Church including boundary wall to north and west
Methodist Church. 1874-76. Coursed and dressed stone with ashlar dressings. Slate roofs. Nave, chancel. North and south transepts and south-west tower. Plate tracery windows, two in the west end with rook shafts with carved capitals and rose window above. The transepts have group of three lancets. Buttresses with set-offs and gablets. The south-west tower has buttressed square base and octagonal upper stage with broached and bell-openings with nook shafts with carved capitals, and a short stone spire. Sunday school built in 1937 attached to north-west side.

Including dwarf stone boundary wall to north and west with decorative cast iron railings and two pairs of stone gate piers with large caps with carved capitals and crochets.

Interior: arch braced roof on corbelled colonettes supporting stone angels. Cruciform on plan with short chancel and transepts.

Ivybridge, Harford Road
Stowford Paper Mills

Paper mills. Dated 1862. Coursed and dressed granite ground, first and second storeys. Red brick above with yellow brick dressings. Large rectangular building. Six storeys. Nine by five bays. First three storeys of nine bay front have only five windows per storey. Round arched iron frame windows with keystones. Right and doorway on each floor with iron fire escape. String course at third floor level inscribed 'Stowford Paper Mills AD1862'. Water tank over roof at left hand (west) end. Engine house, dated 1914, with tall brick chimney, at west end.

Ivybridge, Keaton Road
Rose Cottage

Detached house. Early C19. Red brick with slate hung end walls and rendered corner pilasters. Slate roof with gabled ends. Two storeys. Three bays. Sash windows with glazing bars, first floor, with flat brick arches, ground floor segmental brick arches. Central plastered door case with open pediment, panelled reveals, semi-circular fanlight and panelled door. Brick chimneystacks at gable ends. Hipped roof wing at rear.

Ivybridge, Station Road
Woodhaye

Detached house. Early C19. Stuccoed. Low-pitched hipped slate roof with deep eaves. Two storeys and basement. Three bays. Sash windows with glazing bars in plain stuccoed architraves and with shaped blind cases. Ground floor central doorway flanked by pilasters and French windows onto veranda which has a tented zinc roof on thin iron posts, and a flight of steps at the centre. The wooden balustrade to the veranda is C20. Basement sashes beneath the veranda. Two bay right-hand return. Brick chimneystack at left hand end. Situated on rising ground above the River Erme.

Ivybridge, Station Road
Ivybridge Viaduct

Railway viaduct similar to Blackford Viaduct qv and Slade Viaduct on this line. 1893. Sir James Inglis engineer. Rock-faced granite piers supporting eight round arches of blue engineering brick and with granite spandrels and brick parapets. The granite piers of Brunel's original timber bridge of 1848 survive alongside to the north.

This section from Totnes to Laira (Plymouth) was opened in 1848 under the South Devon Co., which was dissolved in 1878. The Great Western Railway took over in 1876. The broad gauge was replaced in 1892.

Ivybridge, Western Road, Victoria House GV

Detached house. Circa 1840. Stuccoed. Low-pitched slate roof with gabled ends. Rusticated quoins and stringcourse at first floor level. Two storeys. Three bays. Sash windows with glazing bars in moulded architraves with acanthus brackets to the cills. Central doorway with rusticated pilasters, entablature, panelled door and rectangular fanlight. Rendered chimney stack at gable end.

Ivybridge, Western Road
Green Bank and Greenwood

Pair of semi-detached houses. Circa 1840. Stuccoed. Slate roof with gabled ends, and wide eaves at front with lion heads on gutter. Corner pilasters. Two storeys. Three bays each house. Sash windows with glazing bars. Greenwood has moulded stucco architraves and small brackets to cills. Central doorways with plastered porches with heavy entablatures, panelled doors and rectangular fanlights. Rendered end chimneystacks with moulded cornices.

Shaugh Prior, Bickleigh Vale
Shaugh Mill House

Mill house. Circa early C18. Whitewashed stone rubble. Asbestos slate roof with hipped and gabled ends. Two storeys. Three bays. C20 casements with glazing bars. Stair projection at centre. Stone chimneystacks at either end. Hipped roof wing at rear forming L-shaped plan. C20 hipped roof lean-to porch on gable end.

A Trip Around the Town With Henry the Mule

The population of Ivybridge is now 16,000; the town is full.

We are now in Harford Road car park, formerly a car park for the second London Hotel (we will hear more of this later)! Before that it was a tennis court for the same hotel. The town leat once fed Lees Mill, formerly the Union Corn Mill, which was located approximately where the Somerfield Supermarket stands. A mill has been known to stand on this site since 1555. As with all early mills, its use changed with the seasons. By 1713 it was a grist mill. John Allen, owner of the paper mills, purchased it in 1857 only to sell it on to the Lee family at the turn of the century. The leat flowed along Erme Road and under Fore Street, a sluice gate controlling the flow to the giant snail-like object, the old water turbine (1935), on display in the car park, that was used to drive the grist mill, now Glanville's Shopping Centre, as well as generating electricity for the village in the years before the war. This leat was open and ran right outside the Exchange pub. Customers leaving the inn would rarely negotiate the gap successfully! A further interesting feature is the leat which once fed the Lower Mills and which can be seen behind the Duke of Cornwall pub, the water running across the aqueduct feeding the 'shoot wheel' situated in the grounds of Waterside House. Of course we are standing alongside the River Erme (formerly Anne), reputed to be the second fastest river in the country when in full flood. Rising at Ermehead, just above Harford Moor, and joining the estuary at Wonwell Beach, the river used to do a lot of work, i.e. supplying power and water to drive two mills in our, then, village. Now it just does nothing.

Ivybridge became a town in 1977, when Jack Congdon was its first mayor. As we leave the car park we see a memorial stone to the US 116 Regiment, who were stationed here to prepare for the D-Day invasion, 6 June 1944; General Montgomery (Monty) himself came to Ivybridge to meet the garrison..

Many of the soldiers from the regiment who died on Omaha Beach in Normandy came from the town of Bedford in the USA, whose population was decimated. We are now passing Costly Street, the name being derived from 'Course Ley', as it was formed in a very wet field,

Hawthorn House, on the corner, was formerly a dairy run by the Withicombe family, as well as a library. We are now crossing the New Bridge (1826), built to improve road access to the village.

Now we are at the Exchange pub, originally known as the King's Arms (1834). The Second World War saw race riots between black and white soldiers stationed here.

Turning into Erme Road, on our left is Highland Street, where lived the horsemen, gardeners, etc:, who worked at Highland House. The owner in 1839 was one Henry Cotton, who had inherited a large collection of classical paintings by artists such as Reynolds which are currently in Plymouth museum. Another occupant of Highland House was Sir Maxwell Hyslop, but at the time of writing it has been converted into apartments. The second house is the old Police Station, with police cells still in the garden.

As we proceed along Erme Road we pass No. 2, a Georgian house where lives Julian Stockwin MBE, internationally renowned author of historical naval novels including *Seaflower*, *Artemis* and *Mutiny*. At No. 7 lives Mr Ivor Martin, Ivybridge historian and chairman of the Ivybridge and District Civic Society, and finally we approach Raleigh House, where the town's only VC, Col Hartley, was born.

At the end we come to the Whitehouse, now a private home, where Welsh artist George Wynne once lived and which also served as a health centre and meeting-place for the WI and other organisations of the community.

Now we come to the bridge, first recorded in 1280. One can see the boundary stone from Ugborough identifying the meeting point of the parish boundaries of Harford, Cornwood, Ermington and Ugborough. The name 'Ivybridge' derived from this bridge, and the developing village was recognised in the eighteenth and nineteenth centuries and became officially named in the late 1800s. The bridge was mainly for pack-horses – way before Henry! It was widened in the 1700s to accommodate coaches. This

Ivybridge Viaduct, photographed in 1819.

was the easiest crossing point for those travelling westward and was used by monks travelling between monasteries including those at Tavistock, Plympton and Buckfast. Before the bridge was accessible to them they had to cross the river at the Blue Elvin Rock (a very hard rock).

Now we proceed along Station Road, passing the Health Centre (the local cattle market until the late 1950s). The Erme County Primary School replaced an original school, built in 1854 and extended in 1896, where the older inhabitants of the town remember skipping over the wall to help in the market when they should have been at lessons and being given a tanning for their trouble. We now come to the paper mill, notable for being the main employer and the core reason for the development of Ivybridge from village to town. Built here because the waters of the Erme are pure and so ideal for the making of high-quality paper, the mill is little known outside the town and yet is one of our oldest industrial sites, dating from as early as 1500. It started as a 'tucking' or corn mill, graduating to paper milling in the late 1700s. At the time of writing the mill produces very specialised high-quality papers providing the bases of driving licences, lottery tickets and other high-security papers.

We now pass the Chantry on the left, which was the original vicarage for St John's Church and was also the Beaconville nursing/residential home, which housed the Women's Services during the Second World War.

Now we come uphill to Longtimber and Pithill Woods, purchased by the town to prevent excessive felling of our English hardwood species. There are some wonderful walks through our woods, with some very rare plants and wildlife. Through the woods can be seen the viaduct, originally built by Brunel in broad gauge and changed to standard gauge in 1893. The original pillars (now listed) can be seen behind the ones used today. Just above these we see the 68 steps that led to the station, now derelict. The views from the viaduct were reckoned to be the best from any railway in the country.

We then come into Crescent Road, and on our right are the old railway cottages built for the workers. Proceeding to the end of Crescent Road, we see a large old grey building, previously the Dame Hannah Rogers School, built for the maintenance and education of poor children in Devon & Cornwall. Costing £3,700 in 1887, it was used later as a hospital for the physically handicapped and was subse-

Top and above: *The Chantry.*

quently moved to the other end of town at a cost of £90,000. The original old building, reputed to be haunted by various ghosts, was converted into apartments and a small engineering business where the first catamaran yacht was built by the Stibb family.

Now we turn into Blachford Road, named after the Blachford family of Cornwood. Before turning right down towards Highlands House we see St John's Church down to our left. Consecrated in 1882, the original church, built in 1789, was just below the current one. The stone from the old church was used in the 1930s in the building of a row of houses to an Edwardian design, which the locals quickly nicknamed 'Gentry Avenue'.

Now we can cross our bridge and come to London Court, originally the London Hotel and formerly the Swan. Some say that this was the original coaching inn, but it was the old London Hotel at the other end of town which was so used. This London Hotel was the central point of such village activities as dances, rallies, meetings etc.

The Masons of Ivybridge

J. Herbert Mason: the Man and the Medals

John Herbert Mason, after whom the Mason Medals of Upper Canada, Havergal and Ridley Colleges are named, was born on 10 July 1827 at Ivy Bridge, Devon, England. His father was a miller and an importer of wheat from Russia. When Herbert was 14 and at school in London, his parents, Mary and Thomas, decided to emigrate to Canada. So he, his three brothers and one sister joined their parents and, on 14 May 1842, sailed from Plymouth. They arrived at Montreal on 1 July, a seven-week voyage. It is thought that the family first settled at Tollendal, Lake Simcoe, where Thomas bought or built a mill. They later moved to Toronto, where Thomas died in 1847, only five years after coming to Canada. Herbert, just 15 years old, took a job as accountant to the Farmers' & Mechanics' Building Society. He started his career without special privilege – apart from some remarkable genes – and, by sheer hard work, character and good judgement, rose to become one of the most respected and influential Canadian businessmen of his day. (Another brother, the youngest, Thomas G., founded Mason & Risch Pianos.)

In 1855, when he was 28 years old, Herbert again saw opportunity and seized it. It was one of those times – another of those times – when money in the province was in painfully short supply. To deal with the situation, fraternal organisations called building societies were organised, and they were exactly what their name suggested: a group of men would pool their savings to enable one or more of their number to build a house. As the money was repaid, it became available for other members of the group to borrow in turn. After a building society had served its purpose and each member had built himself a home, its books would be closed and the group disbanded.

Thomas Mason and His Descendants

Thomas Mason: born 19 March 1793. Bealsmill(?), Cornwall, married 12 May 1821 to Mary Stephen: born 29 May 1794 Latchley, Cornwall (daughter of William and Grace Stephen) settled in Ivybridge, Devon. Four sons and one daughter.

William Thomas Mason: born 5 January 1824, Ivybridge, Devon (died 6 November 1882, Canada).

John Herbert Mason: born 10 July 1827, Ivybridge, Devon (died 9 December 1911, Toronto, Canada).

Elizabeth Stephen Mason: born 1828, Ivybridge, Devon (died 14 August 1851, Kingston, Canada).

Alfred James Mason: born 1 September 1831, Ivybridge, Devon (died 24 October 1914, Toronto, Canada).

Thomas Gabriel Mason: born 1835, Ivybridge, Devon (died September 1924, Lake Simcoe, Canada).

All sailed from Plymouth on 14 May 1842, arriving in Montreal on 1 July 1842.

Alfred James married Mary A. Newcombe, who was born in Bideford, Cornwall, on 4 June 1835.

John Herbert married Sarah Jane Darracott, whose family came from Plymouth.

The following account of the Masons's voyage across the Atlantic was put together by Susan Woods, a great-great-granddaughter of William Thomas Mason (1824–82), the eldest son of Thomas and Mary (Stephen) Mason.

Atlantic Voyage, 1842

The following is the account of the voyage across the Atlantic by the Thomas Mason family as told by his daughter, Elizabeth Stephen Mason. In transcribing the diary, I have attempted to improve understanding by inserting punctuation and correcting some spelling. While I believe that the words as transcribed are all Elizabeth's, some of them were difficult to decipher. When this was so, I tried to catch her meaning but had to guess on occasion. There is evidence that she, like most of us, sometimes lost her train of thought, and where that happened I have not changed her words.

I have attempted, also, to identify place names, but am only certain about Cape Ray, Anticosti and Cape Breton. I think Cape des Monies is fairly accurate (there is a Pointe des Monts in my atlas) but I can find no trace of the name 'Pellees'. Likewise, the naming of a Mount 'Chad' is doubtful, but I cannot find another name in the area that might be the spot she is referring to. Ditto, her statement on Thursday 22 that they are near 'Feather' Point. That word is really illegible. If a reader has a good local knowledge of the north shore of the lower St Lawrence, I would be grateful for all suggestions!

Elizabeth Mason was 15 years old when she wrote this diary. She drowned tragically in her early 20s at Kingston, Ontario, on 14 August 1851, only nine years after arriving in Canada. She was buried at the Toronto Necropolis on 26 August 1851.

This diary, a wonderful bit of family history, came into my hands through my father, David Mason Woods. It had been given to his mother, Bertha Mason Woods, by her aunt, Bertha Elizabeth Mason, a niece of Elizabeth.

Susan Woods, a great-great granddaughter of William Thomas Mason (1824–82), the eldest son of Thomas and Mary (Stephen) Mason.

Saturday, 14 May 1842
Left Plymouth 7 o'clock in the evening. Mrs. Williams obliged to go to bed immediately, being very sick. I slept tolerably well.

Sunday, 15th
Awoke in the morning early, had a headache and very giddy. Got up about 8 o'clock not at all sick but obliged to lay down in consequence of the headache. Had mutton broth for dinner. After this felt much better. Mother very poorly indeed. In the evening came on deck. Father gave out the hymn, had singing. A Providence Gentleman read John 3rd Chapter and 7th Chapter Romans. After this he gave an exhortation. The meeting concluded with prayer and singing. Took supper and went to bed.

Monday 16th
Another early. Very much better. Mother very poorly. Mrs Williams not been out of bed since Saturday. William and Alonzo did not get up until dinner time. Father, Uncle Iain and Alfred very well. Have beautiful weather and nice breeze and the wind fair. Mrs. Burt with her 3 children have been very jolly. Saw a large porpoise. One ship in sight.

Tuesday 17th
Father poorly in the morning. Got up about dinner time. Mother very poorly. Got up about 2 hours in the evening. Mrs. Burt very well. Herbert and William very unwell. Alonzo made some broth for supper.

Wednesday 18th
Very ill. Mother, Herbert, nor self out of bed for the day. Very rough. Vessel tossed very much. Every female with the exception of Mrs Burt and her cabin passenger Mrs Beard very ill, obliged to be in bed. William partook of some soup and immediately brought it up again. All went to bed early.

Thursday 19th
Did not sleep very well, wind high in the night. Got up early, washed and came on deck. Did not stay long and, being cold, made a plum pudding before breakfast. After this felt much better. Made a good breakfast on fried potatoes, rasher and coffee. Mother got up about 11 o'clock and came on deck. She is much better. Wind favourable and not so high as it was yesterday. Very pleasant on deck. Saw a ship just on the horizon.

Friday 20th
Father poorly. Herbert in bed ill all day with a very sore throat. Mutton chops for dinner. Could not eat any. Wind very high and fair.

Saturday 21st
Very strong weather. Did not sleep 5 minutes for this night the wind being high and contrary, vessel very much on one side and tossed a great deal. Got up about 8 o'clock, breakfasted on cocoa, felt better. Father got up in the morning about 3 o'clock for the sailors were obliged to take down some of the sails. After breakfast I came on deck and saw a ship bound for England. Came so near that we could discern persons on board. Winds being in her favor, her sails were all hoisted and looked very beautiful. Came on deck. It was very cold. Saw scores of porpoises at the stern of the vessel. Some passengers fired at them. Herbert still obliged to keep his bed. Mother rather better while on deck but very sick immediately on going below. Wind contrary and very high.

Sunday 22nd
Did not sleep very night in the night [sic] being very limited as the vessel tossed so much. I got up early had cocoa for breakfast, very much better. Mother better. Herbert still in bed very poorly. Father preached in the afternoon from 50 Psalm and 15th verse. Had a very good meeting singing and prayer. Mr Williams concluded the service. After this, Mr Williams and and all our family took our tea on deck. Very comfortable indeed. In the evening the Providence Gent gave us an exhortation. He was being long and as he said nothing to the purpose it made it rather tedious. He exhorted sinners to come to Christ through faith, never mentioned our repenting and forsaking our sins, that the times of refreshing may come from the presence of the Lord. Very cold in the evening.

Monday 23
Had a very good night. Wind considerably abated and the vessel steady. Had coffee and smoked ham, fried, for breakfast. Mother and Herbert much better. Both came on deck early. Had a beautiful season pudding with boiled potatoes for dinner. Mother made her dinner on mashed potatoes which she took on deck. Very pleasant and the weather much warmer. Commenced making a guard for Herbert. Wind contrary towards the vessel in a different direction. We are now going N.N.E. Mrs.

Williams joined us and all took coffee on deck. Went down about 8 o'clock and discovered that some person had stolen a large piece of smoked ham and about 10 or 11 pounds of dried fish. Captain gave orders the boxes should be searched, but this we did not as Father thought it would be of no service.

Tuesday 24th
Wind very strong and contrary. Rather poorly, did not go on deck until about 10 o'clock. Mother rather better. (This entry in its entirety scratched out)

Tuesday 24th
Very well. Got up took breakfast and made a turnip stew for dinner. Mother still better. Wind squally and contrary.

Wednesday 25th
Very stormy all the night. Got up and made pea soup for dinner which was very nice. Rather poorly in the morning. Mother begged some fish and potatoes for her breakfast which was the first thing that she relished since coming on board. Wind very high all the day. A French vessel came near and spoke to know our longitude.

Thursday 26th
Poorly in the morning. Did not get up until after breakfast and then immediately came on deck where I remained all the day. Mother made a good meal on fish and potatoes. Mrs. Williams much better, comes on deck every day. Winds not so high but contrary. Father very poorly, caught a violent cold.

Friday 27th
Very well. Made a good breakfast and came on deck. We have now been on board one fortnight. Oh, how I long for land. Weather very fine in the afternoon. The wind blew favourable. I trust the Lord will grant us fair wind and weather the last 7 or 8 days. The wind has been contrary so that we have been beating about a great deal. Altho' we have no reason to complain for the Lord has been better than my doubt and fears for he has heard our prayers and hast rebuked the winds and waves when they have been ready to swallow us up. Father still very poorly. Mother better.

Saturday 28th
Very well. Raining in the morning. Had leg of mutton boiled for dinner. Mother much better. Father little better.

Sunday 29th
In the morning 8 o'clock a vessel from Boston America came close to us. Called the Telese and was going to Amsterdam. Laden, with tobacco and sugar she came quite near so that our Captain and theirs conversed for some minutes. The sailors had on red jackets. Had a beautiful plum pudding for dinner with cold mutton. I am thankful to my Heavenly Father that I feel so well and my appetite every day is increasing. In the afternoon my dear father who feels a little better preached from the last Chap. 2nd Peter and the verse – Oh how

Fore Street, Ivybridge, photographed in the early years of the last century.

good it seems to meet together and pray on the mighty deep. In the evening the Providence Gent gave us an exhortation. My thoughts were at Ivy nearly the whole of the day. I could fancy them attending to those means of which I am now deprived. Oh! when I think of the kind friends I have left behind and the many happy hours spent amongst them, strong spirits stir up within me. But I feel comforted when I remember there is a friend who stickest closer than a Brother. I trust the Lord is directing our steps for then I know all things will work together for one good. Mr Williams family and ours took tea again on the deck. The evening very calm in hopes a fair wind which we have not had for days may spring up.

Monday 30th
Got up early and as the morning was beautifully fine, went on the deck before breakfast. A fine breeze and now exactly in our favour. Had a turnip stew for dinner which we enjoyed. Took tea about 6 o'clock and had an excellent appetite. The vessel (although we are going 7 miles an hour) goes quite upright and so steady we can scarcely discern any motion. This being the case it is no wonder we should be so well. Mother has been much better today but is obliged to remain constantly on deck after she gets up until she goes to bed. Mrs Williams is the same but she is sick immediately on coming below and Mother has not been since Saturday. Father's cold worse today.

Tuesday 31st
Weather very calm

Wednesday June 1st
In the morning very calm wind increased towards the afternoon. About 7 o'clock the wind rose so very high that the waves dashed over and one tremendous one came down in our room and frightened us all very much. But to calm our fears Mr Williams agreed for us all to sing Peace, Doubting Heart, after which I felt much more composed. The storm ceased towards night.

Thursday 2nd June
Very damp all day. The sailors went out in a boat to fetch a cap.

Friday 3rd
This is the day which will be remembered by us all. About 3 o'clock P.M. the wind which before was very calm now sprung up very brisk and in a few hours came on to a gale. Waves rolled mountains high and dashed with fearful rapidity over the vessel. Mrs Williams and Mother who went on the deck in the morning did not come below until late. Before the sailors could have time to take down the sails the wind split the jib sail in pieces. Everyone was in bustle and confusion below. We could not sit for the vessel rolled dreadfully and our boxes were dancing in every direction. Mother nor I did not undress for the night. The wind did not cease until Saturday towards 12 o'clock A.M. The Captain nor sailors were in bed for the night and once we all depended the vessel went so much on one side she would never rise again, but the Lord who rides before the storm, shields and calms the roaring seas, heard our prayers and He bid them, Peace be still. It was an awful evening for we did not know whether we would be permitted to see the light of another day. But our God was better to us than our doubts and fears. Fortunately, the wind was in our favour and we were sailing at the rate of 9 knots an hour.

Saturday 4th
In the morning wind still very high and the sea very rough but towards 12 o'clock the wind went down and consequently the sea soon became more calm. Oh Lord as thou hast mercifully preserved us, enable me to dedicate myself afresh to thee. Still continue thy kind providential care toward us. Guide us safe by thy counsel and afterward receive me to glory.

Sunday 5th
This is the 4th spent in this vessel. How different to the Sabbaths spent on shore but as the weather was very fine we are enabled to hold services on deck. In the afternoon Father preached from these words (indescipherable). Mr Williams's family and ours again took coffee on the deck. In the evening Mr Harvey preached but I cannot agree with his views relative to salvation. In fact, he repeatedly contradicted himself and in exhorting sinners to flee from the wrath to come, he tells them simply to believe in Jesus and says there is no such thing required as being sorry for them, past offences repenting, and seeking God with his whole heart. He read the Chapter 5th Acts and the 15 Chap of Corinthians then Mr Williams and father concluded the services of the day with prayer. About 10 o'clock the Captain sounded to discover whether we were on the Banks or not but they find no bottom. However from appearances it is evident we are not far from them.

Monday 6th
Wind rather high in the morning. Mother very poorly indeed, being as usual very sick. Mrs Williams also very poorly. Some say we are now on the Banks but the Captain nor sailors will tell. I trust the Lord will be with us and preserve us. I have no reason to doubt it seeing the deliverances he has wrought out, but might call up my soul to bless and praise his holy name who daily loaded us with benefits.

Tuesday 7
Very fine weather. Was on the deck the whole of the day. Mother better.

Wednesday 8
Surprising to say it is so very cold that no person could stay on the deck. Mother did not get out of bed for the day. Herbert not until the afternoon and then we felt it

so as it was in England one day last winter obliged to take some spirit and water in the evening to warm ourselves and go to bed early.

Thursday 9th
Awoke in the morning early by the sailors telling us there was a large iceberg in sight but as it was so very sharp and cold Mother did not wish me to get up so soon. About 9 o'clock a vessel from Madeira came close and spoke to us. They left there 21 days ago and is laden with wine and fruit. She sailed all round us and was a pleasant sight as they conversed with us some minutes, but she soon left and, as the wind was not favourable, we steered more towards the south. Consequently it was a little warmer.

Friday
Went on the deck before breakfast to see an iceberg which we could with the assistance of a spy glass very distinctly, but it was not so large as the one on Thursday. As the wind continued contrary until 4 o'clock we steered in another direction and all the day it was beautifully warm. Fair wind in the evening so the men turned the vessel. We have been off the Banks the past few days and shall pass them without going on them very much. Hundreds of porpoises passed us.

Saturday
Very cold attended with rain and sleet. I can scarcely fancy it is now June for we do not know what to do to keep ourselves warm. It is very foggy. We are now on but nearly at the end of the Banks. Mother and Mrs Williams went on the deck but was soon obliged to come down. It is now 4 weeks today we left our native land and how many more we shall spend here God only knows but we are all longing to come safe to land but we must be thankful to our Heavenly Father that although the winds have not been very favourable yet the weather has only once been tempestuous.

Sunday 12
Last night being on the Banks, Iain and Alonzo stayed aft until late fishing but they with the rest were unsuccessful. In the morning it was very wet and foggy. Wind directly aft and so it continued all the day. In the afternoon we had service below the deck and all found it good to unite in Prayer and Praise to our Heavenly Father. About 6 o'clock while we were all comfortable and quiet below we were dreadfully alarmed by hearing a tremendous crash which was occasioned by the wind instantaneously turning and broke the yard arm or stern sails in pieces and some went in the sea. Had the men not been in attendance directly the poop would soon have gone under water, but our Heavenly Father did not suffer a hair on our head to be injured. Mother not out of bed for the day.

Monday 13
Awoke in the morning early by the sailors calling on

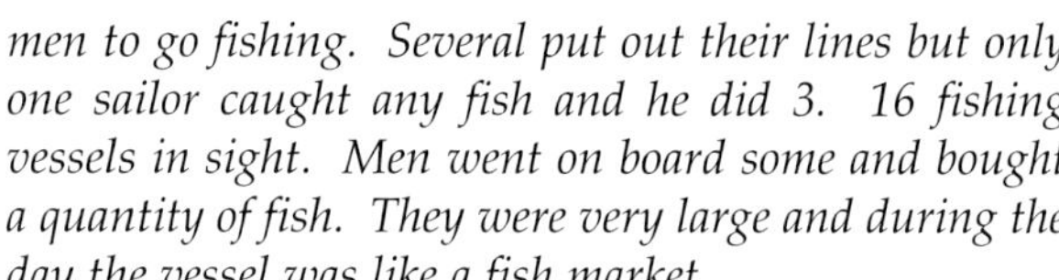

men to go fishing. Several put out their lines but only one sailor caught any fish and he did 3. 16 fishing vessels in sight. Men went on board some and bought a quantity of fish. They were very large and during the day the vessel was like a fish market.

Tuesday
Beautifully calm, wind contrary. In the evening dead calm commenced. A small bird was caught on the vessel and it is quite exhausted. Mother's sore throat a little better. We enjoyed deliciously Newfoundland Banks fish. They really are delicious. In the evening two sailors took a boat and went out for a cap which fell overboard.

Wednesday
A most delightful morning as can be imagined. Not a ripple on the water, the sun shone delightfully. The Captain and a few others sailed some distance in an open boat. A large number of black fish passed us. In the afternoon a line of porpoises, which the vessel divided, passed us. Mother better, came on deck a little while.

Thursday
Very wet all day and foggy. Mother renewed cold yesterday. She has not been out of bed for the day.

Friday 17th
Wind favourable with a very heavy fog all the day. Captain rather uneasy thinking we are near land and, owing to the dense fog, has not been able to make his observation on the sun at 12 o'clock.

Saturday 18th
Winds directly behind us but still very foggy. About 4 o'clock P.M. we were all delighted and surprised to hear the Captain call out 'Land'. They had been keeping a sharp lookout last night and had all the day, but the fog was so dense sometimes we could scarcely see $^1/_2$ mile off. The Captain, prior to his discovery, was very uneasy but we were about 3 miles from Cape Ray. At first it appeared like a cloud but gradually the fog diminished and we discovered the mountains with a great quantity of snow upon them. This is the first land we have seen since we left England and Oh how were our hearts cheered at the sight.

Sunday 19th
Wind very favourable but still very foggy. Saw Anticosti and Cape Breton. We are now looking with pleasure to see Quebec in the early part of the week. Had service below in the afternoon and on the poop in the evening, but it was very cold.

Monday 20th
Wind changed it being now against us. We are opposite Seven Islands.

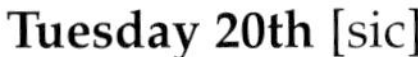

Tuesday 20th [sic]
Wind still against us. We are obliged to be constantly tacking the vessel but toward evening the wind changed more in our favour. About 10 o'clock a pretty little boat with a pilot came close and we took the pilot. Soon after another came near but the Captain soon let them know we were provided.

Wednesday 21
A beautiful day but the wind against us. Obliged to be tacking the vessel every 2 or 3 hours. It is beautiful now on the deck. In the afternoon we were opposite to a vessel wrecked a short time ago called Jane Black. In the evening about sunset we were directly opposite the lighthouse and a little hut at the point of Cape Des Monte Pellets [?]. The sunset was beautiful such as I never saw in England. The mountain I think were the Highlands of Mount Chad [?], were very high and the tops covered with snow. We could see the green trees very plain. There were upwards of 1/2 doze vessels constantly tacking with us. One, the May of Newcastle, came so close that we could discern the passengers with the naked eye but with the assistance of a glass could see them very plain and Oh what wretched looking people. The vessel appeared to be crammed and there was a bag to let down air in the steerage. In the night about 10 o'clock ours was one of 6 vessels that were sailing all together and the wind was favourable.

Thursday 22
A beautiful day but the wind against. We are now opposite a wide Canal near Feather [?] Point and can see a village, farms cleared out in the forest. We can see the sheep walking on the beach.

Sunday 26
Arrived at the Quarantine ground, 1 P.M.

Monday 27
Left it.

Tuesday 28
At Quebec.

Wednesday 29
Left for Montreal.

Friday July 1
Arrived at Montreal.

Elizabeth's Drowning

The following are excerpts taken from two newspaper accounts of the tragic accident that claimed the life of Elizabeth Mason, age 23, daughter of the late Thomas Mason and his wife, Mary. It is not known why Elizabeth was in Kingston. Probably she was visiting friends and had accompanied them on this pleasure jaunt. The accounts of this tragedy provide a glimpse of the style of newspaper writing then practised and, presumably, admired. From the Globe, Tuesday, August 19, 1851:

The Catastrophe at Kingston

Seldom has it been the task of a journalist to record a more distressing incident than the fatal catastrophe briefly announced on Saturday. The death of one person by ordinary sickness creates a blank in many a social circle, and when it comes suddenly and unexpectedly it makes an impression for the moment among the associates of the deceased which nothing else can provide. What then must have been the deep heart-rending feeling in Kingston when the fact was realized that nineteen citizens, known to everybody, and endeared to hundreds by all the ties which bind human beings together – who but a few hours before had left the city buoyant with life and the expectation of pleasure – had in one brief moment been plunged into eternity. Gone – dead – no more to be seen on earth. Let the mind wander in imagination to the dwellings of these nineteen persons and fancy the hopes, the attachments, the affections crushed in a moment by the fatal blow. Think of the high anticipations of pleasure formed days before the event from the promised expedition – think of those who intended to have been of the party but were detained by the inscrutable hand of Providence; of the hasty partings of those who went to return no more; of the instructions left for the day and the preparations for the undoubted return in the evening; of the engagements for the morrow and the next day and the next. Strange that we can hear of such events without a pang – because the scene of misery is a few miles distant! Still more strange that we can banish the thought that the fate of others today may be ours tomorrow.

The Kingston papers furnish but meagre particulars as yet of the sad occurrence. We gather that a pleasure excursion had been made up as a trial trip of a new yacht built by Mr D.B. Jenkins of Kingston for the approaching Regatta, and that the party was composed of thirty-four persons, including fifteen ladies. The Argus *says everything went well until the vessel got within a mile or two of French Creek and about three-quarters of a mile from the shore, when the wind, being light, and the yacht carrying full sail, a sudden flaw of wind struck her and brought her nearly on her beam ends. The little deck being crowded, the unfortunate passengers were all propelled towards the lower side, which completed in a moment what the wind had done, and down she went. The females, rushing to the lower side of the vessel for the most part, plunged into the water and disappeared.*

The Herald *says the screams of the drowning were terrific and shrilling. Friend clung to friend in fatal embrace and sunk together. The water was not very deep where the boat capsized and to this circumstance, under God, is to be attributed the preservation of those saved. A part of the mast remaining above the water, those fifteen clung to and were rescued from their perilous position by boats from the Islands.*

The Whig *says that eight bodies have been recovered (besides four previously), namely: Mr H.A. Mills, Mrs Gaskin, Mrs Olden (Wife of Captain Olden of the bark* Ontario*) and young Olden, the two Misses Height, Mrs Jenkins and Miss Mason (from Toronto). The remains were all carried to the late homes of the deceased through a dense crowd of sympathizers. An inquiry was held on the bodies of Miss Mary Olden and Master Edward Probe and some evidence taken but an adjournment was had to Monday (yesterday) morning. The names of the parties in the yacht were as follows:*

Drowned
Miss Stacey, Miss Mills, Miss Hunter, Miss Olden, Mrs Jenkins, Miss Jenkins, Mrs Olden, Thomas Grist, Mrs Gaskin, Miss Mason, Mr Thorne, Master Olden, May Anne Probe, Edward Probe, 2 Misses Height, Mr H.A. Mills, Mrs George Hunter, Miss Walker

Nineteen in all

Saved
D.B. Jenkins, W.M. Lecky, James Wilson, Thos Height, H.O. Hitchcock, David McCollum, Charles Mills, Charles Mackenzie, Geo. Hunter, Alexander Phillips, Jack O'Hair, Master Scott, H. Johnson (collared), Edward Height, W.M. Jenkins

Fifteen

The Argus *mentions that Mr Phillips (who was saved), on seeing that the vessel was sinking, struck out for the shore; but being impeded by his clothing which was saturated with water and perceiving that the mast of the vessel still remained above water returned to it and with the greatest exertion, regained the wreck. On approaching it he saw a number of passengers hanging on and he mentions that just as he made way to get hold of the boom young Grist was hanging on a portion of it seemingly exhausted but shortly fainted for fell off from exhaustion and disappeared in the dark waves. Mr George Hunter rescued Mrs Hunter and got her into the skiff which was attached to the yacht but being chained to the other it was dragged down along with it.*

From the *Kingston Whig*:

The Late Sad Accident

Verdict of the Coroner's Jury:
'That the deceased, Edward Probe and Mary Olden, came to their death by drowning caused by the foundering of the boat Jeannette *on the 14th. August instant on which they were aboard and the Jury further of the opinion consequently that yachts of the description of the* Jeannette *are unfit for pleasure excursions.'*

There was but little discrepancy in the evidence, a great many witnesses were examined but the public will be satisfied with the record of the testimony of four only. Henry Johnson, sworn, was a musician on board the sailing boat Jeannette *on 14 August, left Kingston 1/4 past ten o'clock. Hiram Hitchcock was the Sailing Master. There were about thirty ladies and gentlemen on board. Among others was a little boy named Probe and a young woman named Olden.*

There was 15 to 20 minutes between the capsizing of the boat and the arrival of rescue boats. Mr Hitchcock had management of the boat at the time of the accident.

There were two sails, the mainsail and jib which were too large in the opinion of some. The persons on board the boat were sober. None swam ashore. Mr Hitchcock is not much acquainted with the sailing of boats. At the time of the accident the boat was sailing with a free sheet and took the wind abeam from the south channel of the St Lawrence. When the shore of Long Island was left the wind coming strongly down the river struck the vessel abeam and before her head could be got round the vessel capsized. Could the mainsail have been lowered in time the vessel would have righted.

[Bodies] *were brought up to Kingston in the United States Steamer* Niagara *and witnesses helped to bring the body of the boy to his home. Remained on the shore at the foot of Long Island till the steamer arrived. It was quite dark at the time.*

Some thought the Jeannette *over sailed, over loaded. Some others thought that she was properly misted and sparred. Boat* Prince of Wales *next morning recovered bodies. Picked up four bodies under the lee bow of the vessel.*

The loss of life was occasioned by the confusion caused by the number of women on board and their crowding together.

Weather was fine and not too rough. Attributed to the women being scared and rendering the men unable to manage her.

Raleigh of Fardel

Fardel was a Saxon Estate and a Domesday Manor. It came to the Raleighs c.1310. It is generally thought that the great Sir Walter was born at Fardel, but in fact he was born at Hayes Barton in the parish of East Budleigh on the Devon/Dorset border. Why his mother travelled so far to have her baby is a mystery, but there is no doubt that she was a remarkable lady.

Born Katherine Champernowne of Modbury and Dartington Hall, her family fought with the Royalists during the Civil War and were defeated at the Battle of Modbury by the Devonshire Clubmen. Katherine first married a Gilbert of the family of Gilbert of Compton Castle, but she and her family lived at Greenaway on the Dart below Totnes. She was the mother of Adrian and Sir Humphrey Gilbert. On the death of her husband she married Walter Raleigh of

Fardel, by whom she had the great genius Sir Walter Raleigh. Professor Hoskins wrote: 'I should like to have seen a portrait of this very remarkable woman and to have known more about her.'

After the death of Queen Elizabeth Raleigh fell foul of King James and was a prisoner in the Tower for 13 years, when he wrote *A History of the World*. He persuaded James to set him free from Eldorado, the city of gold. He failed and on his return was again in the Tower with a day fixed for his execution. We might ponder on how we would spend our last day on earth, when we knew we were to die for certain the next day. Sir Walter occupied himself by writing a poem which he called 'My Pilgrimage', in which he described his journey into Heaven. The poem ends:

And since my flesh must die so soon
And want a head to dine next noon.,
Just at the stroke when my veins start to spread
Set on my soul an everlasting head
Then I am ready like a Palmer fit,
To tread those blessed paths, which before I writ.

Stan Rogers Remembered

In 1928 Plymouth Corporation had a boat moored off Plymouth Sound for smallpox cases. This boat was sitting in a poor state of repair and in this year they bought the land from David Abbot's grandfather to build a hospital. They needed something out in the country and this was ideal, as Lee Mill Estate and the bungalows along the road weren't there. Scott Hospital was there and taking patients with diphtheria and other diseases.

I don't know when Didworthy started but they took all the TB patients, some of the nurses came to work at Lee Mill when Didworthy closed in the early '60s.

When Burrator reservoir was built they had some wooden huts which the workman lived in whilst they were raising the level of the land around the reservoir. The huts where bought and re-erected at Lee Mill as wards, etc., and the hospital opened for smallpox victims in 1934.

There were also some tin buildings in the field behind the mortuary these were used by Plympton Hospital for their smallpox cases. In 1948 the government merged the Plympton and Plymouth hospitals together and Stan took over the tin huts to put his tools in. I can remember the old wooden building and also Stan's tin workshops when I started in March 1974.

Stan and Mrs Rogers started to work at Lee Mill in 1946, he as caretaker, gardener and handyman and Mrs Rogers in the kitchens. They both got smallpox, Mrs Rogers three times, although they were both inoculated. Poor Stan had the awful job of burning all the dressings.

Lee Mill staff on holiday at Bigbury on Sea, 1950.

Scenes at Lee Mill Hospital

Lee Mill Hospital in 1948.

Hunt visit to Lee Mill Hospital.

The tin huts used by Plympton Hospital, 1949.

Bet and Stan Moor, 1998. They both contracted small-pox while working as housekeeper and gardener at Lee Mill Hospital.

Above and left: *Nurses at Lee Mill Hospital.*

Scenes at Lee Mill Hospital

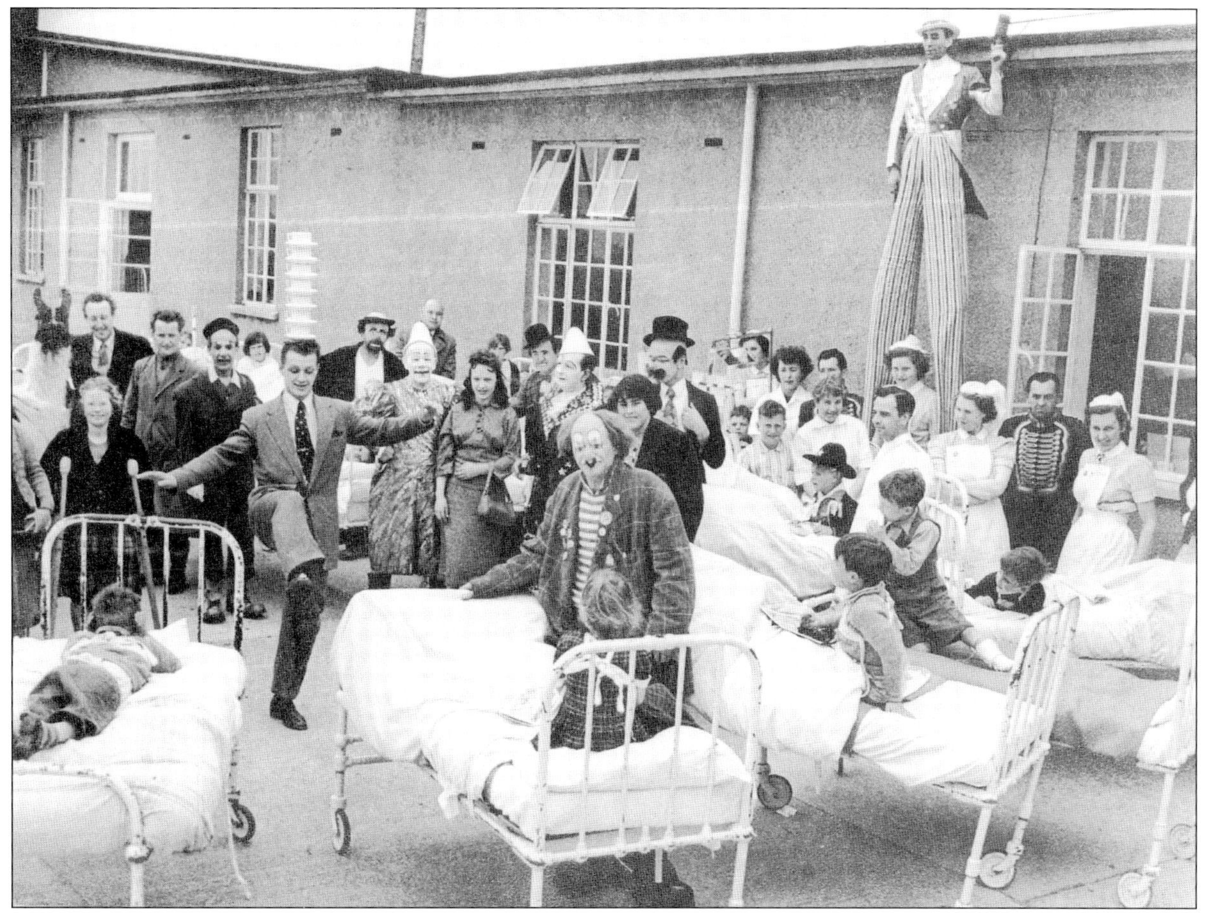

Above and below: *Chipperfield's Circus entertain patients at Lee Mill in 1954.*

Lee Mill staff pose for a farewell photograph.

Lee Mill hospital reunion.

The block building which we knew as the wards were erected in 1939. Freedom Fields maternity ward was hit by a bomb and I think three were killed. So a building was erected at Lee Mill to evacuate the patients if need be. I've never heard of it being used as a maternity unit but I know Flete House at Ermington was used.

I'm a little unsure what was happening in the way of nursing if there weren't any smallpox victims about. I do remember being told at my interview that we were still on standby or if a patient came through the gates we would have to stay for a long period until the all-clear with the smallpox.

The children came out from Mount Gould in 1950 and it was then an orthopaedic hospital. Sister Geach spent a few months of her training and she said that the nurses home was up the west wing. The main building and west wing were joined in the early '70s by the corridor, before that the nurses had to go outside in all weathers and one nurse spent all night up there on her own.

There were also children with polio at Lee Mill, but I think they took them with broken bones as well.

We put the year of 1961 when it went over to the elderly. No one seems quite sure about this.

Stan put in all the shrubs in the grounds and helped build up the wall on the roadside. He grew vegetables on what we remember as the front lawn and also on the verge on the right-hand side of the driveway. He had quite a market garden.

When Stan first arrived at the hospital they lived in the bungalow that our patients used as a day room. I can remember Sister Rogers using it as her own little pad to entertain the doctors, etc. A Mr and Mrs Gillard lived in the bungalow down the driveway and when they moved Stan and Mrs Rogers went down there to live. John and Daphne Willis lived there after the Rogers and then Sister Gheers had it.

Henlake Down Racecourse, 1786–96

In the summer of 1786 Sir Frederick Leman Rogers, 5th baronet, built a racecourse on Henlake Down, his property by reason of its being a part of the manor of Ivybridge. As a young man he had found pleasure in attending race meetings. His journal, written during his tour of England and Scotland, which took up most the year 1766 when he was 21, contains several passages recording how he and his friends had been content to rest for a few days wherever there happened to be a meeting within easy reach. Sir Frederick's enthusiasm for the sport shows no sign of going beyond the interest every country gentleman was bound to have in horses and the necessity to cultivate a discerning eye for performance. At no time in the history of the Rogers family, spread over six generations, is there any suggestion that any one of them was a gambler. It is true that, once or twice, Sir Frederick paid about £12 for a ticket on the national lottery, but the heaviest loss recorded in the journals kept by the baronets of the 18th century is 5s., lost at whist after dinner at Blachford.

In the 1784 parliamentary elections at Plymouth Sir Frederick declined to stand. He had been a member of Parliament since 1780, but now, after four years of proclaiming his independence from strict party allegiance, his political conscience would not allow him to accept nomination. So there was now more time for him to spend with his family at Blachford or at his fine Wotton estate at Stoke Gabriel, and perhaps to think up ways of improving the lot of his somewhat run down manor of Ivybridge. In 1785 plans to build a chapel at Ivybridge had reached the contract stage. The following year Sir Frederick's enterprising mind turned towards a more worldly innovation.

Very little has been known about the Henlake Down racecourse. Messrs Pode of Slade, in their *Notes on Cornwood*, written in 1918, tell of public races once held on Henlake Down in the years 1794 and 1795 at which the squires of Slade and Blachford won silver cups. They say that at the time of their writing the foundations of the judges' stand were distinctly visible. They also felt confident to say that Cornwood people, and others, approached the course by way of Hanger Down and Fourteen Stone Lane, the short stone-hedged lane leading from Hanger Down to Henlake Down. How this information came to Messrs Pode is not revealed, but it would almost certainly come from the family archives relating to their possession of Slade. The Old Series Ordnance Survey map of Devon, surveyed in the first decade of the nineteenth century by William Mudge, has 'Racecouse' named near the summit of Henlake Down, this recognition of its existence being repeated in 1819 by a small unnamed building marked there by James Green on his map of the Exeter to Plymouth turnpike. The information which follows has been uncovered in a search of the Blachford archives relating to Sir Frederick.

The first document of record is 'An Account of the time Mr Greenslade's men were to Labour on Henlake Down a Making the course or racing from June 27th to July 25th 1786'.

June 27–July 1	*38 days' work*	
(Wm Maddock and Mr Hillson @ 1s.9d. a day, others @ 1s.2d. a day)		
July 1–July 8	*452 days*	*£2.6s.4½d.*
July 8–July 15	*31 days*	*£2.16s.3½d.*
July 15–July 22	*76 days*	*£4.14s.9d.*
July 22–July 25	*25 days*	*£1.10s.4d.*
		£13.8s.7d.

paid by Samuel to Wm Maddock

Races were run on the last day of work on the course. Sir Frederick's journal for Tuesday, 25 July 1786, records: 'Spitfire won the Henlake Down Goblet' and that he had paid £5.5s. subscription to Henlake.

Sir Frederick's journal for 1786 also records that on Tuesday, 6 June there were 'Cornwood Races. 20 people at dinner.' It is not understood what is meant by 'Cornwood Races'. The second sentence clearly illustrates Sir Frederick's pleasure in taking part in these sporting events.

In 1787 there is another account for work done on Henlake Down. On 12 and 13 April three men were paid 5s. for 'pulling down the old building' on the first day, and three men for one day's work on the second day, for which they paid 7s.6d. 'To making a mould to set out the building' cost 3s. Other work brought the total cost of the building, with windows, water-closets, etc., to £60.8s.10d. On 20 October in the same year Sir Frederick 'Gave Will Vivian carpenter, in full for Henlake House £1.2s.8d.

Journals for subsequent years show that interest in the venture stayed high enough for the meetings to be held annually for ten years, up to the year of Sir Frederick's death, which was in 1797.

1788 Monday, 12 May	*Henlake Races. Carety won ye Cup.*
1789 Monday, 1 June	*Henlake Cup won by Mr Chappell.*
1790 Monday, 24 May	*Henlake Races. Mr Knighton won ye Bowl.*
1791 Monday, 13 June	*Henlake Races.*
1792 Tuesday, 5 June	*Henlake Races. Mr Kelly won*
Wednesday, 6 June	*Henlake Races.*
1793 Monday, 20 May	*Foster for Henlake course. Cup for last year to Jefferys £13.13s.*
Monday, 17 June	*Henlake Races. Cup won by Mr Worthington.*
1794 Tuesday, 15 July	*Henlake Races. Self steward.*
1796 Tuesday, 5 July	*Henlake Down Races.*

Lord Clinton won ye Cup and gave it to Rivers.

This is not a complete list of entries in the journals, but they are typical. The winner of the cup in the last year of the races, Lord Clinton, was the 17th Baron Clinton of Trefusis in Cornwall and of Heanton Satchville in North Devon. Being a Trefusis he was probably closely related to Sir Frederick's late aunt, Dame Hannah Rogers. Sir Frederick had visited the Trefusis estate near Falmouth on his tour in 1766. Both Lord Clinton and Sir Frederick died in the following year.

Mr Henry Rivers at the London Inn appears to have been the administrator for the meetings. Subscriptions were paid to him at the inn; in 1789 there were 36 persons paying a total of £28.14s.6d. Mr Rivers then rendered his account to Sir Frederick:

Mr Rivers for Advertisements	*£1.10s.6d.*
Buckskin breeches	*£1.7s.0d.*
Sadler's bill's bridle & saddle	*2.4s.0d.*
Holland shift	*10s.6d.*
Carriage of 2 Cups from London last year and this year	*17s.3d.*
Picking the Stones from the Course and levelling the Hoals	*£1.3s.6d.*
Drummer	*5s.0d.*
Collecting at the Door	*2s.0d.*
Lent to Mr Knighton to give Chaing	*3s.6d.*
Total	*£8.2s.9d.*

This left a comfortable balance of £20.11s.9d. for the purchase of trophies.

Mr Knighton appears as steward for a part of the time. In 1789 he was at the London Inn making a list of the names of eight horses, with their measurements in hands and inches, entered to run in a race on 30 May, the prize to be 'a Bowl of 21 pounds'. Sir Frederick had in fact bought two bowls worth £21 each, with inscriptions, from a jeweller named Greenhill of the Strand, London. In 1790 Sir Frederick paid a bill of £42.7s.6, which covered the cost and 2s. for boxes, clearing or leaving a balance of 5s.6d. It seems that each year the cup remained the property of the winner.

The subscribers in 1792 and their payments are listed below, also the account of expenses for the year. We may wonder who wore the buckskin breeches and shift. In 1794 a list of subscribers paying to Mr Rivers has only eight names contributing £13.2s.6d. Sir Frederick paid his usual £5.5s., Mr Pode (of Slade) £2.2s., Mr Dunsterville (of Stowford) £2.12s.6d. and five others. There is no knowing if this is a complete list of subscribers for the year.

There is no record of a meeting in 1797. In June of that year Sir Frederick set out on a journey to Bath. On the way he was taken ill and died, either in his coach or in a house at the roadside, on 21st of the month. He was brought back to Cornwood for burial in the family grave.

There is little likelihood of further information on the Henlake Down races coming to light. The only possible source may be the Rivers family archives, wherever they may be held. When one walks over Henlake Down at the end of the twentieth century, it takes quite a lot of imagination to visualise a racecourse there. Can the site of the judges' stand be detected? Like other ventures into race meetings around Ivybridge – on Ugborough Moor near Hanger-shell Rocks, or the point-to-point meetings at Wrangaton attended once by the then Prince of Wales (later King Edward VIII) – there is little to be told beyond knowledge of their actual existence.

Mr Henry Rivers's Account for Henlake Down Races, June 1792.

Subscriptions paid to Henry Rivers

Sir F.L. Rogers	*£5.5s.0d.*
Stapleton, esq.	*£1.1s.0d.*
Wm Clark, esq.	*£2.2s.0d.*
C. Hague, esq	*10s.6d.*
Lt Bickford	*10s.6d.*
Mr Watts	*5s.0d.*
John Kelly, esq.	*10s.6d.*
Lang, esq.	*10s.6d.*
J.P. Carpenter	*£1.1s.0d.*
B. Dunsterville	*10s.6d.*
Lt Brown Navy	*10s.6d.*
Mr Saunders	*10s.6d.*
Mr John Longmead	*10s.6d.*
Revd Mr Fortescue	*10s.6d.*
John Lapens, esq.	*10s.6d.*
John Pode, esq.	*£1.1s.0d.*
John Crode, esq	*10s.6d.*
Westropp	*10s.6d.*
Cornvile Hunt	*10s.6d.*
Capt. Shuttlevorth	*10s.6d.*
Mr Julian	*10s.6d.*
Richard Freeman, esq.	*10s.6d.*
Mr Chappel	*5s.0d.*
Mr Bateman	*5s.0d.*
Mr Mills	*5s.0d.*
Mr G.C. Skinner	*5s.0d.*
Perring	*5s.0d.*
	£20.19s.6d.

Cash paid by Mr Rivers

Saddle Furniture	*£2.12s.6d.*
Pair of Buckskin Breeches	*£1.7s.0d.*
A. Shift	*10s.6d.*
Advertisements	*7s.0d.*
Clearing the Course	*5s.0d.*
Cash given a drummer	*5s.0d.*
Cash given to Sir F. Rogers to Purchase a Bowl	*£15.12s.0d.*
	£20.19s.0d.

Note: It was in fact Sir Frederick, 4th baronet, who bought the lottery ticket in 1776, the year before he died.

The information on Lord Clinton's title comes from the Presidential Address given by Lord Clinton, 22nd Baron, to the Devon Association in 1995 (*TDA* 1995, vol. 127).

Ivybridge Corn Mills, 1322–1976

Early References to the Mills

Documentary evidence dating from the sixteenth century to the early years of the twentieth century shows that for more than 400 years there were water-driven corn mills working in Ivybridge on the site which only relatively recently has become known as Glanville's Mills.

In the sixteenth century the manor of Ivybridge was held by the Bonvile (Bonville) family. The mansion house and most of the land were on the west side of the River Erme in Ermington parish, but the manor also held land nearby in the parishes of Cornwood and Harford. In October 1522 Humfrey Bonvile, lord of the manor, leased a house he owned in Stowford, Harford parish, to William Cannycote and his wife, one condition being that Cannycote would grind all corn for his own use at the mills at Ivybridge. In the following January, Humfrey leased another house at Stowford to Henry Withycombe with the same condition regarding the grinding of corn at Ivybridge Mills. These are the earliest known references to the Ivybridge corn mills.

A document held in the Blachford archives concerning a lease of land at Lukesland in Harford reveals that there had been a corn mill at Stowford as far back as the thirteenth century, the miller being William Godrich. One may doubt whether the population of Ivybridge and Harford in the thirteenth and fourteenth centuries could have sustained two mills. As far as the present writer is aware, Stowford mill does not reappear until the eighteenth century. It may be that after William Godrich, Stowford mill was turned to other uses, leaving the way clear for the lords of Ivybridge to establish their corn mills lower down the River Erme.

On Humfrey Bonvile's death in or about 1576, Ivybridge manor passed by gift to his younger son, John. The indenture dated 18 April 1576, confirming the family's consent to this inheritance, states that the manor had two corn mills and one blade-mill. The corn mills were probably for grinding wheat and barley; the blade-mill appears in later documents as an 'edge-mill', which would be known now as an 'edge-tool mill'.

John Bonvile died in 1588. The inquisition post mortem taken at Modbury by the escheator George Fortescue declares John's daughter Agnes to be his heir, and states that in Ivybridge there are three grain mills and one edge-mill. This may mean that a malt-mill had recently been added to the wheat and barley mills, a probability supported by later references to the three mills.

Agnes Bonvile died in 1622 and her heir was John Crocker, the eldest son by her first marriage. Being 'deeply endebted to divers persons for great sums of money', John Crocker sold Ivybridge in 1628 to Robert Trelawney, a merchant of Plymouth who became mayor of the borough in 1636. The price paid was £2,010, but after he had taken possession Trelawney complained that he had been overcharged and that amongst other discrepancies the mills, valued at £16 by the year, were found to be 'not worth above £12 by the year'. Crocker countered by saying that as the valuation had been carried out by a relative of Trelawney's and another he could see no justification for the complaint. No record has been found of the case being brought to court.

About the year 1620 Agnes Fountayn, as she then was, and John Crocker, her son, had granted permission for William Hunwill, a local fuller, to build a tucking-mill 'on the North part of a parcel of land neare unto the Leat or Water there that runneth and descendeth from the Mill there called Ivybridge Mills'. The fuller was allowed to use water from the leat but: '... leaving; therewith standing always sufficient water there in the Ancient Mill leat to run and descend to the Grist Mills there near adjoining called Ivy bridge Mills.

The draft agreement, dated 1 January 1621, then goes on to explain how a little timber bridge across the leat is to give access to the tucking-mill from the highway, to pass a 'Shoppe' (smithy) then held by Andrew Blaze, who also owned the meadow (Blaze's Meadow), about two acres, on the south side of the highway. No other mention of the tucking-mill appears in the archives, but the term of the lease is the lifetime of William Hunwill and his wife Joan, with remainder to their son Robert for his lifetime. William died in 1625 and his son Robert in 1642, so it seems that no successor was found to continue the business.

During the time of the Commonwealth John Drake was lord of Ivybridge. This was by reason of his marriage to Prudence Williams of Ivybridge, whose uncle, Thomas Williams, had bought the manor from Robert Trelawney. In 1655 John Drake granted a lease to Sarah Welch, widow of Christopher Welch, of a quillet of land in Ivybridge Woods, where, long before, Christopher had built a house, the quillet 'lying and adjoining to the highway there that leadeth from Ivybridge towards Woodland on the west side over against the headweir of the mill leat there'. Sarah also took on lease the common ground lying between the quillet and the bridge called Ivybridge. This clearly defines the course of the mill leat from the headweir, which still exists, with a short part of the leat alongside Erme Road in Ivybridge. In the late-seventeenth century and throughout the eighteenth, tenants with leaseholds in the vicinity of the mill were obliged as part of their manorial services to give one day a year 'to cleansing and ridding' the mill leat, or pay usually about six pence in lieu.

The Millers at Ivybridge Mills, 1691–1785

On John Drake's death in the early 1680s his son William inherited the manor. Within ten years misfortune of some kind overcame him and in 1691 he appears to have realised that he would have to sell. Later events suggest that he may have become incapable of managing his affairs. A survey carried out in 1691 placed a value of £26 a year on the mills, naming the miller as John Hele, but early in 1692 John Olliver, a miller, was granted a two year lease at a rent of £15 a year. In the spring of that year the manor was sold to John Rogers, a merchant of Plymouth, whose seat was at Wisdom in Cornwood.

On taking possession John Rogers made a new survey of his recently acquired estate. He valued the mills at £474, with a yearly rental value of £26.3s.4d. John Olliver was allowed to stay on at £15 a year, which he was still paying in 1697.

John Rogers blessed his son John's marriage in 1698 by making over to him the beneficial interest in the manors of Ivybridge and Blachford and other properties in Plymouth. The settlement gave John the younger the power to grant leases, which, with regard to Ivybridge Mills, he did with a degree of eccentricity if not always with success. In March 1700 (new style calendar) Arthur Edgcombe, a Cornwood mill wright, was granted a lease for seven years at a yearly rent of £12. He was to repair all the millstones when necessary, but John Rogers would maintain the walls and roofs (helliers) and replace when necessary the barley mill runner. John Rogers would also pay 20s. a year for Edgcombe to keep a dog or bitch for John Rogers's pleasure. The indenture says there were three mills: wheat, barley and malt.

Before he could settle into the mills Arthur Edgcombe died. John Rogers found another miller, John Fox of Ugborough, willing to take a lease for seven years from 20 September 1700 at a yearly rent of £13.15s. Otherwise the terms and conditions were much the same as with Edgcombe, except that John Rogers did not pay anything for the maintenance of the dog.

Again the tenancy was short lived, with John Foy surviving less than four of his seven-year term. In the summer of 1704 John Rogers signed articles of agreement with Walter Hannaford, a miller of Holbeton, for a 99-year lease on three lives at a yearly rent of 20s., the lessee to pay a consideration on entry of £100 in two instalments. The lessee would also do suit and service to the courts of Ivybridge manor, and keep a dog for John Rogers's pleasure. All this proved too much for Walter Hannaford; the unsigned indenture of lease is endorsed 'Void not being able to get on with the bargain'.

Failing to find a local miller to take on his mills, John Rogers looked elsewhere. On 25 July 1705 Thomas Alford of Newton St Patrick in North Devon signed a lease for the 'three greist mills called Ivybridge Mills' for a term of 99 years on three lives at the yearly rent of 20s. He would pay £100 on entry, would do suit to the courts of Ivybridge and would keep a dog for John Rogers's use. But Alford could not fulfil the conditions of the lease and on 21 February 1707 (old-style calendar) John Rogers paid him £3 'to surrender the lease and clear out'.

A local man now came forward to work the mills. Richard Chambern, a miller of Ermington, signed a lease on 5 March 1707 (old-style calendar) on the same terms and conditions as Alford's except that the consideration of £100 should be spread over ten years. He also covenanted not to lease or rent another corn mill within 20 miles of Ivybridge whilst he remained the miller at Ivybridge. This tenancy was to last until after Richard Chambern died in 1731 or 1732, leaving his wife Jane in possession.

Mrs Chambern stayed on at the mills for about four years after her husband's death. The marriage had produced four daughters but apparently no sons (Ermington parish registers), and it probably became increasingly difficult for her to carry on the business. On 8 January 1736 she surrendered all her rights to the lease, and on the following day John Tabb of Cornwood, a carpenter who had paid the quarter's rent due the previous Christmas, having 'procured Jane Chambern, widow, of Ermington to surrender her rights etc. to the millhouse and mills to Sir John Rogers', was granted a lease for a term of 99 years dependent on his life and that of:

> *... Jane his now Wife'. The yearly rent remains at Twenty shillings and John Tabb is to keep the dog. He is to repair the mills and keep them in good repair, and he further covenants not to lease or rent another mill within twenty miles of Ivybridge.*

John Tabb came from a family of millers. James Tabb was a miller at Cornwood between 1718 and 1740; Sampson Tabb, a miller from Modbury, had moved to Yeo Mills at Wisdom in 1691. Since Ivybridge Mills seem to have been in need of repair when Mrs Chambern gave up, John Tabb, with his skills as a carpenter and his mill background, gave promise of being an ideal tenant.

Ivybridge Mills were occupied by the Tabbs for 50 years. It was probably their son John who married Mary Macy of Woolborough at Ermington church in 1770, but it was John Tabb the lessee and his wife whom Christopher Savery, the Rogers's steward, in November 1784 tried to oust from the millhouse. A Mr Hellier had already indicated that he was willing to take on the mills, make some alterations and do some repairs. John Tabb at first refused to quit, and it was not until 5 September 1785 that Mr Hellier's lease was executed on payment of £20 consideration. He had already cut down some timber on Rogers's property (without leave, apparently), and had arranged for Mr Bent, the local builder who was shortly to begin building the chapel at Ivybridge, to start work on alterations to the mills.

Some time before April 1786 John Tabb died. Mr Savery had then to inform Sir Frederick Rogers that Mrs Tabb, the widow, refused to leave Ivybridge Barton house, where she and her late husband had been allowed to remain for a little while until they could find other accommodation. It had been reported to Mr Savery, incorrectly as it turned out, that Mr Bulteel, lord of Ermington, who was also chief lord of the fee of Ivybridge manor, had encouraged Mrs Tabb to stay.

The Plymouth Dock Co.

Relatively few Ivybridge title deeds of the nineteenth century are held in the Blachford archives. The sequence of events concerning the mills has to be sought in other documents – stewards' accounts, rentals, correspondence. Mr Hellier's indenture of lease has not come to light, but there is no reason to suppose that it differed very much from earlier leases. What is clear, however, is that some time in the first or second decade Mr Hellier assigned his lease to a company based in Marlborough Street Dock (Devonport), known as the Plymouth Dock Co.

A survey of the Ivybridge estates made by Mr Christopher Savery in May 1818, when Sir John Rogers was contemplating selling the manor, lists the Water Greist or Manor Mills leased to the company on the lives of William T. Hellier, aged 54, Josiah Hellier, aged 52 and Mary Gushing, aged 48 years. The mills are given an estimated yearly value of £35 at the conventionary rent of £1.

Ivybridge Mills were given a new name, Union Mills. Towards the end of 1825 Mr Servington Savery (Mr Christopher's son) negotiated a new lease with those he called the Dockyard Co. – acting through a Mr Shaw, settling for a payment of £120 and an exchange of 'lives'. A locally resident manager was put in to run the mills. This was Mr Mason in 1825

ESTABLISHED 1905
ALL OFFERS SUBJECT TO REPLY BY RETURN OF POST AND IF UNSOLD.
DIRECTORS H. E. BRADSHAW, H. J. DYER

From LEE & SON (IVYBRIDGE) LTD.
MILLERS
WHOLESALE & RETAIL
Flour, Corn, Seed, Manure & Forage, Timber & Builders Merchants

IVYBRIDGE MILLS, Ivybridge. 1st August 1958

TELEGRAMS, "LEE, IVYBRIDGE 4 & 5." TELEPHONE NO. 4.
REGISTERED OFFICE, IVYBRIDGE MILLS.
YEALMPTON MILLS, YEALMPTON PHONE NO. 8.
KINGSBRIDGE PHONE NO. 2767.

To Mr.
Wakehams Rook,
Cornwood,
IVYBRIDGE. 129

July. 21.	To 14 lbs Dehydrated Dog Meat	@ 1/5d		19	10
	3 Udder Cloths (striped)	@ 1/8		5	0
	3 Udder Cloths (Plain.)	@ 1/7d		4	9
			£1	9	7

JOHN P. HIDDLESTON

LEE AND SON (IVYBRIDGE) LTD.

A bill from Lee & Sons, dated 1 August 1958.

and in the 1830s. In the 1830s he received numerous complaints from Mr John Selden, who had recently opened the King's Arms in the highway a short distance east of the mill. The inn had become very popular with the local inhabitants, and the complaint was that the mill company were negligent in not covering over the mill leat which ran in front of the inn. It may, perhaps, be presumed that some of Mr Selden's best customers failed to avoid the leat on leaving the inn.

In 1840 Mr Morice Cole was the manager (Ermington Tithe Apportionment) and in the 1850s he was followed by William Baron (1856–62), and then William Wyatt in the 1870s (Kelly's directories).

On 7 August 1878 the *Exeter Flying Post* carried the advertisement:

> *To be let by tender, for a term not to exceed five years, the newly erected water Flour Mill, containing four pairs of stones with machinery complete, also a garden attached, and known as Union Mill, situated at Ivybridge in the county of Devon. To view apply at the Mill between the hours of eight a.m. and six p.m. For further particulars and conditions of letting apply to Mr Charles Lee, 15 Marlborough Street, Devonport, to whom Tenders are to be sent in writing not later than the 31st Day of August. The Directors do not bind themselves to accept the highest or any tender.*

It is not known if any tenders were received. Not until 1889 do *Kelly's Directories* show a change of occupier: 'Richard Pooley, corn merchant and miller (water), 10 Fore Street' (Ivybridge), repeated in 1893. In 1902 the *Directory* entry reads: 'Mrs Jane Pooley, 10 Fore Street, corn merchant and baker'. The Pooleys must have been Dockyard Co. tenants because the company was still paying the yearly rent of £15 to Rogers in 1893 (Ivybridge Rentals).

Henry John Fice Lee of Ivybridge

It was probably 1902 when Henry John Fice Lee bought the mill. Mr Lee was born at Yealmpton on 30 October 1861 and had come to Ivybridge as a baker and pastry cook, having his own business in Western Road. There is a record of Mr Lee having work done at the mill in 1902 (Mr Fice's Account Book, by courtesy of Mr Reg Vincent). About this time Messrs F.&H. Holman closed their paper mill, which had been established adjacent to the corn mills in the early years of the nineteenth century, and restricted their business to their premises at Lee Mill. Mr Lee took over the abandoned site and by 1905 had made further alterations to the corn mill buildings and installed a modern façade facing Fore Street.

From 1905 to about 1927, W.G. Heath, a Plymouth electrical engineer, occupied a part of the mill buildings. He used the water of the mill leat to generate electricity with which he was able to supply at least a part of Ivybridge.

The late Harold Webber gives a thumbs-up to saving the turbine from Glanville's Mill (Lee Mill), where he worked for many years. The turbine is now preserved in Harford Road car park.

Ivybridge mayor Tony Barber and deputy mayor Ivor Marin opening Ivybridge Museum in 1988.

Tony Barber and Ivor Martin with some of the exhibits in the town's museum.

Farmer Nigel Hawkins found a 400-year-old canonball while clearing weeds from his stream.

A full account of Mr Heath's enterprise has been written by the late Mr Edwin Harvey, one of Mr Heath's first apprentices.

The name 'Union Mill' was dropped and the mill became known as Lee's Mill, trading as 'H.J.P. Lee, Miller'. The business was later made into a private company, directed by members of the family. Mr Henry Lee became a prominent figure in the community life of Ivybridge.

Friends of Ivybridge Museum

The society was formed in 1987 by the then town mayor, Tony Barber, and deputy mayor, Ivor Martin, with a subcommittee of councillors and interested parties. The Council had purchased premises, i.e. two cottages. The idea was for the Historical Society to use them with help from local arts and crafts clubs who would exhibit and sell their wares and look after the admissions, with help from FIM members.

After the initial opening exhibition, which was enormously successful, the full Council decided at a public meeting that they could not afford the upkeep of the cottages, so sold them again, not giving us the

Toys From Our Past

Reconstruction of old schoolroom, Ivybridge Museum.

A young gardener with his garden roller.

Some children's favourites, Ivybridge Museum.

Prepare for take-off!

All aboard!

Right: *A fine carriage and pair.*

chance to try for grants and fund-raising. This left us with artefacts which we exhibited in the Town Hall in glass cases, putting on various special displays, e.g. the Second World War. Then, because the Magistrates' Court wanted to use the Town Hall, we were without a home, so were invited to use a spare classroom at Erme School until it was needed for the children. We then moved into the attic at the same school and became Ivybridge Historical Society, and this worked very well and we still continued to put on special events, e.g. the History of the Local Paper Mill. One very successful idea was using the children from the school to portray old pastimes, re-enacting old games, etc. We were also very busy visiting all our five schools with our artefacts and talking about various projects connected to the National Curriculum. The children certainly seemed to get a lot of benefit out of these visits. We also talked to groups of grown-ups and began to make sound archives, etc., from our senior citizens. We built up a considerable collection of documents and photos for our archives and attended various local events, putting on displays at agricultural shows and staging veteran vehicle parades.

In 1992 we joined up with the local Amenities Society, which was formed in the 1960s to stop the destruction of the Erme Valley from indiscriminate development.

Under the title of Ivybridge & District Civic Society we had regular meetings, visited other museums and events and had talks on various interesting subjects, not always historical in content.

We produced booklets on various subjects from our area and sold them through different outlets.

The local comprehensive school used our archive for the special projects the youngsters took for their final years and produced some very interesting papers. We also had papers on various walks in and around our town to help visitors enjoy our area as much as we do.

We had people enquiring about their family tree from as far away as Canada and Australia, and worked on those of the Americans who were here during the war years when Ivybridge witnessed race riots in the main street. Some of our local ladies were very shy about passing on information referring to this period! I wonder why?

We also have a collection of horseshoes dating back to the eleventh century.

Reminiscences of William Cotton

An extract from the will of William Cotton of Ivybridge, made 28th day of May in the Year of Our Lord 1862.

1823 – On the 18th February I was married at Bodium Church by cousin The Revd F. Borradaile, who had recently taken holy orders, to Mary Ann, eldest daughter of the Revd James, rector of Thorpe Abbots, during the absence of the incumbent Sir Godfrey Thomas.

After the ceremony we went to Brighton and returned to Ballam Hill in April. In October we went to Worthing from thence to sale at Abbey where I bought a set of drawers, an ebony table and a tortoiseshell cabinet.

I now let my house at Ballam Hill on lease to Mr Alexander Provost for 21 years at £325 rent and purchased a cottage at Leatherhead in Surrey, on the banks of the River Mole a picturesque and beautiful situation. My friend Edward Carey, architect, undertook to make the necessary alterations and additions, which consisted of a library 30 feet by 25, with ground floor and pendant copied from the Presence Chamber at Hampton Court Palace, which was built by Cardinal Wolsey. The purchase of the Freehold and cost of new buildings etc amounted to £5,000.

1824 – Having passed the site at Worthing, whilst our new home was building, we went early in the Spring of this year to Devon for three weeks. Harriet Collins and my cousin William Borradaile was staying with us during the Epsom Races.

1826 – My brother John was now articled to Messrs Henry and Charles Berkley, solicitors at Lincoln Inn, and Edward entered himself as ? Commoner at New College, together with his cousin, Robert Hudson, but neither of them stayed long enough to take a degree.

In May we went to Oxford and Blenheim, and in August (1826) to Penzance, accompanied by wife's sister Harriet Collins. We sailed from Portsmouth in the Brunswick *steamboat taking our travelling carriage with us. At Plymouth we stayed two days at the Royal Hotel and saw the grounds of Mount Edgcombe and the pictures at Saltram.*

Crossing the Tamar at Saltash Ferry we posted through Liskeard, St Austell, Truro and Helston to Penzance, where we spent three months with my wife's cousin Mrs Edward Scoble, widow of Captain Scoble RN at Poltair House, commanding a beautiful view of Mounts Bay.

I, in company with Captain Giddy RN visited all the Cromleys stone circles and druids' remains in the neighbourhood of Poltair. With his assistance, was enabled to clear away the site and trace out the original entrance to the Castle, of which I forwarded a plan to the society of antiquaries, of archaeology and at a meeting of geological society of Penzance… and this led in.

1827 – To my preparing for the press and printed 25 copies (for private distribution only).

I also builded a cottage for my sisters (Mary, Charlotte) in the (Leatherhead House).

Highland House, where William Cotton once lived.

1833 – My sister Charlotte was married at Leatherhead to William Hall Esq MD of the same place. Early in this year, my youngest sister Mary Cotton was married at Clapham Church, by Chancellor of the Diocese to Nathaniel Fred Edwards, Lieut of the Royal Navy and youngest son of John Edwards Esq of Worthing Park, Hampshire.

In June, my wife and I joined them in Devonshire at Whitehill, a cottage near Kingsbridge, which was let to them for a few months by Mr & Mrs Stanley Lowe.

1837 – I was glad to avail myself of an opportunity I had long desired to West Rattery, willing and able, the former residence and patrimonial estates of my mother's family.

June 20 1837 at a service in Winchester Cathedral we learnt of the decease of King William IV and then proceeded to Exeter. From Haldon Hill we had one of the finest prospects in England. At Chudleigh I called on the Revd Gilbert at the vicarage – a tall man in his 86th year whose father, also vicar of Chudleigh, had married one of the daughters of Waltham Savery of Slade. I found the much respected Vicar walking in his garden and I had such an interesting conversation with him regarding my mother's family (this worthy old gentleman died at Chudleigh in September in his 88th year).

From Ashburton to Totnes the road runs for the most part by the side of the River Dart and is exceedingly picturesque, and executed in me a strong desire to live in Devonshire. The quaint old town of Totnes delighted us much.

We found my sister and her husband at Whitehall Cottage near the village of Churchstow, Devon. To the village of Rattery of which my maternal grandfather was Vicar and found in the church and burial monuments to the memory of several members of the Savery family. The Manor of Rattery was sold by King Henry VIII to Richard Savery of Totnes in 1544 and remained in the family for more than 400 years.

1839 – This year having let my house at Leatherhead we moved into Devonshire, having purchased the lease of Highland house in the Parish of Ermington and district of Ivybridge, a village much loved for its beauty and its outstanding scenery on the River Erme.

The house was built in 1792 by Col Webber of Exmouth, and the property, containing about 14 acres, was held on a lease for a term of three lives from Sir John Leman Rogers of Blachford.

I spent £500 in alterations and improvements and we took possession towards the end of the year (1839). It is known that this property in Ivybridge belonged to Sir Francis Drake, the circumnavigator, whose daughter, Prudence Drake, married my ancestor William Savery of Slade in 1690, and her portrait painted, is now hanging upon the walls of my hall at the present time.

1840 – Queen Victoria was married February 10th to her cousin Prince Albert on St George's Day. My wife's sister Mrs Collins was married from our house to George RN of Lepson House, Plymouth.

In the winter, we had a remarkable heavy fall of snow, with a strong east wind which drifted the snow in places and rendered road impassable for several days, the snow between 4-5 feet deep opposite our drawing-room window, and the mail coaches from Plymouth were detained at Ivybridge being unable to proceed further.

1843 – My wife's cousin and her husband paid us a visit in Devonshire, and in July we dined with them on board their yacht the Sitana, on a three-year cruise in the Mediterranean (a cousin of Mary Anne, she was a most gifted artist).

1848 – This year I offered to give to the town of Plympton my collection of books and oil paintings, engravings and drawings by the old master to an Institution in memory of Sir Joshua Reynolds providing a suitable building be secured for its reception and a sufficient fund for its maintenance. On September 14th I met Lord Morley at Mr George Eastlake's at Plympton to discuss the matter and to ascertain how far the Mayoralty House, which had been offered by the Trepay family, would be a suitable building for the purpose. On the 22nd of the same month, I was presented with the freedom of the ancient Borough Town of Plympton and a long correspondence took place between Mr Eastlake, myself and the Town Clerk of Plymouth, Devonport and Stonehouse, as it was thought that without the concurrence of the three towns, nothing could be done at Plympton alone as a considerable outlay would be required. The larger towns, however, refused to co-operate if the collection was located at Plympton, and the project was ultimately abandoned for want of the adequate ???.

1850 – Having failed in my wish to establish at Plympton an Institute dedicated to the memory of Sir Joshua Reynolds in his native town, I was resolved upon giving my collection to the public library (was the Plymouth Library) as certain conditions... by what gift I sought to prevent the sale and disposition of the Rogers collection of works of art and preserve memorial of my family and name.

Went we as usual to London in the spring. In the autumn we went to the celebrated Madam Moisella concert at the Teignmouth Theatre and dined with Colonel and Mrs Radford to meet Lord and Lady Morley.

1851 –Dined on the 9th January

1852 – I offered to endow the Chapel of Ivybridge with my Leatherhead property, consisting of a freehold house and garden called The Priory and let for a term of years at £120 per annum, if Lady Rogers (of Blachford) would build a parsonage house and to me and my heirs, the alternate right of presentation. This proposal was accepted by Lady Rogers and her son, Sir Frederick: the Revd R.P. Cornish was appropriate to the perpetual Curacy and took possession of the new parsonage, having added considerably to the house and grounds.

1853 – On the first of June, Library at Plymouth was opened by the Earl of Derby.

1854 – Early in the year, I published 'Sir Joshua Reynolds and his works', from his manuscripts in possession of Mr Robert Palmers (members and relation of Sir J.R.) and others. Also a catalogue of the portraits he painted completed from his own memoranda.

1854 – February 10th I read at the Ivybridge Institute a lecture on the life and genius of Sir Joshua Reynolds, illustrated with engravings from his principal works by Mr Andell, Watson, Fisher and others.

July 1st 1859 – My niece Juliann Edwards was married at Modbury Church to Captain Charles Louden Barnard of the Royal Marine Artillery, the 3rd Admiral Barnard of Stonehouse.

On December the 6th I read a lecture on the cartoons of Raphael to the member of the Ivybridge Institute, in April being invited to attend a meeting in the Town Hall of Plympton to consider the siting in the town of Plympton a public testimonial to the memory of Sir Joshua Reynolds. I was appointed a member of the committee, a satisfactory result, but I drew up and printed a short account of the Ancient Borough Town of Plympton, from memoirs of the Reynolds family. This little book I published solely with the view to assist the Reynolds testimonial, but as that seemed to be abandoned and [illegible] *Plympton was dissolved in the following year, I proposed having a marble bust of the Great Devonshire artist executed for the Plymouth Public Library. A subscription list was opened for the purpose and then collected, which was the price for which Mr Behnes offered to them a bust in marble from the model in the Council Room of the Royal Academy. 1860 – Dear little Lila, the youngest child of Mrs Edward Younge, died at Highland House after an attack of measles on the 13th of January and was buried in the church yard at Ivybridge (Lila was the youngest child of Eliza Collins, sister to William Collins, Mary Anne – she married Edward Young at Camberwell in 1842, William Cotton gave the bride away. During 1858 both Eliza and Edward Younge died and dear little Lila came to live at Ivybridge with Mary Anne and William.*

Note: the Reminiscences end abruptly – the last entry reading:

Nov 13th 1860 – Received the intelligence of my brother Edward's death by drowning, while bathing in the sea at Brighton in the colony of Victoria, Australia.

Mary Anne, William's wife, died in 1861; William Cotton died January 1863

There follow extracts of letters between William Cotton and his cousin, Robert Hadson.

1849, Friday 17 August, Page 39–40: If I had succeded in my Plympton venture, I may have been able to have let Highland House, and gone to lodgings or taken a less expensive place. But as it is I am living here to the full extent of my income, or rather beyond it, and as you know have experienced considerable difficulties in passing money from time to time as I have required to do.

PS I am sorry to say that chlolera has made an appearance at Ivybridge. There have been four fatal cases: two healthy woman who were at work at the paper mill the day before yesterday, were taken suddenly ill the same evening and died the next morning.

I took the chance at a meeting of the inhabitants yesterday to form a local board of health and take measures for the protection of the people and cleansing of the drains, gutters, etc.

1849, 21 August, Page 41: We have had three more cases of cholera in Ivybridge but none for the last three or fours days.

1849, 27 August, Page 44: We still have much sickness in the village, though no more cases of cholera

1849, 2 or 4 September, Page 48–49: Poor Miss Cooper is in a bad way and bad state of health and unable to do to much (Miss Cooper was an old and valued servant)

PS We have much sickness in the village and had several deaths, and is a very sad case to be a resident clergyman. I was obliged to say prayers for the sick myself at the bedside of a poor little girl, the daughter of our gardener last week, who died the following day. We have written to the Bishop on the subject of our spiritual distribution, and I immediately received an answer to the effect that the Bishop could only forsee a residence of the incumbent where there was a house provided with the endorsement.

1849, 30 November, Page 54: I have now, my dear Robert, to communicate a more melancholy piece of intelligence. Which I am sure you will be sorry to hear, we have lost poor Miss Cooper, a most faithful and attached servant for more than 30 years.

THE GREAT WESTERN AT IVYBRIDGE

The GWR came to Ivybridge in the guise of the South Devon Railway and opened its station in 1848. Early trains were hauled by contractors' locomotives belonging to Green's of Newton Abbot. Soon the GWR began to work the trains themselves all the way to the western terminus at Penzance – via the Cornwall & West Cornwall Railway Co.'s lines on the broad gauge. Unlike today's standard 4ft 8ins between the rails, a distance of no less than 7ft was the norm.

The GWR absorbed all our local lines in 1878 (Ivybridge opening for traffic in the summer of 1848) and handed them over to British Railways (Western Region) at midnight on New Year's Eve 1947. British Railways (Western Region) – whose staff called themselves 'GWR' more often than not – eventually closed the station to passengers in 1959 (2 March) and to goods in 1965 (29 November). The last man to lock up was Tom Pettifore.

Today there is much to be seen. The stunted piers of Brunel's viaduct still stride across the valley of the River Erme at intervals of 66ft, the tallest rising 108ft 6ins above the tumbling waters. The timber and ironwork which supported the track are, of course, long gone. Any single component, however, could be replaced in under one hour and without the need to remove the line from traffic. It was built to take a single line of broad-gauge track. The present viaduct dates from the doubling of the main line and the conversion to standard gauge in 1892. It is, of course, several yards to the south of earlier lines of rails. While the track was still single Ivybridge provided not only a passing loop but also a number of sidings controlled from a signal box or cabin to the west of the station site (towards Langham).

The early station building was of red deal upon oak frames with a slated roof of the 'Brunel Chalet' pattern similar to that still in use at many stations in Berkshire, Oxfordshire and Wiltshire – Charlbury springing to mind – the tops of windows having a semicircular soffit and a verandah roof giving shelter to the face of the building. Similar windows adorned the three houses that were built for the signalman, stationmaster and ganger just to the south of the station site. They shared with the station a panoramic view of the whole of Ivybridge.

The red-brick standard GWR goods shed is still in place, though its connection to the main lines was taken out of use in 1968 (14 January) and a private siding with revised connections to the main line put in. A utility corrugated iron loading shelter was installed shortly afterwards. The siting of the goods yard and sheds shows the relative importance given

Ivybridge Station and viaduct, c.1910.

The London mail train snowbound at Langham, March 1891.

Staff at Ivybridge Station in the late 1800s.

to goods traffic. While Station Road (for passengers) was shorter, paved earlier, lit earlier and even given a paved footpath earlier, it was a test of stamina whether one took the steps (still there) or the road compared with the gentle walk to the 'goods end'. The early goods lock-up store (stone built) next to the early wooden station proved to be far too small for the traffic when the lines were doubled. New passenger buildings followed on the enlarged platforms. They were linked by a footbridge of plate girder construction, so enabling passengers 'NOT to CROSS the LINE except by way of the FOOTBRIDGE nor to TRESPASS on the LINES of the RAILWAY', as the cast-iron notice boards put it. Traces of the two packers' (or platelayers') huts can still be seen to the east and west of the station site, together with the outlines of the cattle and loading docks. Milepost 235 is still prominent on the side of the 'up' line (nb 'up' means facing Paddington and 'down' facing Penzance in this part of the world). The early 'lamp hut' (for storing lamps for both signals and rolling stock and the long burning oil to fuel them) I have not been able to site accurately, although I believe it to have been close to the west end of the down platform.

Apart from the 'stopper' trains that called to pick up or set down passengers in the days of the GIB, a number of famous trains passed through in revenue and fame earning service. On the morning of 9 May 1904 the 'City of Truro' in charge of an Ocean Mails express (American mails having landed by tender at Millbay Docks in Plymouth) became the first steam locomotive to exceed 100mph, though according to the many drivers that I have spoken to the real risks and dangers were faced before the sprint down Wellington Bank in Somerset was attempted.

They considered the banks and sharp reverse curves betwixt Hemerdon and Dainton to be far more dangerous at the permitted speeds, let alone 'with the lever (regulator) in the roof'! Perhaps the most famous passer-by was the Cornish Riviera express, usually referred to as the '1030 Limited' or even the 'Ltd'. This train first ran in the same year as the first 'ton' by a steam locomotive – 1904 – and was a successor to both the earlier 'Zulu' (named after the speed of the Zulu Impis in the African Wars) and the 'Cornishman', to be reintroduced as a through service from the Midlands and the North of England by the LMS (sometimes referred to as the 'lose 'em, mix 'em & smash 'em railway). For many years it offered the longest non-stop (Paddington to Plymouth and vice versa) run on any railway anywhere in the world. Its successor, in the form of an HST-1C125, pounded through with twin power plants whining through the cuttings either side of the viaduct.

The heavy freight was usually a 1,000 ton clay train with a pair of class 37 diesels on the front. More often than not one of these would be 'William Cookworthy', complete with the flags of both Cornwall and British Rail on its yellow nose, not to mention the 'head to tail logo' of Cornish Railways

Ivybridge Station during the Second World War.

Tom Pettifer locking up for the last time in 1965.

Ivybridge viaduct after restoration.

on her engine casing, for this locomotive worked from St Blazey freight depot in the heart of the china-clay country of Cornwall. Earlier freights included the following:

'The Drake' (Bristol to Laira passing about 2.00a.m.)
'Tre Pol & Pen Flyer' (Marazion to Bristol passing about 7.00p.m.)
'Cornishman' (Paddington to Penzance passing about 5.00a.m.)
'Tamar' (Paddington to Laira passing about 4.00a.m.)
'Searchlight' (Penzance to Paddington passing about 6.00p.m.)
'Biscuit' (Reading to Laira passing about 4.30a.m.)
'Rasher' (Swindon to Laira passing about 7.00p.m.)
'Western Flash' (London West Depot to Penzance passing about 3.00a.m.)

A daily 'pick-up goods' would call each weekday to pick up and set down the 'station track', as well as shunting the yard as required. Sometimes such shunting moved cattle or other livestock from the loading dock on the first stage of its main line journey – often to the largest stockyards in the UK at Banbury.

'Namod' freight trains and those conveying livestock usually travelled much faster than the general run of freight trains. Milk trains, too, and those carrying gold in special bullion vans needed high-speed paths through the working diagrams of traffic. This meant that slower local trains had to be shunted to one side in refuge sidings. One was provided at Ivybridge in the up direction, giving space for 45 wagons as well as engine and brake van. The nearest refuges in the down direction were at Hemerdon and Brent. In the early part of the twentieth century clay trains were loaded (and coal and timber discharged) at Cantrel sidings close to the clay dries under the Western Beacon. The steam-operated Red Lake Railway had a rope-worked incline to the exchange sidings to enable fuel and timber to reach its works on Dartmoor. Clay, however, was piped down to the dries and 'exported' in solid blocks in timber open wagons with a tarpaulin sheeted over in a ridge tent shape. The rail connection to the works is long gone and the site is now Western Machinery & Equipment Co. Ltd, part of the Dutton Forshaw group.

At random intervals Ivybridge was visited by trains known as 'Farm Specials' – in short, a farm on the move by rail. Livestock, fodder, machinery, working horses, together with the family (and more often than not the farmhands) would move from one part of the country to another following farm sales. Regular stops for milking, feeding, watering and mucking out in refuge sidings en route all had to be planned for, as well as regular changes of locomotive and the train's crew. One other group of special trains (or even individual bullion wagons) called at Ivybridge to pick up supplies of the specialist paper produced in the mills.

During its stewardship at Ivybridge the GWR brought in a great many innovations to Ivybridge, including telegraph services, more efficient postal deliveries standard (or London) time, cheap coal for industry, householders and the companies set up to produce gas and electricity; machinery for the farmers and the mill owners; national newspapers on the day of publication; cheap slate for roofs and mass-produced beet by the barrel load. Fast and efficient exports of livestock, milk and other produce followed. Above all, the station enabled people to both visit and travel from almost any part of the United Kingdom – at one time no part of England was more than ten miles from a railway station. Manufactured goods of all kinds became as readily available in Ivybridge as in the town of their manufacture. It was the norm for goods to be ordered via the station telegraph to be delivered the following day by horse and cart from the railway station to the customer. The railways were, of course, by definition, common carriers, meaning that they had to be prepared to carry any item of freight or livestock in a suitable conveyance provided the price was paid.

Railway services also extended to the provision of lorries and .buses operating as feeders and distributors to its rail network. Operation was by timetable and under control of the local stationmaster, who was bound to ensure that the bus did not leave before the train arrived, and vice versa. The GIB introduced its own internal air services linking South Devon and South Wales for both rail and special passengers as early as 1951, the journey time between Ivybridge and Cardiff being cut from six hours 20 minutes to one hour 55 minutes in that year. The service was operated in conjunction with Imperial Airways, the forerunner of British Airways.

Company servants and officers of the GIB appeared to exhibit a great deal of pride in their work. I feel that this was due to a number of factors, evidence of which can be seen in a local context. In the heyday of the GWR a job with it was both secure and comparatively well paid. Staff were uniformed and well trained and in many cases using the very latest of technology, e.g. automatic train control started on the GIB in 1906 – British Rail eventually got around to fitting a similar system in the 1950s. Medical and educational services offered by the company, together with incentives for promotion and innovation, were second to none.

A new station was opened at Ivybridge in 1994, 40 years after the closure of the original.

Church and Chapel at Ivybridge

Mr Christopher Savery's Account for 1785 records that on February 26, acting in his capacity as Sir Frederick Leman Rogers's steward, he had attended one Mr Bent at Ivybridge about his building a Chapel there, a plan for which Mr Bent had brought with him. It is apparent from this meeting that for some time before February 1785 Sir Frederick and Mr Savery had discussed the feasibility of building a chapel at Ivybridge, and that a plan had already been drawn up.

Two explanations may be offered for why, in 1785, Ivybridge should have a chapel which (although not stated) would be of the established Church. The village was at least two miles from its Parish Church at Ermington, taking paths across meadows and over Filham Moor, with two crossings of the River Erme over which, at that time, there were no stone bridges. But such a distance from a Parish Church is not rare in the parishes around Dartmoor, which are large and have scattered and isolated populations. In times past various devices were used to relieve this inconvenience. Many so-called 'church houses' still survive, built to give rest between morning and evening services to parishioners from some distance away. In the fifteenth century the Bishops of Exeter would sometimes grant licences for divine service to be held in the private chapel at the house of the lord of the manor or other wealthy landholder, which is what happened at Ivybridge, at Filham and at Fardel, amongst others. There is also the well-known sanction by Bishop Bronescombe in 1260 allowing the inhabitants of the hamlets of Babeny and Piswell in Lydford parish to use Widecombe Church for baptisms, marriages and burials. That in 1785 Ivybridge was a village already growing in size and population and deserving of special treatment for church-going facilities sounds reasonable but may be hard to prove. So far as Mr Savery's accounts of work done at Ivybridge, and the surviving title deeds, may be relied on, the village did not begin to expand beyond its seventeenth-century size until the last 15 years of the eighteenth century.

The second explanation comes from the Church itself. John Wesley had stormed through the South West in 1743, and by the end of the century his Methodism seems to have gained a strong foothold in Ivybridge and its neighbourhood. Without having purpose-built places of meeting, the Wesleyan teachers made close contact with the people. The clergy of the established Church found their congregation dwindling, and judging by the letters written some years later to Sir John Rogers, who was then lord of the manor, they thought that the presence of a local chapel would draw people back to the Church. In 1785 the one man who possessed the power and the means to make this possible was the lord of the manor who owned all the land at Ivybridge, and was seen to show concern about the welfare of the village.

Apparently finding Mr Bent's plans acceptable, Sir Frederick chose a site on part of the old Clyff's Tenement facing onto the road leading from the bridge towards Cornwood. This was in Cornwood parish and meant that if built there the chapel would be within the ministry of the vicar of Cornwood. Sir Frederick's home was in Cornwood, but whether the choice was deliberate because of that can only be guessed.

Mr Bent was given permission to take all the timber he needed from the local woods. The chapel was built and ready for use in 1789. It seems the work had been supervised by Mr Henry Rivers, the proprietor of the London Inn, who, 20 years later, was still waiting for some arrears of payment due to him. It is not clear how the building was paid for or by whom. Sir Frederick's Journal records that the first services were held on Sunday, 11 October 1789, and that he attended the service on 25 October at which 'young Mr Forster preached'. It would be unreasonable to suppose that having provided the

The old church, Ivybridge.

Ugborough Church.

The old and new churches, Ivybridge.

The old church.

land and then honouring the village with his presence at the service he had not put money into the project.

The first 20 years passed without notice. It is likely that no chaplain was sought for Ivybridge during the early years. But the village was now growing fast; an extrapolation from a count made in 1817, when the population was found to be 477, suggests a figure of about 400 in 1809. This was the year when the Revd Robert Savage, rector of Harford, felt it his duty to draw Sir John Rogers's attention to the present inadequacy of the chapel, and 'to take the liberty' of informing Sir John that, through lack of accommodation, Ivybridge inhabitants were either neglecting public worship altogether or were frequenting meetings in the village presided over by illiterate and ignorant teachers. Mr Savage implored Sir John to consider favourably a proposal to enlarge the chapel by a north aisle (see Mr Savage's letter).

Sir John, busy elsewhere, appears to have been slow in acting on the Revd Savage's request to have the chapel enlarged. It was not until 1812 that Mr Savery began working on the idea with Mr James Green, who at that time was employed in planning a little street with cottages on the other side of the road opposite the chapel, a street which became known as Green Street. A builder named Goodridge was committed to the task of enlarging the chapel in 1814, and, like Mr Bent in 1785, Mr Goodridge was given permission to take as much oak as he needed from the woods. Some writers on the history of the old chapel say that the north aisle was added in 1836, but an appraisal of the chapel in 1847 supports the earlier date.

It must have been about this time that the Revd Duke Yonge, vicar of Cornwood, produced a circular letter asking for financial support in enlarging the chapel. Mr Yonge rarely dated his letters, but a copy addressed to the Revd Richard Strode of Newnham has survived. The Revd Strode married Miss Harriet Rogers in 1810 and died in 1821. According to the letter, Sir John Rogers had expressed his willingness to subscribe £500 towards enlarging the chapel. If Sir John did give this amount of money it could scarcely have been for less than a north aisle, and perhaps for the gallery which it is known the chapel contained.

The time had now come for Ivybridge to have its resident chaplain. Mr Henry P. Beloe was appointed in June 1815. His financial prospects, set out in Mr Yonge's circular letter, depended largely on the pew rents he could extract from his congregation. But in November of the same year Mr Beloe had to inform Sir John that only trifling subscriptions had been received, which, he said, was partly due to the villagers wanting to know if Sir John was going to

The interior of St John's.

transfer the land from himself to trustees, since they apprehended (probably mistakenly) that this legal nicety affected their rights in the choice of a chaplain. In the following March Mr Beloe was forced to write again to Sir John. This time he had to report that Ivybridge was in great confusion, every person being so miserably poor that he had received no more than £11 for nearly nine months' duty. He thought the only solution lay in effecting an endowment which would then lead to money becoming available from outside sources. He took this opportunity to inform Sir John that 'Old Rivers' was bankrupt, and that so much iniquity and fraud had been uncovered he would be turned out of the inn.

The haggling over endowment was to go on for over 30 years. In the meantime, the chapel had not been consecrated and the ground on which it stood still belonged to Sir John Rogers. Without an endowment from him or any other benefactor, Queen Anne's Bounty could not help, neither could any money be extracted from parliamentary grant. Both of these lifelines would also require at least £100 to be raised in Ivybridge. But the inhabitants of Ivybridge only added to Sir John's problems. They did not want the chapel to be consecrated, and yet they were reluctant to put money into it whilst Sir John held title to the land. It may seem strange today that the success of a chapel of the Church of England should depend so much on the lord of the manor.

Mr. Beloe's appointment in 1815 was evidently by sanction of Sir John. Whether the Revd Yonge approved of the choice is not known, but within 18 months he wrote to Sir John's brother, Captain Robert Henley Rogers RTJ (Sir John being unavailable) telling him that the curate was behaving strangely and was thought to be mad, preaching unscrupulously and departing from true liturgy. Before the year 1816 had ended Mr Beloe was dismissed by Mr Yonge.

This act by Mr Yonge precipitated a quarrel between him and Sir John over whose right it was to appoint a curate. Sir John supported Mr Beloe and claimed the right of appointment as owner of the land on which the chapel stood. Mr Yonge claimed the right was his as vicar of the parish in which the chapel was situated. The village favoured Sir John's right. A petition dated 9 October 1816 and presented by 27 leading inhabitants of Ivybridge asked Sir John not to have the chapel consecrated because it would pass the right of appointment solely to 'the rector' (in fact Mr Yonge was the vicar) by his application to the bishop. They wished the right of appointment to rest with Sir John, provided they, the inhabitants of Ivybridge, approved of his choice.

The result of all this unpleasantness was that Ivybridge went without a chaplain for a whole year. Mr Yonge blamed Sir John and wrote to him in April (1817) complaining that the chapel was closed and no divine services were available to the inhabitants, who were drifting away to the Wesleyans. Furthermore, Miss Powell had nowhere to send her children to Sunday school (Miss Powell had a little school at her house, believed to be at the east corner of Chapel Place in Fore Street). The Revd Robert Savage of Harford had his say by telling Sir John that the people were giving up paying the rent for their pews; this was the money upon which the procurement of a chaplain depended.

The closing of the chapel must have been a great disappointment to Sir John. In an endeavour to increase the prospect of financial help from outside, a count was made in October 1817 of all the families which might be expected to form the congregation, regardless to which parish they truly belonged. To those who know the area, the count for some settlements may seem surprisingly high.

About November 1817 the Revd Francis Humberstone accepted the living and stayed until the following September. Then may have come Mr Thomas Phillips from Plympton. A somewhat incomprehensible letter from Mr Phillips written in March 1823 says he is willing to return to the chaplaincy, which he had left after two years there, because a gentleman of Calvinistic principles had been introduced and certain dissenters had made it impossible for him to continue. Sir John seems to have declined Mr Phillips's offer of reconciliation. There seems to have been no dearth of applicants for the post, but few have left any record of actual appointment.

Mr Christopher Savery retired in 1823 or 1824 and his place as steward was given to his son, Servington. He is unlikely to have had the same influence on Sir John or on Ivybridge as his father. In September 1824 Mr Daniel Neuter or Nanter, apparently of Shilstone, was appointed chaplain. On his departure in September 1825 he advised Sir John to find another chaplain to stop another drift away to the Wesleyans.

The Wesleyans in Ivybridge now had their own chapel or meeting-place. In 1812 Mr Savery had found them a piece of ground at the head of a dirty lane towards Miss Powell's 'backside' with a promise that the lane would be improved. It could be argued

The crooked spire of Ermington Church.

The Congregational Chapel.

The Revd James Craig, who was minister at Ivybridge Congregational Church in the early-twentieth century.

that the Wesleyans had a salutary effect upon the Church inasmuch as their success forced the diocesan authorities to be concerned about Ivybridge.

The Bishop of Exeter was in fact getting quite concerned about Ivybridge. He asked Sir John to hurry up with the endowment so that the chapel could be consecrated. Sir John replied that he was willing to endow if he could be given assurance that he would have perpetual right of nomination. This assurance seems to have been given, so that it was now up to Sir John to secure an endowment and to win the support, shown financially, of the inhabitants of Ivybridge.

In 1827 the Revd Thomas Brown of Devonport was appointed chaplain. This was probably the best choice yet made in the history of the chapel. Mr Brown was to remain at Ivybridge until 1840. The prospects for consecration began to rise. In April 1833 Mr Brown heard from the Bishop that in the circumstances known to him the Bishop would accept an endowment of £5 from Sir Rogers if the parish would make the pew rents £70 per annum. Mr Brown was fairly confident the parish would raise £70, and that Mr Savery would arrange about applying to Queen Anne's Bounty. So another population count was made, based on the 1831 census, on a wider basis than in 1817, and the seating capacity of the chapel was analysed. The greater the expected congregation the more money could be expected from Queen Anne's Bounty, and from government grants.

The consecration of the chapel by the Bishop was fixed for Monday, 30 September 1833, and Mr Savery had all the deeds ready for execution. But something prevented the ceremony from taking place, and it was not until Monday, 5 October 1835, that consecration actually came about.

Ivybridge chapel was now properly established in the eyes of the diocesan authorities. In 1836 the Ecclesiastical District of Ivybridge was formed, with boundaries regardless of topographical features, if defined at all. On 17 April 1838 at the vestry meeting it was decreed that the chapel should henceforth be known as the Church of St John at Ivybridge. From the date of consecration the chapel could be used for baptisms, marriages and burials in the ground around. It could also begin to keep its own written records.

The Revd Thomas Brown was followed in July 1840 by the Revd J. Duncan Cork of Exeter College, Oxford. He was to stay for eight years. It was during his incumbency that Sir John Rogers died. Sir John had spent most of his time living in a hotel in Bond Street, London, and he died there on 10 December 1847. The body was brought to Teignmouth by train and from there carried to Cornwood, passing by the church at Ivybridge. After the funeral there were complaints that the bell at Ivybridge had not been tolled as the cortège passed. The Revd Cork had to explain to Frederick Rogers, who had succeeded his brother to the baronetcy, that the bell at Ivybridge church was only a dinner bell and not suitable for tolling.

Sir Frederick, the seventh baronet, had spent all his adult life as a civil servant in London, at the Audit Office in Somerset Place. He retired on pension when his brother John died, and moved to Blachford with his wife and family. In his middle sixties, Frederick did not find it easy to become a country gentleman and lord of the manor, with the constant demands, financial and otherwise, which his social position attracted. His replies were likely to be negative. In 1849 he turned down a request to provide a parsonage for Ivybridge on the grounds that he was fully committed in looking after Cornwood.

On the departure of the Revd Cork in 1849 the curacy was again vacant. In August of that year cholera broke out in Devon and the disease reached Ivybridge. Added distress was caused by there being no clergyman available to bury the dead. One resident of the village decided on action. Highland House was occupied by Mr William Cotton. A wealthy man with no occupation, he had come to Ivybridge with his wife in 1839. His mother was Catherine Savery, of the Rattery branch of that family. First he wrote to the Bishop. Then, on 16 August, he wrote to Sir Frederick telling him of his letter to the Bishop and requested Sir Frederick to have the leat which ran at the back of the village cleaned out. Having lived in Ivybridge for ten years Mr Cotton would be fully aware of the somewhat primitive conditions which existed in the village.

A new curate was appointed in October 1850, with popular assent. The Revd Robert Atherton had been assistant curate at St James's, Navy Row, which promoted an evangelical style of preaching not to his liking. Mr Atherton was quick to appraise the situation at Ivybridge, and in August 1851 he sent his analysis of the troubles and his suggestions for their remedy to Sir Frederick. Before Sir Frederick could decide what to do he died at Blachford on the following 8 December.

Lady Sophia Rogers was left all the Rogers estates. Unlike her late husband, she took an active interest in the welfare of Ivybridge. Her concern for the church was shared by Mr Cotton. Together they took up Mr Atherton's theory that a parsonage would help to stabilise the running of the curacy. The complicated arrangement between Lady Sophia and Mr Cotton which followed has never been clearly resolved. An explanation offered in 1877 after all the persons concerned were dead says that Sir John Rogers had charged his Blachford property with an annuity of £20 in favour of the incumbency then in his gift, and that Mr Cotton wished to endow the incumbency more adequately by the gift of an estate at Leatherhead in Surrey, to take effect after his death

The opening in June 1916 of Butter Brook Reservoir, which cost £17,000

and that of his wife, and that on 31 December 1856 he granted an annuity of £20 to Lady Rogers on the same terms. When the annuity should commence Lady Rogers would be relieved of the £20 annual charge on the Blachford estate. In return for all this, Mr Cotton would be given an alternate right of presentation. It was also said that (in 1877) the Leatherhead estate was the property of the living. Mrs Cotton died in 1861 and Mr William Cotton in 1863, leaving no issue.

It was Mr Cotton's intention that a parsonage should be built. Lady Rogers provided a piece of land between the old Bicton Wood (Victoria Park) and the meadows called Beacons. Water would be piped from a little reservoir built below the railway on the side of Henlake Down. The house was ready for occupation in about 1860. Before very long it was found that the house was too large for the curate to maintain on his income, and it was let out to others who came with greater means.

Mr Atherton did not stay long enough to occupy the parsonage. In the years between 1856 and 1872 a succession of curates came and went. Then the Revd George W. Anstis arrived and he was to remain a highly respected figure in Ivybridge for 37 years. He lived in a house in Station Road. Old age and infirmity forced him to resign on 14 October 1909, the Bishop telling him that his pension would be £70 a year.

It was Mr Anstis who, in his first years at the church, realised that the structure was in a very bad state of repair. It was, in fact, found to be beyond repair. One writer (Miss Beatrix Cresswell, 1912, 1922) claims the church was struck by lightning, but there is no record of this ever happening. A new building was put up on land just west of the old church and was consecrated by the Revd Anstis on 27 June 1882. In the same year Ivybridge became a vicarage.

The old chapel was allowed to decay, held in affectionate regard by at least some of the inhabitants of Ivybridge. A motion to have the walls taken down in 1890 was passed with some opposition and the resolution was sent to the Bishop for his opinion. The reply from the Archdeacon favoured retaining all the building with some 'few hours work by a mason' to make it safe. Mr Simpson of Torrhill (on the Exeter road) said he would guarantee the expense. In 1890 one visitor to Ivybridge was induced to write that:

... while it may be admitted that the building possesses no architectural merit, its artistic beauty is incontestable. The walls and tower have been largely overgrown with masses of ivy, and to anyone approaching the village from the direction of the railway station, the appearance is most singularly picturesque.

The ruins were finally demolished in 1925 by a firm of local builders. They paid £5 for the stone, which they used in their building of some houses in Ivybridge.

Suggested references:
Louise Ryan, *An obscure place* 1973, Plymouth. Mrs Ryan gives some information on the building of the chapel but does not state her authority
Tony Barber, *Aspects of Ivybridge* 1988, Ivybridge.
St John's Church records held at West Devon Record Office, Coxside, Plymouth.
Beatrix P. Cresswell, *Notes on Devon Churches* 1912, 1922.

The Church of St John the Evangelist

Davidson describes the church in 1847:

At this village which is in the parish of Cornwood, is a chapel of ease of recent date said to have been enlarged about 40 years ago. It consists of a large area with no architectural pretensions. The roof is supported by three columns in the middle. The windows exhibit some attempt at the pointed style with pieces of stained glass. The pulpit and pews are modern. The Font is a marble basin. There is a gallery and organ. In front of a side gallery are the arms of Rogers impaling Lemian of Norfolk.

The ruins comprise a south-west tower with a western doorway, and the interior shows that it had a nave, north aisle, and chancel. The building seems to have been very poor, and the ruins are now by no means safe.

Letter from Robert Savage, rector of Harford, to Sir John Rogers:

To Sir John Rogers at Blachford
Lukesland and Grove
November 18 1809

Sir,
I take the liberty of representing to you the want of sufficient accommodation in the Chaple to Ivybridge for the Inhabitants many of whom have in consequence been induced rather than neglect entirely Public Worship to frequent the Meetings in the village over which preside the most illiterate and ignorant teachers. As the village is rapidly increasing both in size and population, it is proposed to erect with your permission and assistance an additional Aisle to join the Back of the present Edifice sufficiently spacious to contain the Extra inhabitants and the Poor in particular: the erection of which with some trifling alterations, would it is considered amount to the sum of £300 or thereabouts including arrears due to Mr Rivers on the building of the Chapel some years since. Mr Yonge a Vicar of the Parish of Cornwood in which it stands, Has I understand promised to contribute One hundred Pounds towards the necessary addition. I have therefore to solicit your aid on the occasion not doubting your ready compliance

with my request to promote the object in view. Mr Rivers will I am persuaded cheerfully undertake the superintendence of the new building, and will lay before you an Estimate of the expense likely to be incurred in erecting the Aisle should the matter be brought to bear. It is proposed to commence the building next Spring. Your answer will determine our future proceedings and will I trust be favourable.

I have the honour to be
Sir, Your most faithful humble
Robert Savage

Undated circular. Copy to the Rev Strode of Newnham:

Sir,
The increasing Population of Ivybridge has induced Sir John Rogers at an expense of nearly £500 to enlarge the Chapel at Ivybridge. A Chaplain is appointed who performs divine Service twice a day; expecting when everything is settled to receive from the Rents of the Pews about £60 a year. The Bishop refuses to consecrate the Chapel unless something like an endowment can be previously established, he has proposed that if a subscription be raised of £250 he will support with his influence a petition to the Trustees of Queen Anne's Bounty without doubt of success to obtain £200 which with what may be expected from Parliamentary Grants and he would consider as an Endowment that would justify him to Consecrate – The Amount of our present subscriptions shall be subjoined. I am not ashamed to beg, in the behalf of the Religion and Constitution of my Country, supported too as I am in this Case by the Cause of Humanity when so many Poor Creatures would be almost destitute of Sound Instruction in Religion and Morality and in danger of being drawn aside into fanatical schism, without this assistance. If to this good End, I can obtain your charitable Help, I can only add my prayers that your Alms may ascend for a memorial at the last day.

I am, your Humble Servant
Duke Yonge

Undated letter postmarked 2 March 1816 from Revd Beloe to Sir John Rogers:

Dear Sir,
As I am ignorant at the present time where you may have your head Quarters I shall direct this letter to Teignmouth whither I had intended to have gone for a few days, but this place has been and still continues in great confusion – every person is so miserably poor that I am unable to get any settlement from them having only received Eleven pounds for nearly nine months duty – I am therefore anxious to endeavour to effect the Endowment as speedily as possible and request you to let me receive your opinion upon the Trustees – I should venture to propose the following list:

Sir John Rogers
Revd Mr Yonge – necessarily
John Bulteel Esq.
Revd M.R. Froade
R. Rosvear Esq.

and as a Compliment the Bishop should be asked if he would present his nomination – if this should meet with your approbation I will immediately collect what money I can and place it in their hands, and I am inclined to hope that you will not make any objection as it will be the only means of securing that income which was stated in the advertisement – I have fixed upon these persons because in the immediate neighbourhood and therefore more easy of access upon any occasion.

Old Rivers had his last meeting yesterday and proposed to be permitted to carry on the Inn!!! Such scenes of iniquity and fraud have been discovered that it is almost unnecessary to add his appeal was rejected – The Squire's Creditors meet on Friday and he will most probably share a similar fate with his father – he however is much to be pitied having been duped where he could not expect design.

In case you should have heard that I am about to accompany Sir Richard King to the East Indies I take this opportunity to aprise you that I declined the offer although very handsomely tendered to me.

I remain, Dear Sir,
Your obliged and faithful
Henry P Beloe

Sir John Rogers drafted his reply on the same paper, agreeing to the proposals. There followed a letter from Ivybridge residents to Sir John Rogers:

Ivybridge 9 October 1816
To Sir John Rogers at Blachford

Honourable Sir,
We the undersigned take the liberty of addressing you respecting our Clergyman Mr Beloe who from his misconduct has been dismissed our Chapel by the Revd Mr Yonge being so situated we beg leave to say that it is our wish not to have the Chapel consecrated if it should meet with your intire approbation as otherwise it will be forever put out of our power to choose for ourselves a Clergyman as then it would be in the power of the Rector at all times by an application to the Bishop to appoint whomsoever he pleases, and as the Chaplain will have solely to depend on the Inhabitants we particularly wish to know if it meets with your entire approbation, one having the power of choosing to the best of our Judgment a respectable Chaplain for ourselves.

We have the honour to remain with the greatest respect
Your obedient humble Servants

J. Sanders — *Francis Pinches*
John Hodder-Medland — *Hector Bleue*
James Cox — *Richd Spuring*

Scouts

Cubs with Mr T. Maddock, Dartmoor, 1928.

Summer camp, Bolbury Down, 1928.

Scouts

Summer camp at Newton Ferrers, 1929.

On Dartmoor with Mr Maddock, 1928.

Generations of cub scouts and leaders get together to mark the seventy-fifth anniversary of the movement, c.1982.

John Cripps	*John Blackmore*
Philip Bowen	*John Finches*
James Richards	*Wm.Saunders*
Henry Rivers	*John Selden*
John Rivers	*William Pim*
R. Wingett	*Mark Bird*
R. Phillips	*John Hawkins*
R. Leamen	*James Ford*
A.G. Goodridge	*John Windsor*
Jas. Williams-Taylor	

P.S. Your reply as soon as possible will oblige to J. Sanders.

Sir John's replied that he regretted Mr Beloe's behaviour should have induced the withdrawal of confidence from those to whom the power of nomination to the Chaplaincy may be vested and that strict enquiries were made and the most satisfactory answers were received on the subject of Mr Beloe's character.

Ivybridge Chapel

3 October 1817, Endowment of Ivybridge Chapel

In January 1817 the population of Ivybridge had been assessed at	477
Stowford Grist & Paper Mill-houses at 1/8th mile distant	35
Stowford House & Cottages 33 at ½ mile distant	
Westover, Langham, Woodland village at ½ mile distant	79
Villages at Cadleigh, Tor Hill, Trehill & Filham about 1 mile.	146

	770

N.B. The most distant of these villages are more than 2 miles from any Church and in consequence of this a Methodist Chapel has lately been built and is much frequented at Ivybridge and it is reported that another is intended to be built in or near Ivybridge.

Population estimate – undated, probably 1836–37:

1. Population of 4 parishes, taken in May 1831:

Ermington	1,471
Ugborough	1,468
Cornwood	720
Harford	210

	3,868
	----------------

2. Population of parts near Chapel and likely to form a Congregation

Ivybridge	757
plus Cadleigh	26
Hunsdon 11; Brew 5; Yeo 7; Pithill 13	36
Rutt 9; Westover 8; Dunaton 33; Langham 7	57
N & S Filham 116; Lukesland &c 20	136
Turnpike gate 7; Newland & Wadland 9	16

	1,184

During the summer months from 30 to 40 persons sojourn at Ivybridge from Plymouth, Devonport and Stonehouse, who attend the Chapel.

3. Capacity of Chapel? 650

4. What portion will be given free sittings?
About 200 sittings in and under the Gallery and in the Aisles might be given.
5. What rate of pew rents?
From £6 to £4 for each sitting.
6. The amount of Endowment independent of Pew rents?
The answer must be left to the Bishop and yourself.

(The document is an unsigned copy.)

London January 8, 1837. Draft letter from Sir John Rogers to the Bishop of Exeter.

I have the honour to acknowledge the receipt of your Lordship's letter of the 23rd ult. forwarded to me from Teignmouth, and am flattered by your Lordship's sanction of the improvement and enlargement of the Chapel at Ivy Bridge. A sum of about £100 is, I believe, already in the hands of the Vicar of the Parish of Cornwood, as a contribution towards its endowment. By this subscription an additional £100 can be obtained from Pinkham's trust. These £200 could procure £300 from the Governors of Queen Anne's Bounty. If the population of the place is above 500 I understand the Governors may be induced to give a lot of £300 (and should it far surpass that number two lots of £300 each) out of the Parliamentary Grants. The inhabitants of the village were some time since computed to exceed six hundred, but I will get a correct report of their present amount. The rent of the seats, estimated at about £60 per annum clear of repairs, together with the interest of the above sums, would render the duty worthy the attention of a respectable clergyman. It would likewise afford a great pleasure to encourage by every means in my power the establishment of a Classical School for which the situation of Ivybridge, from the salubrity of its air, the accommodation of stage coaches, its convenient distance from Plymouth etc appears to be peculiarly eligible, and might create another source of emolument to the officiating Minister. I learn from the Secretary to the Governors of Queen Anne's Bounty that the names of three Clergymen of the Diocese and three Laymen of the County to be appointed Trustees should be transmitted for ratification and he considers there would be no objection to my having the right of nomination to the Chaplaincy subject to the approbation of the Vicar Mr Savery, who had an interview with your Lordship at Exeter, and understood your Lordship to approve of this arrangement has discovered another Trust (Marshalls) from which probably £100 or £200 more may be obtained. It will I suppose be necessary for me to convey in fee the land on which the Chapel is built to Trustees appointed by your Lordship, may I therefore be permitted to place your Lordship's name at the head of the following list which I presume to offer for your Lordship's consideration, and I beg also to be favoured with your Lordship's opinion whether it would be right and proper to propose the same Trustees to the Governors of Queen Anne's Bounty:

Revd Duke Yonge, Vicar of Cornwood
Revd Robert Savage, Rector of Harford
Revd George Baker, Rector of S Brent
Sir J.L. Rogers
Edmund Pollexfen Bastard, Esq.
Richard Rosvcar, Esq.

Secretary of the Governors to Revd Thomas Brown, Ivybridge, 6 January 1837. Bounty Office, Great Deans Yard, Westminster:

Informing Revd Brown that his curacy of St John's Ivybridge is to be augmented with £200 out of the Royal Bounty and that Interest will be allowed him at 3½ per cent per annum.

Whenever you may propose to invest the above Augmentation in a suitable purchase of Lands or Tithes, you will be pleased to send to me an account thereof, and the names of three beneficed Clergymen of the Diocese, and of three Laymen in the neighbourhood to be inserted in a Commission of Enquiry. If you propose the purchase of & Copyhold, it must be of inheritance, at a Fine certain, and the consent of the Lord of the Manor must be obtained, it being necessary that you should be admitted to a Copyhold to the use of yourself and successors for ever. The Governors object to heritable lands.

Slip of paper. Two years Endowment of chapel due from Sir J.L. Rogers at £20 per annum due £40.0.0 Mis. 1837

16 1836. Sir John paid to Mr Hodson for QAB as

described by M. Brown	*£100*
Quarters interest to Mis. 1836	*£1.5s. 0d.*
One years int. on £80 to Mis 1837	*£4.0s.0d.*
	£105.5s.0d.
Due Mis. 1837 to Sir John	*£65.5s.0d.*
One years int. due Mis 1838	*£3.5s.0d.*
	£68.10s.0d.
Less one years endt. Due same time.	*£20.0s.0d.*
	£8.10s.0d.
A years int. due Mis.1839	*£2.8s.6d.*
	£50.18s.6d.
Less a years endt. Due Mis. 1839	*£20.0s.0d.*
Due Mis. 1839 to Sir J.L.R.	*£30.18s.6d.*

Revd Thomas Brown to Sir John L Rogers, Ivybridge, 16 April 1840.

My dear Sir, In accordance with your wishes I beg leave to state to you the particulars touching Ivybridge Chapel as follows:

The Endowment you know to be £20 per annum and has been applied since it was first due to the liquidation of the £100 advanced by yourself to meet in conjunction with the £100 given by the Pincocombe Trust that £200 granted by the Governors of Queen Anne's Bounty. The Pew rent has varied from £44 to £52 upon the entire seven years, out of this the Clerk's stipend £3 and the Sexton's salary £1.8s. are to be deducted and the expenses of collecting. All the repairs of the Chapel of whatever kind, Sacramental Wine and all contingencies devolve on the Minister such as Visitation ..?.. etc. The Surplus fees are from £3 to £4 per annum. The interest granted from the Bounty office which becomes due in April and October respectively is £13 per annum. These I believe are all the particulars connected with the benefice.

Very faithfully yours,
Thomas Brown

July 1840. Revd J. Duncan Cork is appointed to the Incumbancy of Ivybridge:

Ivybridge Church
Letter from Revd R. Atherton to Sir Frederick Rogers.
Ivybridge, 16 August 1851

Sir Frederick,
As you are patron of the Chapelry of St John Ivybridge, and interested in whatever affects, or is likely to affect the prosperity of the place, I beg to lay before you some matters respecting the state and prospects of the Chapelry before I submit them to the Lord Bishop of the Diocese. It is my earnest wish to hand down this District to my successor better than I found it, and I cannot doubt that in any effort to secure this Sir Frederick will give me his warmest support. I need scarcely tell you that the Chapel at Ivybridge was consecrated by the Bishop of Exeter in the year 1835, and was intended to provide for a population of 67 from the parish of Cornwood, of 875 from the parish of Ermington and of 190 from the parish of Ugborough, i.e the Chapelry was to provide for the Spiritual wants of

1,132 persons. Though released from the duty of attending to this large number of people, the parishes of Cornwood, Ermington and Ugborough have never contributed, as far as I am aware, either jointly or severally, to the support of the Clergyman at Ivybridge. I leave others to say whether there is or is not a just claim upon them. The following are the only existing sources of income to the Clergyman
1. A provision of Twenty Pounds (£20) a year made by the late Sir John Leman Rogers Bart at the time of consecration.
2. The sum of Twelve Pounds twelve shillings and sixpence (£12.12s.6d) a year from the Governors of Queen Anne's bounty that would be discontinued if a parsonage were built.
3. The produce of pew rents, which from a variety of causes has been small during the last five or six years and is not likely to be improved for some time to come owing to the removal of certain families and
4. A very small sum from Surplice fees.

The late Sir John vested a further sum of £40 at the time of consecration, in addition to the endowment, but the interest it produces is to be spent on repairs and forms no part of the Clergyman's stipend.

It is necessary to state here that the Incumbent is responsible for everything connected with the Chapel – for the payment of Clerk and Sexton, for cleaning and repairing the Chapel, and for all incidental expenses that may arise. If writing of myself I should not allude to these things without at the same time testifying to the kindness that has been shown me by yourself, by Mr Cotton, by Mr Hartley, by Mr Warren and by Mr Duffin and others, but I write for the District not for or of myself, and I foresee responsibility that it would be difficult to provide for without some change. The schools for example, owing to Miss Fincher's death have just given rise to great anxiety. Something must be done to supply her place, but we are at a loss how to act for want of funds. Any change as it appears must involve an expense that we are not yet prepared to meet. I mean to try what can be done among my Plymouth friends next week. Again, in a short time, I say a year or so, the Chapel will require considerable repairs of which the roof already gives an intimation and parts of the Churchyard that are not yet cleared will require to be opened. It is difficult to see how the expenses of the next few years can be met (i.e. if some change does not take place) without trespassing upon kindness that has already done what it can.

You will naturally ask what remedy is proposed for this? One person has suggested the formation of an Endowment fund, which is very good no doubt, but where can we look for help? Others have suggested an appeal to some of the 'Societies' for Church Extension, but I was told on application that they could hold out no hope. It has occurred to me, however, that there is one Plan left that would help us if approved by yourself and sanctioned by the Bishop. There may be an idea in some minds ever since the Consecration, that Ivybridge would one day become a parish entitled to the tithes of a District that are now paid to the Mother Churches. If this could be it would relieve many of our difficulties, besides securing several very important objects. If it (a Chapelry) were a parish the Clergyman would be brought more directly into intercourse with people than he is now – the whole parish would have an interest in the Church, the schools would be parochial not private, and much of the responsibility that now rests on a few would be share by all. Besides it might then be possible to retain a Clergyman in the village. I should like information on a few points before anything is done and shall be glad if you or Mr Rogers will kindly assist me in obtaining it. We should know before going to the Bishop how far the law would sanction the erection of this District into a parish:

To what extent, as far as rates & are concerned, we should if a parish be Independent of the Mother Churches: And

What fees tithes & now received by the Clergymen of the parishes out of which the District is formed could be taken by the Incumbent of Ivybridge?

We need not add how important the influence of the Church is to the temporal prosperity of a place and how desirable it is to find some bond that will more firmly unite the people to their pastor. The settlement of the Church question might draw persons to the Village, for one of the first questions strangers ask is about the Church and its Clergyman.

I shall be only too happy if this plan or any other can promote the permanent interests of Ivybridge, and remain Sir Frederick

Yours very truly, Robert H. Atherton.

Colonel Campbell, who was vicar of Ivybridge in the 1920s.

To: Sir Frederick Leman Rogers Bart.
23 August 1851. Letter from Revd Robert H. Atherton to Sir Frederick Rogers. Thinks it will not be difficult to get Ivybridge St J. Chapelry made into a parish without coming into collision with the Incumbents of Ugborough, Cornwood and Ermington.

Ivybridge would then qualify for an Endowment of £150 from Government. Then it would not be difficult to get a parsonage built.
August 1849. Cholera in Ivybridge. Four died in one day. No clergyman to bury the dead.
October 1850. Revd Robert H. Atherton appointed Incumbent at St John's Ivybridge.

Bittaford Carnival

Above and right: Members of the Coker family

Percy Coker at Bittaford Carnival, 1937.

Bittaford Carnival

Above left: *Bullen's car before being decorated for the carnival.* Right: *The car decorated!*

Hospital staff during Bittaford Carnival, 1936.

Awaiting decoration, Bittaford.

Ivybridge carnival in the 1940s.

Ivybridge Carnival

Celebrating the coronation of King George VI in 1937.

Carnival float.

Ivybridge Carnival

Above, left and right: *Pam House, Carnival Queen.*

Children's fancy dress, St John's Road, 1953.

The Women's Institute in national dress from around the world.

Ivybridge Carnival

Flying the flag for Britain!

Ready, get set... The mum's race about to start.

The PHAB (Physically Handicapped and Able Bodied) float

Ivybridge Carnival

The Ivy Pageant, 1950. Left to right, back row: *Ivy Kingsland, Pat Withycombe, ?, Barbara House, ?;* front row: ?, ?, Mrs Stockland.

The Ivy Pageant

Ivybridge Carnival

The Ivy Queen, Mary Turner, and attendants.

Entries in the fancy dress competition.

Ivybridge Carnival

Fancy dress contestants in the 1940s.

Pets Parlour carnival entry, 1974.

The Ladies' Circle dressed as honey bees.

Clowning around, Ivybridge Carnival.

Ivybridge Carnival royalty.

Ivybridge Electric Supply Co., 1905–41 – Recollections of Two Ex-Apprentices

Edwin Harvey

In 1905 the then Ivybridge Urban District Council invited the late Mr W.G. Heath, electrical engineer of Plymouth, to establish an electricity undertaking in the district.

The first generating station was set up in a part of Messrs H.J.F. Lee's mill off Fore Street. The nature of the engine or generators is not known.

Distribution of electricity was by means of underground cables, the system being two-wire direct current at 200 volts. The cables were laid throughout the village streets, including a separate cable for street lighting.

The underground cables were terminated in a wooden distribution box near the Ivy Bridge in Station Road. From there overhead lines were erected on short wooden poles, giving distribution to Exeter Road, Station Road and Beacon Road ending at 'Ottawa'.

In Station Road the line extended up the hill and crossed the river by means of insulators and brackets fastened to the old viaduct. Much trouble was experienced by electrolysis on the insulators due to dampness from the railway. On leaving the viaduct the line connected Stowford House and Ermewood.

The underground cable from Fore Street extended to 'Greenwood' in Western Road. Another underground cable extended to Blachford Road near the vicarage gate, and from there an overhead line ran to the then Dame Hannah Rogers School. Much trouble was experienced after storms with fallen trees and branches.

In those early days many consumers' supplies were unmetered, a fixed charge of 10s. a quarter per lamp being made.

The demand grew and in 1916 a 35bhp Tangye suction gas engine and pump, together with an Armfield water turbine and a 365 ampere hour battery were added in an adjoining building known as Union Mills.

The engine and turbine were coupled by means of endless belts to their respective Mather & Platt 4-pole shunt wound generators.

The water from the river Erme was used by Lee's Mill during the day and by the electricity works at night and at weekends; special automatic magnetic switchgear was fitted to enable this to be done.

The suction gas engine was used to charge the battery and meet the evening peak lighting load.

With the increased price of anthracite about 1926 a cheaper grade of fuel was tried with disastrous results, which eventually led to the purchase by the company of the old paper mill near Factory Bridge about 1927.

The great advantage the old mill offered was its large water-wheel which replaced a smaller wheel in 1896, being some 22ft in diameter and 11ft in width and said to develop 80bhp.

Between the years 1927 and 1930 the old system was improved, the battery removed from Union

Stowford mill before the 1914 fire.

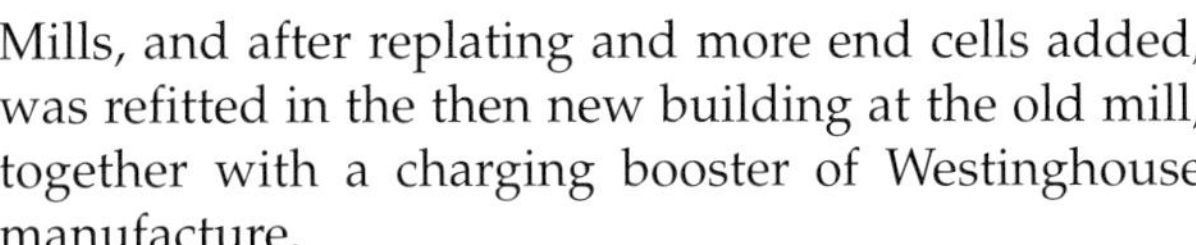

Mills, and after replating and more end cells added, was refitted in the then new building at the old mill, together with a charging booster of Westinghouse manufacture.

A 60kw shunt-wound Mather & Platt generator was connected to the water-wheel by means of belts and gearing and ran at 600rpm. The voltage on the system was then raised from 200 to 230.

The average output from the 60kw water-wheel generator during the winter months – September to March– was 28kw, max 40kw.

This output gave, on average, 120 amps at 230 volts, corresponding to a water flow of about 18 cubic feet per second over the wheel. The water flow dropped rapidly during a dry March until June and the rest of the summer gave about 6kw output.

In November 1930, after a heavy rain storm, a raging flood swept through the weir, which resulted in a complete shut down of the plant.

A friendly understanding between the company and the paper mill resulted in a temporary connection allowing interchange of power between the systems, so allowing the battery to be recharged and maintaining the supply.

With the help of local unemployed men and the company's staff the hole in the weir was repaired using iron bars and concrete, and the plant started up again. To avoid a similar shut down two 60bhp Gardner petrol-paraffin four-cylinder vertical direct-coupled sets from the former Okehampton station were installed.

These engines had a separate carburettor to each cylinder, were fitted with magnetic ignition and were started with a starting handle. This proved difficult and the sets were fitted to start electrically. Then, in an endeavour to stabilise the voltage output, a water-cooled magnetic brake was fitted to the water-wheel generator. The load continued to increase and a supply was extended to Woodland, Godwell, and to Mr Hart's poultry farm on the Ermington Road. The petrol paraffin engines were taken out of service and diesel engines with their generators were installed.

The final blow came during the Second World War with a disastrous fire, which burnt out the old mill and wrecked the generating plant. A supply was then provided from the Plympton RDC high-voltage network – in any case this supply was needed to meet the increased demand caused by the American Forces camps then based in Ivybridge.

So when you press that switch and flood the house with light, heat, sound or television, think of the early band of pioneers who gave South West Devon the lead in Hydro Electric Power.

Members of Staff

The engineers in charge, handymen and apprentices in the early days were Percy Heath, Samuel Phillips, Harry Lee and Jack Millman. In the 1920s they were William Friend, James Pulleyblank Bank, Jack Tidball and Henry Northmore; and in the late 1920s to early 1940s Robert Clarke, William Fox, William Hurrell, Edwin Harvey, Alfred Moysey, Ronald Worth and Kenneth French.

The Lower Mill

Public interest in the history of the Lower Mill, which used to be approached from Keaton Road in Ivybridge, revived in the spring of 1985, when the brick and stone aqueduct that had carried water to drive the water-wheel on which the mill depended for power was about to be demolished as part of the development of Waterside House, a residential home for the elderly. A short history of the aqueduct based on what was known about it at the time was instrumental in persuading the Department of the Environment to list the surviving structure as 'a building of special architectural or historic interest'.

Similarly drastic action in the same cause had been necessary in May 1976. The first clearance of the site for development meant that all the old mill buildings, then very much decayed, had to be removed, and work was about to begin on the destruction and removal as scrap of the water-wheel. The wheel was still in a fair state of preservation, and by tremendous effort on the part of a number of Ivybridge people and others, it was dismembered and its iron frame taken to Plympton for storage until ways and means could be devised for its restoration in Ivybridge. Although as time goes on the practicalities of restoration become more and more difficult, the intention has never been entirely abandoned.

Mr Berry's Woollen Factory

The story begins in the 1820s, at which time the village was part of the manor of Ivybridge, held by Sir John Rogers of Blachford, sixth baronet. A bachelor, Sir John spent little of his time on his estates but gave over their management to his stewards, Mr Christopher Savery and his sons, Messrs Servington and John Savery. It is in the Saverys's accounts and bills of cost for work done, submitted once a year to Sir John, that most of the early history of the mill has survived. But reconstruction of the history from the sometimes vague details presented in the accounts has its difficulties, and the present writing may contain errors of interpretation without, it is hoped, distorting too much the general run of events.

On 17 June 1822 Mr John Savery met two gentlemen of the name of Berry at Ivybridge respecting the building of a woollen manufactory at Ivybridge. The Berrys were serge and blanket manufacturers at Chagford and Ashburton, and they also owned a woollen mill at Buckfast, close to the abbey. Almost a year later, on 5 April 1823, Mr Servington Savery came to Ivybridge and had a long conference

The horse and cart was used to transport the 'half stuff' between mills.

Watercolour of the bridge and mill

Christmas dinner at the mill.

Mill manager Tony Traill is presented with a barometer outside the main office of Stowford Mill. Also present are Mr Freemantle, Mr Northmore, Mr Drummer Leigh MBE, Mr Ward and Mr Christopher.

with one of the Berrys about the siting of the proposed factory and about the taking of water for a leat from the Erme. They met again on 14 April and examined the spot chosen by Mr Berry for his factory, and on 8 May he marked out the ground. The proposed line of the leat was the subject of a long discussion on 16 June, since water from the Erme would have to be taken at a point lower down the river from the outfall of the leat which served the Union corn mill and Mr Pim's paper mill.

Negotiations went on all through 1823 and 1824, and it was not until September 1824 that Mr Berry's lease could be prepared. His buildings were to include a wash-house and a stretch-house, and he would require a road. The yearly rent was agreed at £16 (Mr Savery had hoped to get £20, ten per cent on the value of the land) for a term of 99 years dependent on three lives, and there would be an additional payment of either £1 or 10s. a year for 'the Spot proposed for the Fulling Mill'. The absence of mention of further meetings suggests that Mr Berry was in occupation and working the factory early in 1825.

There is no information on what kind of cloth the Ivybridge factory produced, nor on how the enterprise prospered. An Ivybridge rental states that John Berry was insolvent in 1830, but on 31 July 1832 he was back negotiating the building of a cottage, the site unfortunately not being mentioned. The Ermington parish Tithe Map of 1841 shows the site of a 'Manufactory Yard' on 26 perches of land where the Lower Mill stood, leased to and occupied by John Berry, and a house and garden close by occupied by Mr William Squance. On the few facts available it is reasonable to assume that the factory was in production from 1825 until at least halfway into the 1840s.

In 1848 the Ivybridge mill was put up for sale. An advertisement in the *Exeter Flying Post* for 21 September in that year provides the only description we have of the mill as it was in the 1840s.

Ivybridge. To be sold by public auction at Rivers' Hotel in Ivybridge on Monday October 2nd 1848 at 3 o'clock in the afternoon, by Messrs.Widdicombe & Son, all that excellent WOOLLEN FACTORY with the working Gear thereto belonging, Smith's Forge, Lathe etc together with a Cottage attached.

Also attached near to the above, a neat and comfortable sized Cottage fit for the residence of a Manager: Flower and Vegetable Gardens, with a large Stable, convenient Offices and a Labourer's Cottage; also a large piece of Ground (about 120 yards from the Mill) now used as a Garden, purchased by the original Proprietor for the erection of another Mill, having a powerful fall of Water, the whole containing about Oa.3r.20p.

The Factory consists of Four principal Floors and a Garret, with two large Store Rooms, the Mill Floors being 60 by 35 feet, two of which are fully geared with Line Shafting, and Bevel Gear, has a never failing and bountiful supply of Water, the whole of the River Erme being available. It is substantially built of the best materials. The Water Wheel is 24ft high and 10ft wide, from 30 to 40 horse power, and is, as well as the whole of the Gear and Premises in a first rate repair.

The Premises may be either used as a Woollen Factory, or can easily be converted into a Paper Mill, or any other Manufactory requiring great Water Power, and are very advantageously situate in the village of Ivybridge within half a mile of the South Devon Railway Station thus offering great facilities for the easy and speedy transit of Goods.

The Property is held under Lease from Sir. F. Rogers, for the residue of a term of 99 years, determinable on the deaths of 3 healthy lives aged 52, 50 and 31 years respectively, subject to a Yearly Conventionary Rent of £16 and a Heriot of £2 on each Life with the right of perpetual renewal. For viewing the Premises, apply to William Squance thereon, and for any further information to Messrs. Widdicombe & Son, of Hay, Ugborough, to Messrs. R. & B. Sherwell of Ivybridge, or to Mr Berry the Proprietor of Chagford.

If there were any bids, later events suggest they were unsuccessful.

Mr John Allen's Lower Paper Mill

Stowford paper mill, above the bridge at Ivybridge in Harford parish, was founded in 1787. Owned successively by several proprietors, the mill was bought in 1849 by John Allen, an entrepreneur with many business interests. The mill had been fitted out with new machinery by one of the previous owners, and before long Mr Allen found that the water taken from the River Erme which a leat carried to the mill for papermaking and for power was no longer sufficient for the mill's needs. On 20 July 1850, Mr Servington Savery informed Sir Frederick Rogers, who was now the seventh baronet and had inherited Ivybridge from his brother, that: 'From insufficiency of Water Power in the Higher Mill to work the machinery I heard of Mr Allen's intention to purchase or take the Lower Mill in aid of the upper one.' What Mr Savery had heard appears to have been correct, for in March 1851 a lease to Mr Allen for the Lower Mill was ready for execution, and on 14 April the purchase was settled by Mr Allen on payment of £200 'consideration money to Sir Frederick'.

It is likely that Sir Frederick had bought back Berry's lease in 1850.

Mr Allen used the Lower Mill in later years, and probably from its conversion to papermaking in 1851, for the production of what is known to papermakers as 'half stuff'. Rags and old sails were pulverised at the mill and afterwards the partially made paper (half stuff) was taken by horse and cart to Stowford for processing into finished paper.

After John Allen's death in 1877 his sons, Edward

The large beater used to smash up the cloth.

Each receving a clock for services to the paper mill are Sid Ingram, foreman, and Bill ?.

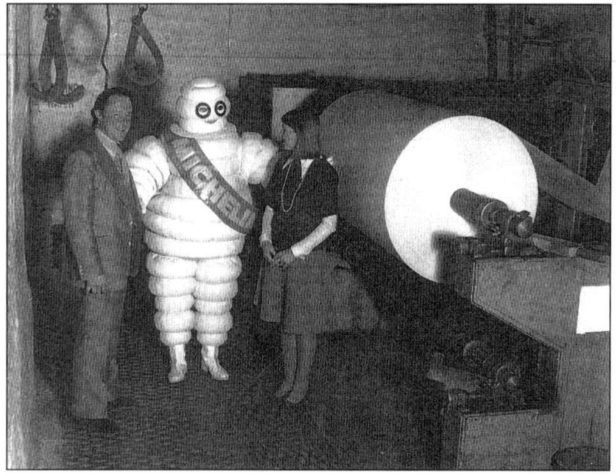

The Michelin Man, alias Sid Ingram, visits the mill.

and John, carried on the paper-making business, first as a family partnership and later as a limited company. In 1915 the mill was sold to a partnership of Clapperton brothers and others and they in turn sold to the well-known paper makers Portals Ltd. of Laverstoke in Hampshire in 1923. By that time, however, Stowford Mill had been very much enlarged and was capable of performing all the processes of paper making. The extra capacity of the Lower Mill was no longer required, although the upper floors of the building were still used for the storage of rags.

Ivybridge Electric Supply Co.

The Ivybridge Electric Supply Co. acquired a part of the Lower Mill, together with the use of its water power, in about 1927. Since 1905 this company had been generating electricity on a very limited scale for the village in a small stone built building alongside Mr Henry Lee's corn mill, sharing with the corn mill the use of the water from the mill leat. But in 1926 the cost of working the plant at Lee's Mill had become uneconomic, so that the availability of the Lower paper mill, with its very powerful water-wheel, came at just the right time.

Ivybridge continued to be supplied with electricity from the Lower Mill until 1941, when rags stored in the upper floors caught fire and the plant was partly wrecked. By then the demand for electricity in the village was beginning to exceed the capacity of the local company, partly because of a US Army camp which had been set up here, and the opportunity was taken to close down the local works and in future supply Ivybridge from Plympton.

Decay set in on the abandoned fire-damaged buildings and nature quickly took over. In 1974 it was only with some difficulty one could break through the dense growth and rediscover where had been a significant part of the industrial life of Ivybridge for about 116 years.

The Lower Mill Leat and Water-Wheel

Mr Berry's choice of site for his woollen-mill necessitated his taking water from the Erme about one-fith of a mile upstream, the head weir across the river and sluice gate to the leat being a measured two chains (44 yards) below the outfall of the corn mill leat. For part of its course an agreement was reached for it to pass through the garden of Mr Roger Phillips, a tenant of Sir John Rogers who held on lease two acres comprising a garden, a field and the house in which he dwelt. He was sometimes referred to as 'Gardener Phillips',and the house still has the name 'Garden Cottage'.

The weir was originally of boulders and probably changed very little until flood water caused severe damage in November 1930. It was then rebuilt with concrete reinforced with iron, local men giving a helping hand in its reconstruction. The leat still runs, but is to some extent silted up. Where it runs through what was Roger Phillips's garden it is 6½ feet wide and has red brick sides up to what was probably the normal water-line. Control of the flow of water at the weir was by an iron gate, raised and lowered by pinion gearing of which only the much-worn axle and pinion remained in 1975, the gate having been replaced by a fixed wooden shutter. At distances along the leat there were three sluices which could be withdrawn when the water got too high or when work was being done on the wheel, surplus water being returned to the river which at these points was several feet below the level of the leat. As the leat approached the mill the ground dropped considerably, so that the required slower fall of water was maintained by taking the water over a series of stone and brick arches which gave a head clearance under of six feet or more. To reach the overshot wheel the launder turned at a sharp angle, and there appears to have been some difficulty in restraining the water from overflowing at the arches, which fault eventually caused a deterioration of the brick-work. The tail-race was also set at an angle to the line of the wheel's rotation, and this too caused trouble under the wheel since the water could not get away quickly enough. The tail-race was covered over in later years when the building was extended over it, and it continued to take water to a low power undershot wheel at Mr Allen's engineer's shop built by him in the 1850s close by the bridge which crossed the Erme on the Ermington road.

But the leat and aqueduct we see now are almost certainly Mr Allen's and his sons' work, much of it carried out in 1896, the date shown in iron figures on one of the arches. What the leat looked like in Mr Berry's time, and what kind of launder he used where the aqueduct stands, we shall never know. In the early twentieth century the leat was cleaned out every Sunday, and people living in Keaton Road whose gardens backed onto the leat were allowed to draw water from it on Sundays, ready for 'wash day' on Monday.

The earliest description of the water-wheel at the Lower Mill is that of 1848, when it is said to have been 24ft high with a width of 10ft, producing 30–40 horse power. This may have been the wheel installed by Mr Berry in 1824, but the dimensions are intriguingly those of a wheel put up for sale at Filham silver-lead mine (Ivybridge Consols) in 1845, the buyer of which unfortunately we do not know. What is known, however, on reliable authority, is that the Lower Mill wheel was replaced by a larger, more powerful wheel in 1896, according to the late Mr Edwin Harvey, 'some 22ft diameter with 11ft breast to develop 80bhp'. It is likely that the leat was improved in 1896 and very possibly at the same time the aqueduct was built. Mr Robert Clarke, who was engineer-in-charge in the 1920s to 1930s, wrote (from 35 years' memory) that the wheel was very wide and with 12ft radius 'the torque was enormous', each bucket, he believed, holding 40 gallons.

Probably the most reliable record of the wheel put in in 1896 , the one ''rescued' in 1976, in an inventory made in 1915 of premises and plant owned by Stowford Paper Mill, which includes at the Lower Mill 'Overshot iron water-wheel with wood buckets and spokes 24ft diameter 10ft breast; 9 inch centre shaft and 2 pedestal bearings. Stone-built race'.

A function of the wheel that at present has a very cloudy history into which more research is required, concerns the water supplied to the mill during its paper-making period. Probably late in the Allens's time, water from the high ground at Stowford passed either by natural streams or by man-made channels through the estate of Torr Hill, later known as Uphill, to a collecting well on Filham Moor. This open well, protected by a circular drystone wall, could still be located in 1989 in the fields between Filham Moor Lane and the A38. From this collecting point the water was conducted by iron pipe under the fields and across the bed of the river to a filter bed near the wheel-pit. The cleaned water went to an adjacent tank sunk in the ground, from whence it was pumped to a high-level teak tank situated near the launder, the pump being activated by a drive taken off the water-wheel. A coal fire heated the water to the temperature required for paper making. Surplus water from the filter bed flowed back across the Erme by a second pipe alongside the supply pipe. Both pipes may be seen in the river bed now that the concrete cover has broken away. The filter bed could be clearly seen in 1974.

Acknowledgements
The early history of the Lower Mill came from documents held at West Devon Record Office in Plymouth, kindly made accessible by Mr Alistair Passy and Miss Elizabeth Stuart, then Senior Assistant Archivist. The history of Ivybridge Electric Co.'s occupation of the mill is taken from the late Mr Edwin Harvey's paper written and given limited private circulation in the 1970s. Mr Harvey also gave a lot of information on the working of the mill and leat. Some information was been taken from a letter written by Mr Robert Clarke in 1976 to Mrs Pat Healey, who, more than anyone else, was responsible for rescuing the water-wheel in that year. Mr Colin Harris of Stowford Paper Mill kindly lent the 1915 inventory for inspection at one of the local history exhibitions staged in Ivybridge.

THE DAME HANNAH ROGERS SCHOOL AT IVYBRIDGE

Hannah Trefusis was the daughter of Thomas Trefusis of Penryn, Captain RN, later Admiral and Commissioner for Victualling the Navy in London. She was baptised in the Church of St Gluvius, Penryn, in June 1719.

On 2 October 1742 Hannah married John Rogers, the eldest son of Sir John Rogers of Blachford, 2nd baronet. On Sir John's death on 17 January 1744 John became the third baronet, and with Hannah he made Blachford their principal home.

Schools

Ermington Council School c.1910.

Mr Lake with his schoolchildren. He was the longest serving head of Station Road School.

Ivybridge Station Road School and staff c.1910.

Schools

Infant class at Station Road School in the 1920s.

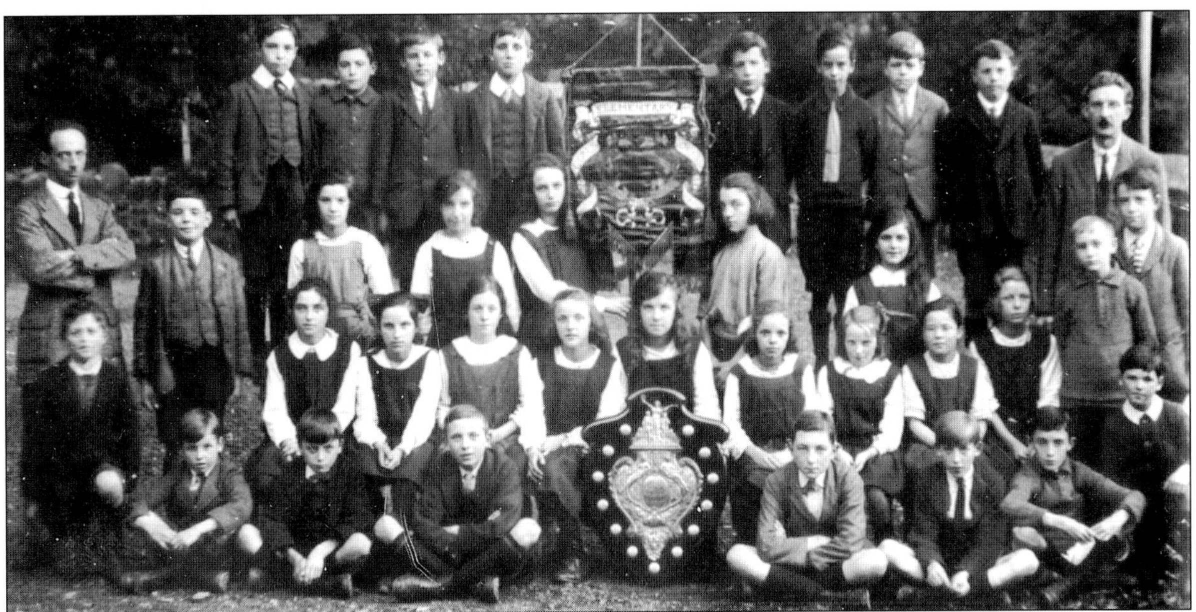

Mr Luxton and Ermington Council School Choir, 1921.

Left: *Ivybridge Mills and School from the air*

Schools

'Gay Nineties' Christmas party, 9 January 1947.

Ermington School football team 1923-24.

Schools

Playgroup, 1975.

Right: *The Highland playgroup, 1980.*

Clowns from the circus in Plymouth visiting Erme School in the 1980s.

Schools

The Mayor of Ivybridge with the winners of an Easter painting competition. Included are Emma Pudney, Jay Day and Holly Humphrey.

Actor John Nettles and a rabbit at Ivybridge County Primary School.

Visiting Japanese student teacher Mutsuko Nakashimado from Fukuoka, near Tokyo, shows Woodland Park Primary School third-year pupils how to drink a cuppa Japanese style!

Christmas visitors to Erme School, 2008.

Santa at Erme Primary School, 2004.

Schools

The Boys' and Girls' Brigades 1st Company, June 1996. Left to right, back row: *Louise McMurrich, Matthew Godward, Matthew Webster, Christopher Patrick, Timothy Farndell (L/Cpl), Jamie McMurrich (Cpl), Andrew Farndell (Sgt), Craig Lewis, Adam Knight, Matthew Swift, Sarah Parkinson, Michelle Edwards;* fifth row: *Sarinha Lavercombe, Connie Davis, Elizabeth Flemwell, Laura Ravenscroft, Kayleigh Hiberd, Amy Fletcher, Philp Gwyer, David Samuels, Nicholas Patrick, Paul Dunn, Sophie Chatfield, Hayley Swift, Hannah Trafford, James Bingham, William Davis, Paul Bingham;* fourth row: *Lucy Rowlands, Rebecca Craig, Leanne Stanley, Rhian Lewis, Robert McNichol, James Rowlands, Ben Hurrell, James Rundle, Daniel Trafford, Carla Ricardo, Isla Hutchinson, Terri Godward, Luke Parkinson, Joe Parkinson;* third row: *Julie Godward, Eileen Webster, Linda Farndell (OIC Juniors), Richard Short (OIC Company), Mark Davies (Chaplain), Terry Farndell (Captain), Mark Beavil, Kelly Short (OIC Anchors), Jennifer Webster. The cadets in the front two rows are not named.*

The Girls' Voluntary Air Training Corps at Station Road School (now Erme School). Left to right, back row: *Anglia Mullins, Pamela House, Marie White, Valerie Turpin, Kathleen Jago, Peggy Pearse, Audrey Winston, Jean Pollard, Eileen Pearse, Doreen Sandercock, Clare Hodge;* second row: *Joyce Tregembo, Dorothy Ford, ?, Dorothy Spry, ?, ?, Miss Kent (officer), ?, ?, Daphne Freemantle (officer), Doreen West, Mildred Holmes, Ernestine Short, Betty Brady, Barbara Priddle, Dot Jones;* front row: *?, ?, Marg Hingston, Vera Hingston, Kath (evacuee), Louisa Willcocks, Marg Gilley, Eveline Wilcocks, Joyce Singleton, Queenie Sergent, ? Lang.*

Sir John and Dame Hannah had no children. In her will, made in 1764, Hannah left the sum of £10,000, part of the fortune she had inherited from her father and from the legacies left by her mother's brother, Mr Samuel Addis of Whiteford in Cornwall, in trust for her husband, Sir John, to have the interest earned on the money during his lifetime, and after his death the capital sum and unspent interest, if any, to be used by the trustees to found a school for the maintenance and education of poor unfortunate children of Devon and Cornwall, or for whatever other benevolent purposes the trustees may decide.

Sir John Rogers died in 1773, but it appears that the trustees were not able to put Lady Rogers's wishes into effect until 1787, when they appointed a master and mistress at a salary of £30 per annum and rented a house near Plymouth to house up to 45 children between the ages of 8 and 18 years. Dame Hannah died in March 1766 at Plymouth and was carried to Cornwood for burial in Cornwood Churchyard.

The school's connection with Ivybridge began in 1887. The lease at Plymouth had expired and the trustees found that its renewal at 1887 values would cost more than the funds would permit. The Rogers family had kept a close interest in the school since its foundation, and in 1887 Lord Blachford, the 8th baronet, provided land at the junction of Crescent Road with Blachford Road, formerly part of lands known as Tisdale's Tenement in Cornwood parish but within the Manor of Ivybridge, whereon a new home and school for the girls in the trust's care was built for the princely sum of £3,700 and was ready for occupation in May 1888. Water was supplied from Henlake Down, piped down under the railway from a reservoir built for the purpose. From 1888 until after the First World War the school trust was used for training orphan girls for domestic service, but it was found financially impossible to continue on these lines. In any case, the majority of the girls did not go into domestic service!

The school buildings were then modernised and equipped to operate as an orthopaedic hospital school, the first of its kind in the South West. It was opened in 1925 under the supervision of the Ministries of Health and Education. By 1947 other orthopaedic hospitals and schools had been opened in the two counties of Devon and Cornwall, and following the introduction of the National Health Service, the trustees decided to seek new uses for the trust fund.

A short account of the school's years at Ivybridge and its removal to larger premises at Westover is given by Tony Barber in his *Aspects of Ivybridge*,1988.

In his will Sir John Rogers requested that the three portraits extant in 1773, those of Dame Hannah, Samuel Addis and Thomas Trefusis, should be hung in the room used by the trustees at the school in Plymouth. Two portraits now hang in the entrance hall at Westover. Neither is signed by the artist, although one may be accepted as being that of Dame Hannah, the other of an unnamed gentleman, most likely Mr Samuel Addis.

IVYBRIDGE VERSES

Ivybridge

This pretty little moorland town where sleeps the bracken hills and tall trees shade the rushing brook beside the paper mills.

Here leaning on the old stone bridge in quiet evening hour you often hear the church bells chime from yonder distant tower'

In Ermington's gay orchard lanes spring forth the pale primrose the old church with its leaning spire, square cottages in rows.

Bittaford Venn Cross to and fro, Run whistling trains all day long.
Down from the moor through pipes is running liquid china clay away.

Cornwood homely inn and village, wooded walks and meadow stiles, with its stately mansion peeping over the pasture land for miles.

Away upon the River Erme, Sunny Harford stands alone, oft lost on the misty moorland, with rough hard granite stones.

Charmed with thy beauty Ivybridge the pretty street, the heather ridge, Borne by the breeze of the road long, the sweet voice of the mill girls' song.

The Ancient Longtimber Legend

Up on the distant, high hilled plains of Dartmoor
The rolling thunder speaks of coming rain
The growling clouds and sudden slash of lightning
Mean stormy weather's on the way again.
A wind whips through the woods and down the ages
Liberating leaves from Longtimber's great trees
They melt into the mud making mould and history
Releasing clouds of ancient memories...

300 million years ago this coarse grained granite
Forced up by heat into Devonian slate
Made batholithic domes on the empty skyline
Temples to gods and giants without date.
Into this wilderness of space and stone
Before music, before time, before words
Came daring men with bony handled axes
Shadowed by women, their young and shaggy herds.
The Beaker people cultivated Dartmoor
And with their tools they made the land obey

Broke fields, grew crops, became first farmers;
Knew loss and hope, feared dark at end of day.
Their fear of death awoke imagination,
They asked 'where are we from?' and 'who am I?'
Built a thousand kistvaens, menhirs and stone circles
Fingers of granite pointing to the sky.
These stone-age steeples haunt Glittered Dartmoor
Bearing witness to man's discovery of the deep
And when the rain teems off these magic henges
It carries with it the secrets that they keep.

Dirty, drizzly Dartmoor days
Make the lichen run
From Rider's Rings new magic's made
In time without the sun.
Cuckoo Ball and Drizzlecombe
Cry endless tears of stone
Filling the Erme's nine tributaries
Name them one by one:
Dark Lake, Red Lake, Dry Lake,
Flow Erme, flow softly
Hook Lake, Left Lake, Stall Moor Water
Flow Erme, flow softly
Hortonsford Brook, Piles Brook, Butter Brook
Flow Erme, flow softly
From blanket bog and mire marsh
Through Hart's tongue, wort and gorse
Comes streaming this strange alchemy
From a primeval source.
It makes the mushrooms magic
Gives sphagnum healing powers
Feeds stonecrop, skullcap, ladyfern
Whatever it touches flowers.
Through solid rock the enchanted Erme
Comes gushing off the moor
Tumbles into Longtimber Woods
With magic at its core.
Birch, alder, hazel, sallow,
Grow, Longtimber, grow
Rowan, hawthorn, oak,
Grow, Longtimber, grow
Larch, holly, sycamore
Grow, Longtimber, grow
The Erme flows through Longtimber's trees
Upwards from root to bough
The branches, bark, the buds and twigs
Are soaked in magic now.
So when you gather kindling
Or logs from trees felled there
Remember the wood,s enchanted
And treat it with great care.
For if you burn Longtimber wood
And murmur the tributary names
Your hearth will burn much brighter
And you'll see the Beaker people in the flames.
I'm going up Longtimber woods
I'll only stop to kick the leaves away
(And wait to watch the water clear I may);
I shan't be gone long – you come too.
I'm going up to see the leaves turn golden
The leaves that have the veins of stone
Might weigh them, throw them in the river
I shan't be gone long – you come too.

Martin Bailey (with acknowledgements to Robert Frost)

A Legend

Stowford is a pretty place,
Its sou'western view sublime
And to find a healthier spot
Would take you all your time.

Ah! I have passed some happy days
In that house upon the hill.
Oh yes, it's haunted anyways;
That makes it better still.

Ages and ages long ago
Here Tom Treneman did dwell
A great and mighty hunter he,
'A fifteenth-century swell.

He used to smoke and drink a lot.
His friends it did astound
For to keep his spirits up
He lowered spirits down.

Tom always from his word departed,
He had no virtues rare;
His friends were broken-hearted
With sorrow and despair.

'Twas said he was a wicked lot
No horseman could him check.
He rode his horse until it dropped
Fell off and broke his neck.

Treneman's Basin (right), *Ivybridge woods.*

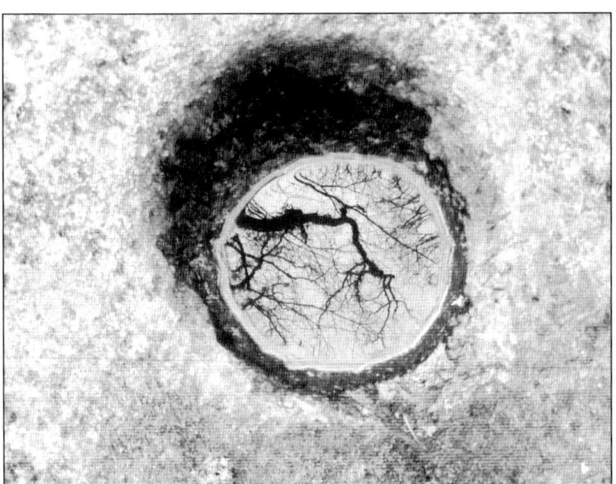

The mystical appearance of Treneman's Basin.

Treneman's Basin, 2009.

Alas! Tom Treneman was dead,
No grief for him was spared,
In a coffin he was laid
That's all his friends they cared.

Of course he must be buried
At Harford, so it's said,
In a vault within the Church
They laid him with the dead.

After the funeral was o'er
And before the mourners went
His ghost was back once more
Which caused astonishment.
A boy sat in the kitchen
A'turning of the spit,
Before a roaring fire
When he nearly had a fit.

For there he saw his master's 'Ghost'
In its deathly shroud.
Tho' frightened to death almost
The youngster cried aloud:

'Hullo, Master, you're come back
Before any of the rest;
D... d... don't touch me,
Master I'm doing my very best.'

The Spectre took him by the heels
And carried him through the hall
Into a room upstairs:
He dashed his brains out on the wall.

I think with me you will agree
This tale is awfully sad,
While standing here just drop a tear
In memory of this lad.

After this awful tragedy
Of the Ghost they were afraid
So it was necessary
To have his spirit laid.

In those prehistoric days,
Tom's Spirit could not rest;
He oft appeared, not always
To those he loved the best.

So in the witching hour of night
Twelve parsons, so I learn,
With halter 'round his neck
Led him to the River Erme.

In 'Black Ann Pool' it is laid down
A task he's to attain.
It'll take some time, I'll be bound
Before on earth he roams again.

To make a bundle of sand.
With sand to make the beams.
A hopeless task you'll understand,
Nor to be done by any means.

This legend I have tried to tell
It will please you all I hope
So now I must wish you all farewell
Tom's crying for more rope.

Author unknown

To the Gate Dressing Judges

We had planned a picture
Of our 'Singing School', you see,
But yet again the weather
Has spoilt our painting glee!

The figures are all floppy,
The banner won't stand high,
And two wet and soggy teachers
Can only stand and sigh!

So we have taken a photo,
So hopefully you'll see
Something of what it could look like
If only it was sunny!

The 'We are a Singing School' banner (above) was supposed to arch over the picture and all the little head were supposed to stand up, but unfortunately the weather has put paid to our plans. Hope this picture gives some idea of what it should look like!

Janet Weston and Helen Johns (the two wet teachers!)
Stowford School

Roads and Turnpikes

In Ugborough parish, as well as in some other parishes in Devon, there are roadside stones placed at road junctions or crossings and which bear on each of their four sides the initial letter of the name of the place to which that side is directed, the letter being carved in relief (E. Mason Phillips, *The Devon Historian 5*, 1972, pp.16–17). Mr Mason Phillips believed these stones to be of the seventeenth century. Not long before his death I discussed these stones with Mr Mason Phillips and suggested that perhaps they had been put up to assist the postboys and other travellers on the post road at what would then have been very narrow crossroads or junctions on winding roads. In Sir John Rogers's affidavit for the Turnpike Dispute in 1758 he mentions a stone with the letters 'P' and 'A' carved on its sides which stood at crossroads east of Ridgeway, the letters standing for 'Plymouth' and 'Ashburton'. At that time Ashburton was the seat of the postmaster responsible for that part of the post road. The stone is also marked on a map of old Plympton, undated, but evidently prepared in association with the dispute. Surviving stones in Ugborough Cross-in-hand, Filham: Sign-of-the-Owl, Wrangaton to Kingsbridge road.

Exeter to Plymouth: a choice of roads, 1743

When Sir John Rogers was preparing to return from his honeymoon in February 1743 he asked his 'confidant', John Elford, for advice on which way he should take. John Elford replied:

> *... we think Totnes or Ashburton the best road and at least eight miles nearer than Oakhampton and if you come that way we propose to meet you at Ivybridge and as it will be near the full of the moon the Tydes will serve as we imagine but if not it will be no great difficulty to come up Lypson Hill as you will be so near home, if you think proper to come the other Road we shall then meet you at Horrowbridge.*

The plan was to have a cheese and wine party at Ivybridge if they met there, presumably at the Royal Oak.

Manuscript in the Dartmouth Papers

In the time of Charles II, 'The Western Road' (one of the six great roads in England).

PLYMOUTH			
Dartmouth	*Ashburton*		*24 miles*
(p)	*Totnes*	*Exeter*	*20*
(p)	*Honiton*		*15*
	Chard, Crewkerne		*19*
	Sherborne		*13*
	Shaftesbury		*16*
	Salisbury		*19*
	Andover		*16*
	Basingstoke		*18*
	Hartford Bridge		*9*
	Staines		*16*
	LONDON		*16*
			201 miles

Note that ye stage in every Road exprest upon ye perpendicular Lyne are the Deputed and chief places upon whom wee send ye constant Baggs of Letters, and Those also in ye Branches w'ch are thus marked (p).

The Post goeth to Plymouth the 3 usuall post nights arriving within 3 days and returneth in equall Tyme.

An Account of the Measurement of the Road between Ivybridge and Ridgeway and the Road mended in the Summer of 1759:

11 November 1759, Measure of Road – Ivybridge to the 'George' by James Wills.

	poles	feet
From the End of Ivy Bridge to Mr Combes Meadow Gate not made	47	5
From thence to Woodland Common made	212	5
From thence to Havylands Cross not made	111	
From thence to Mr Maddicks Stile not made	77	
From thence to the Walnut Tree made	6	
From thence to Mr Waddicks Ruddle made	100	
From thence to Chapley Barn not made	125	5
From thence to Beachrate made	100	
From thence to Western side Leamilbridge not made	38	
From thence to Mr Walter Whyatts Budle made	176	
From thence to a Well near Smithalee not made	82	
From thence to nigh Foss not made	200	
By Foss made	61	5
From thence to John Mannings work not made	91	
Mr Mannings work made home to a Gate	139	
Mr Heles work by Sandover Shop made	204	
Mr Rogers from an Ash treeto the Cross near the Sign of the George made	158	

Total not made 792 poles 5 feet) 1,949 poles 5 feet
Total made 1,157 0
The whole is 6 miles 29 poles 5 feet

13 November. Paid James Wills for measuring of the Highway from Ivey Bridge to the Cross nigh the sign of the George in Ridgway the sum of 3?

Plymouth Turnpike; bids for renting the Toll Gates 1767

Gentlemen,
I propose to take Crabtree Turnpike Gate at Three Hundred and Ten pounds per annum and the Ivybridge Turnpike Gate at Seventy five pounds per annum to keep proper Lights to pay monthly and one month in advance to continue the same during the Term you shall think proper to Grant as a Security for the above payments.
I am, Gentlemen, your most Obedient and most humble Servant, Nat Bartlett

Plymouth
29th April 1767

Gentlemen,
I propose to take the Toll Gates and if you think proper at Three hundred and Eighty pounds a year, for three, five, or seven Years, and pay the rent every month to the Treasurer.
I am Gentlemen Yr Obedient and humble servant

John Aloy
April 29th 1767

Toll Gate Rents; Advertisement in the *Exeter Flying Post*, 21 April 1836 p.3

Plymouth and Exeter Road. Tolls to let.
NOTICE is hereby given, That the TOLLS arising at the Toll Gate called the BITTAFORD BRIDGE GATE, upon the Turnpike Road leading from Ivybridge to Ashburton in the County of Devon, will be let by auction to the best Bidder, on Saturday the 14th day of May next, between the hours of 10 and 2 o'clock, at the Guildhall in the Borough of Plymouth, in the manner described by the Acts passed in the reign of his late Majesty King George the Fourth, 'for regulating Turnpike Roads' which Tolls produced for the last year the sum of £369, and will be put up at the same.
Whoever happens to be the best bidder at the same time give security with two sufficient sureties to the satisfaction for the Trustees of the said Turnpike Road, for payment of the Rent agreed for, and at such times as they shall direct.

Hen. Woollcome. Clerk.
Plymouth, 11th April 1836

The same text for 'Crabtree Gate with Stop Gate' £975. 'Ivybridge Gate' £433. Adverts repeated 28 April 1836. 8 June 1833 Bittaford Bridge Gate up for auction – £385, last year.

Plymouth Eastern Turnpike; Statement of Accounts, 31 Dec 1846 – 31 Dec 1847

Revenue from Tolls	*£2066.18.4*
Repair of Road	*440.0.0*
Land purchased	*8.1.4*
Salaries: Clerk	*36.15.0*
Surveyor	*80.0.0*
Interest on debt	*2220.0.0*
Debt paid off	*750.0.0*

(This was the last full year of account before the railway reached Plymouth.)

Roads and Communications (West Devon Record Office 149/146)

14 August 1827 To Travellers and the Public in General Roads measured by Henry Couch Creagh of Plymouth, Surveyor, within the past 10 days
Distance of Stages from the Guildhall at Plymouth over the Laira Bridge and New Road, through Totnes and Newton Abbot to Exeter

	miles	f.	p.
From the Guildhall at Plymouth to the Fawns Inn at Erme Bridge	11	0	38

	miles	f.	p.
Fawns Inn to Seven Stars Inn at Totnes	12	0	30½
Seven Stars at Totnes to the Globe Inn, Newton Abbot	8	2	24½
Globe Inn at Newton Abbot to the Clifford Arms, Chudleigh	6	0	33
Clifford Arms, Chudleigh to Exeter	10	0	0
	47	5	6

-

Distance of Stages from the Guildhall at Plymouth through Ivybridge and Ashburton to Exeter.

	miles	*f.*	*p.*
From the Guildhall at Plymouth to the Rogers Arms, Ivybridge	10	5	38
Rogers Arms, Ivybridge to the Golden Lion Inn, Ashburton	13	2	7
Golden Lion, Ashburton to the Clifford Arms, Chudleigh	9	2	28
Clifford Arms, Chudleigh to Exeter	10	0	0
	43	2	33

Difference in favour of the Road through Ivybridge and Ashburton *4m 2f. 13p*

Sworn before Edmund Lockyer, an Acting Magistrate for the County of Devon.

1822. Extract from a Cash Expenses Book (Sir John Rogers, 6th bart)

A journey from London to Ivybridge and Blachford.

June 12	Turnpike to Stanes	1s.6d.
13	bill at Stanes	8s.3d.
	baiting Blackwater	1s.8d.
	Turnpikes	1s.4d.
14	Bill at Basingstoke	9s.2d.
	Baiting Andover	1s.8d.
	Smith	1s.0d.
	Turnpikes	1s.3d.
15	Bill at Amesbury	9s.0d.
	Baiting at Hendon	1s.0d.
	Turnpikes	10d
16	Bill at Wincanton	8s.6d.
	Baiting at Ilchester	1s.8d.
	watering Ilminster	6d.
	Turnpikes	1s.2d.
17	Bill at Yarcombe	6s.6d.
	Baiting at Honiton	1s.8d.
	Turnpikes	9d.
	Carriage, Luggage from London	12s.6d.
	smith	1s.0d.
18	Bill at Exeter	9s.0d.
	Turnpike	2d.
19	Bill at Chudleigh	6s.6d.
	Baiting at Buckfastleigh	1s.6d.
	Turnpikes	6d.
	Baiting at Ivybridge	1s.6d.
	paid Mrs Winsor	7s.0d.
	Carriage Luggage to Blachford	1s.0d.

Entries in the Journals of the Rogers of Blachford telling how they travelled in the 2nd half of the eighteen century.

Sir Frederick Rogers, 4th baronet

1767 Wednesday 11 February [probably returning from Wotton, Stoke Gabriel]

Expenses at Totnes	4s.
Expenses at Ivybridge	1s.
Stage Coach	13s.6d.
Post chaise from Plymouth (probably to Dock)	6s.6d.

1771. Sir Frederick frequently dined at Ivybridge, sometimes on his way to or from Wotton. Sometimes he hired a post chaise.

1772. Friday 1 May. Dined at Ivybridge on our way to Dock. Very good roads and weather. Dinner 14 shillings.
1775. Friday 1 September [probably from Bock]. *Ordered the Coach to return to Blachford but rained so hard put off our journey.*
Saturday 2 September. Again ordered the Coach to return But rained so hard could not come away till 12 o'clock. Got to Blachford at ½ before 3.
Tuesday 5 September [Blachford] *Cloudy morning; Glass fallen Wind SW. at ½ past Eleven set out in the Chariot Lady R self to dine at Black Hall. Came away at 6 pm got home at 8* [probably Black Hall near Avonwick. Donn's map 1765 says Black Hall was the estate of Fowell, Esq.].
1776. Monday 18 March [probably Blachford]. *At 8am Captain Vincent Lady Rogers and self set out for Exeter to the Assizes. Got to Ashburton at ½ past Eleven at 2 pm got to Chudleigh and Dined; set out again at 4. Got to Exeter at 6. WNW fine for travelling.*
Saturday 23 March. at 10 we set out on our return to Blachford; at 2 pm Dined at Ashburton; got home ½ after 7. Tolerable good light.

Sir Frederick Leman Rogers, 5th baronet:

1781. Saturday 24 November. Set out after dinner for London. Gave Coachman at Chudleigh £1.1s.
Monday 26 November. Arrived at London at 54 Pall Mall at dinner at ye Cockpit in Evening.
1782. Friday 21 June. Set out for London with the

Plymouth address to his Majesty. Set out at 7PM.
Sunday 23 June. Arrived at Bates' Adelphi Hotel at 2 o'clock PM. Dined at New X Coffee House.
Monday 1 July. Left Hackney Wick for Devon. dinner at Harford Bridge. Journey down £ 14.
Tuesday 2 July. Lay at Chudleigh.
Wednesday 3 July. Returned to Blachford. dinner.
1783. Thursday 23 October. Used my travelling chaise first time at Blachford.

Unexplained Happenings

There have been various reports of happenings in the old Dame Hannah Rogers School from those who were children in the 1960s. They claim to have seen different apparitions, including a girl bouncing a ball, with sound effects. If the children called out to an adult, however, the girl would disappear. A woman who was one of the children involved still insists that this really happened.

Even since the school was converted into flats and apartments those tenants who have known its history of hauntings have been curious about the various sightings.

Also there have been unconfirmed sightings at the bottom of Highland Street, where some people have had unexplained feelings of somebody being behind them when walking in the area where it joins Erme Road. I have been unable to find a reason for this, although there was once a Police Station in this area and Highland House itself has quite a history.

There is a house in Erme Road which at one time, it is said, was visited by the ghost of a relative of one of the tenants. This apparition was seen and heard by residents for quite a few years after the woman had passed on, and allegedly used to put the kettle on ready for their early morning cuppa!

Some residents of Charles Hankin Way enquired at the Town Hall about various happenings in that area, possibly relating to Filham House, which is supposed to have been a monastery in the past.

Perhaps the most startling tale, however, is that of Nigel and 'the flapper'. Nigel and Roger, together with two friends, Gary and Mark, were no strangers to sightings. Living in Lower Broadford, they had seen several apparitions, including a figure looking out of the upstairs window of a house known to be empty, and had heard unexplained noises which sounded like parties. In 1976 Roger awoke one night to feel a hand crawling up his body on the outside of the bedclothes. Years later this same sensation was also experienced by Nigel. Both had leapt out of bed but had found nothing.

But all of these experiences were surpassed one evening in 1986. The lads were, and still are, interested in the Second World War and combat survival, and had adapted the small Larkins Wood, now called Flappers Wood, accordingly. During one of their usual games of soldiers in combat, Nigel and Gary entered the woods to ambush Mark and Roger. On entering they were startled by the apparition of a large black creature which they both described as strange in appearance, being too large to be a dog and too small to be a pony. They continued with the game for about 15–20 minutes when Roger experienced a feeling of unease and, when he glanced towards the right, saw what he took to be Mark standing in a gap in the hedge. He called out a number of times, 'What are you doing over there?' The figure, silhouetted against the dark sky, did not move or reply. Roger then moved towards the figure and was approximately five feet from it when he realised it was not Mark but an evil presence dressed in a long, dark, hooded cloak with just a black hole where the face should have been. The figure raised its arms above its head and shouted, at which Roger took to his heels and headed for home, followed closely by the apparition. He remembers a horrible flapping sound behind him, either from the cloak or from the creature's hands, but was too terrified to look back.

When he arrived home it was, unusually, locked, and he threw himself onto the lawn, not daring to

The gateway to the Flapper's woods.

Reconstruction of the Flapper's appearance in the gap in the hedge, July 1992.

Suddenly a tall monk-like figure appeared in the gap in the hedge. Roger fled in terror towards the farmhouse.

make a sound, listening to the awful noise of the flapper (as he later called him). When the others returned they found him in the garden and got him to say what had happened.

Figuring there was safety in numbers they decided to return to the woods with torches. On arrival at the gate to Larkin Wood they stood motionless and silent, but their bravado was short lived when they heard breaking branches and twigs. They then decided to call it a day, or night, as it was by then, and leave well alone.

Even today if you speak about it to certain members of the group you get a peculiar reaction. My daughter and I have visited the woods and, without being told exactly where this happened, when we approached a certain area it was as if we had stepped into a fridge – and this was on a really hot summer's evening. Nigel later confirmed that that was the relevant area.

He had dropped his cigars in the woods but would not go back to find them and would not even let me do it for him. He was really stressed out about it so we went in the next day to retrieve them.

Murders Most Foul

Rotting corpses in chains once hung on a gibbet in a churchyard in Stoke Damerel, making it a place to be avoided as it was reputedly haunted by a saucer-eyed ghost.

In 1787 the murder took place of a clerk in the dockyard with the usual blunt instrument. Two men, John Richards of Ivybridge and a William Smith, were arrested, tried, found guilty at Heavitree in Exeter and hanged. Their bodies were then brought back to Plymouth by sea.

There were thousands there to witness, on Easter day 1788, the bodies hung in an iron cage in Stoke Damerel churchyard (now gone), where they stayed for seven years, slowly decomposing. Smith's remains were eventually taken away and buried, but Richards's remains disappeared one night never to be found. It was thought they were dumped in the sea and floated away on the tide.

The chapel where bodies used to hang.

After 50 years had passed grave robberies were discovered and suspicion fell on one John Jones. When his house was searched after his arrest, finds included two bodies in sacks in his kitchen, 100 or so teeth in a cupboard and eight human heads. John Jones and his accomplice were sentenced to be transported to Botany Bay for seven years, while a Mary Thompson was acquitted.

In 1884 a killing occurred in the South Hams that scandalised Victorian high society. The daughter of landed gentry, Miss Laura Dimes, aged 24 and newly married, was found dead in a pond at Blackawton with hardly a mark on her body except for a small bruise on her temple. The main suspect was her new husband, who was supposedly in New Zealand on a business trip but was later discovered to have been skulking in a cottage at Modbury. However, he was cleared of any involvement in her murder when the case was brought before magistrates. No satisfactory explanation was ever offered as to how or why she had met her death. The husband, Hugh Shortland, had, in the past, conducted all his business from the London Hotel, formerly Mallet's and later converted into flats. Shortly after the murder an employee of Hugh's turned up at the hotel to collect his mail. Hugh was thought to have had access to a deadly poison from New Zealand that left no trace, and there was evidence that the couple had rowed shortly after marrying in secret, possibly about money, as Hugh was in debt over his business ventures. It was rumoured that Hugh, with his employee, had hatched the plot to kill his wife and inherit her money.

Ivybridge Streets Then and Now

End of Erme Road to Fore Street (1951), right-hand side going down to Western Road:

Beers Riverside Store; High street Westminster Bank; Luckcraft butcher's shop; Backhouse TV & radio shop (now estate agent); private houses; Butterworth's baker's shop (now Dunn's); Co-op store; opening to a chapel (now town hall); French hairdresser; Dingle's store; Salter's drapery shop; Luxton's ironmonger's; Post Office and sorting office; Curson's & Sons plumber's and builder's; private houses; White Horse inn; archway to back of shops; White's shoe shop; Pavitt greengrocer (now Bunker's fish café); chemist; Henderson's tuck shop (was a pork butcher); two private houses; Bryant's baker's shop; Pawley (greengrocer); Sam Phillips's Wayside Café (now hairdresser); Maddock & Sheperd (ironmonger); entrance to Highland Gardens (now Ivybridge Motors); Grosvenor House (doctor's house and surgery); Gregory's second-hand furniture store and shop; Sunnyside guest-house; private houses to Imperial inn; private houses to fire station and entrance to St John's Road

Western Road, right side up to Fore Street:
Kimberley villas; Percy Roberts's grocery shop; Park Street; corner of Park Street, Hoare's bus office (now vet's); small cottages – Caroline's small drapery shop (Clare Street); Mr Steer (baker on corner of Clare Street); Mrs Sambell's grocery shop (on opposite corner of Clare Street); private houses; masonic hall;

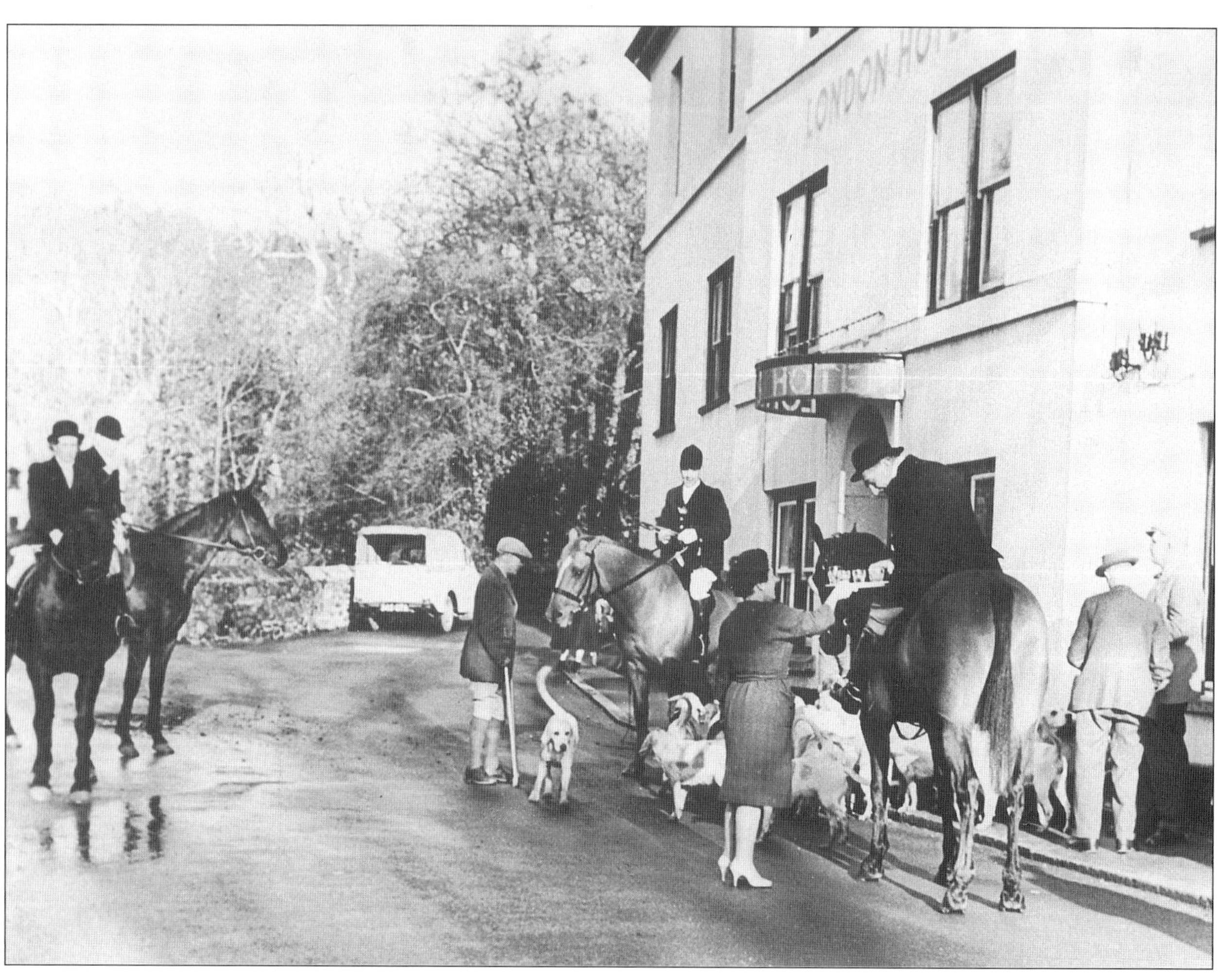

Hunt meeting at the London Hotel.

Above: *'Darkie Days' at the King's Arms.*

Left: *The Duke of Cornwall, Keaton Road.*

Outside the King's Arms in Fore Street, c.1900.

The Imperial Inn annual outing, 1921.

Circus elephants on their way to the big top taking their fill of water outside Lee's Mill.

A parade to celebrate the coronation of King George VI in 1937. At the head of the procession are John Bull with his British bulldog, PC Bright and Mr Love, the postmaster. At this time the Police Station was in Highland Street, where the cells can still be seen in the garden.

a private garden with a big tree, which is now the car park and public toilets; Methodist chapel; Allen Cottages; Harris cottages; Edwin Harvey's electrician's shops; Endicott's dairy-farm; private house; Friend's garage; Tom Pearce (butcher); John Congdon's private house next to newspaper and confectionery shop owned by Mrs Blackler and rented by J. Congdon; Moysey's paint shop (painter & decorator); Lloyd's Bank; The Tannery (two shops owned by Mrs Harvey); Miss Friend's drapery shop; an art gallery; archway; Mrs Howdle's fish & chip shop – later run by the Andrews as a grocer shop; saddle & harness shop; opening to Glanville's Mill, (coal, coke and animal foodstuffs); private houses; Co-op butcher's shop; King's Arms; public toilets.

So over the bridge to Mr Widdecombe's dairy and coalyard opposite the Bridge Inn and the Congregational Church, which is now a large plot of grass (was a high walled garden belonging to the London Hotel)

From Mrs Henderson, 1990. Western Road from Clare Street towards Plymouth:
Vincent undertaker in house; Green's Café and sweet shop; Snell's bakery; Carline's cottons (clothes, etc.); Venn's Bakery; Wellington's garage.

Western Road towards Exeter:
Bowden's garage; Imperial; Martin's builders in house; Labour Exchange where D. Bowden is now; Yabsley builders in house; doctor's surgery (now Grosvenor House)

Fore Street towards Exeter:
Friend's, then Hefford shoe shop (now takeaway); Blacker's paper shop; Pawley's veg ; Bryant's bakery; Bowl's sweet shop; Geddes (chemist); Roberts's fruit shop; White's shoe shop; Yaddicott butcher's; White Horse; Carson's (plumbers, etc.); Post Office; Salter's (clothes, toys, etc.); hardware; Edwards's general stores; French hairdresser; Co-op grocery; Burt's baker's; Backhouse electrical; Hillson butchers

Fore Street towards Plymouth:
Spargo Smithy (corner of Costly Street); Withycombe Dairy; King's Arms; Co-op Butcher; Lee's Mills; Baker Sadler; Andrews's general stores; Simmonds's fish & chips; tannery (rear of Elizabeth's); Lloyds

Bank; Moysey (paint and paper, etc.); Blacker's then Bowdon's paper shop; Pearce butchers; Friend's garage; Endicott dairy; French sweet shop

Erme Road:
Beer's tobacconist & sweet shop; Lee the tailors;

Park Street:
Hoare's garage; Partridge horse breakers; Baker (milkman).

Memories of Green Street

There was a double toilet to serve the houses, that is two toilets with a dividing wall and separate doors. I remember them with a flush water system and a long wooden seat with a large hole into a pan. As a child it did seem rather a long drop!

As you went into Green Street from Blachford Road, Maltacott's dairy was on the left, then a small area with a few old apple trees. On the right there was a house where Mr and Mrs White lived around 1945. Next to this was a courtyard with a house. Carrying on down the right-hand side were 'linhays' built under the gardens. Steps led up to the gardens.

On the left was the first house where a Miss Purdy lived; next to this was another where the Walks lived. Next door, at No. 5, my family, the Fullers, resided. Before that my grandmother Fuller's parents lived here – Walker and Livinia Baskerville – and before them Livinia's parents.

Alo in the street lived Thomas and Livonia (Stead) Phillips. The Baskervilles and Phillips were from Lutton Cornwood. Louisa Head was born in 1815 at Woodlands, Ivybridge, where her father was a wheelwright. The Heads originated from Shaugh Prior back in 1676. I have photographs of these families taken before 1900, one picture of the families in the garden of Green Street – the Mill at Stowford could be seen from these gardens. I don't know when Green Street was built but I do know people were living there from 1861; my family were there from that time until the houses were considered unfit. The houses were two up and two down, with water fetched from a cold-water tap outside. Wash-day was a nightmare but the homes had a warm feeling about them.

Members of the Phillips/Baskerille clan photographed in a garden above Green Street. Left to right, back row: *?, Mrs Varcoe, her daughter, Will Ball, Mrs Laura Ball, Sergeant Ball, Miss Laura Ball;* second row: *William Baskerville, Walter Baskerville, Lavinia Baskerville, Maria Fuller;* front row: *George Fuller, Elsie, William, Dorothy.*

Memories of Ivy Cycles

It is now 100 years since Bowden garage was started in 1898 by W.H. Bowden. He started on his own by selling his own make of bicycle on the Western Road by the Imperial Inn. When Bowden's first started it was worked by him and his son and a couple of helpers. The bikes were completely made in the workshop and were fairly expensive, though none has unfortunately survived. The badge was the trademark of Ivybridge and they were called Ivy Cycles and sold for 20-25 guineas. The business then moved opposite to much larger premises, but even that is now a housing estate. Another choice gone for residents.

Drake

Alec Rogers, 1988

As a Westcountryman with generations of ancestors lying in the churchyards of Holbeton in Devon and Milbourne St Andrew in Dorset (one of whom was named Drake!), I feel it is right and proper that the so-called new evidence that has been recently brought forward regarding Drake could well have been left where it belongs. For instance, it has been said of Vice Admiral Drake and his Westcountry captains that they were all pirates. If they were, which is extremely doubtful in the modern sense of the word, would it not have been a much finer exercise to have examined, for example, Sir Francis Drake's attitude toward the coloured men with whom he came into contact. A very topical subject, but totally neglected, as far as I am aware. In a letter to his parents, a young man serving with Drake had this to say:

But our Captain Drake counts the image of God nevertheless His image, cut in ebony, as if done in ivory, and in the blackest Moor he sees the representation of the King of Heaven.

Or consider this, taken from E. Bradford's *Life of Drake*:

So much nonsense has been written against Drake, that it is well to quote a tribute from the Spaniard who

This window in the mill manager's house portrays Queen Elizabeth I bestowing the knighthood on Francis Drake.

Ivybridge at War

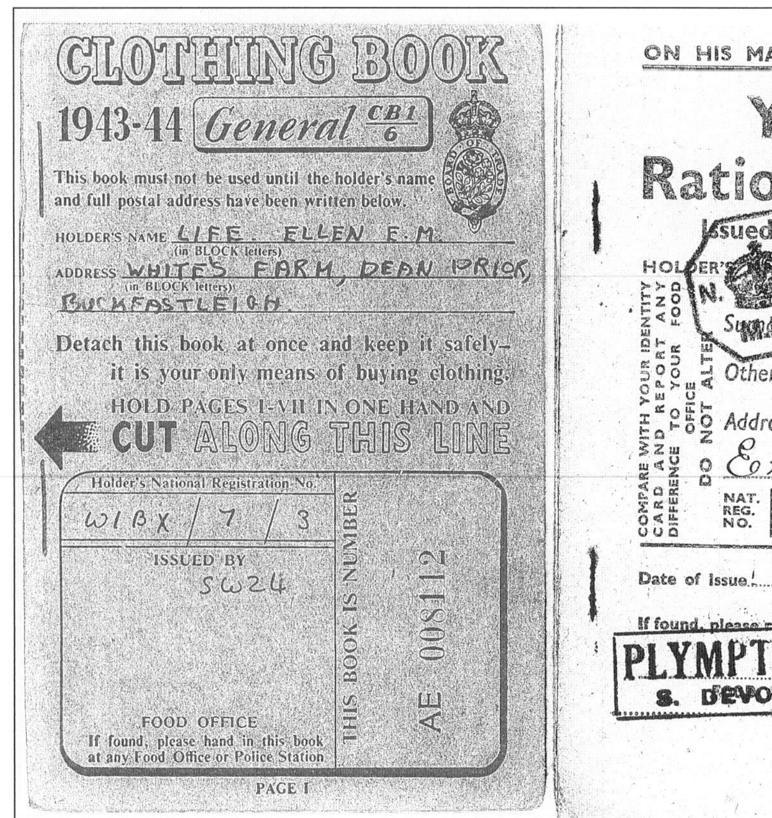

CLOTHING BOOK

1943-44 General CB1/6

This book must not be used until the holder's name and full postal address have been written below.

HOLDER'S NAME LIFE. ELLEN E.M.
(in BLOCK letters)

ADDRESS WHITE'S FARM, DEAN PRIOR, BUCKFASTLEIGH
(in BLOCK letters)

Detach this book at once and keep it safely – it is your only means of buying clothing.

HOLD PAGES I-VII IN ONE HAND AND CUT ALONG THIS LINE

Holder's National Registration No. WIBX / 7 / 3

ISSUED BY SW24

THIS BOOK IS NUMBER AE 008112

FOOD OFFICE

If found, please hand in this book at any Food Office or Police Station

PAGE I

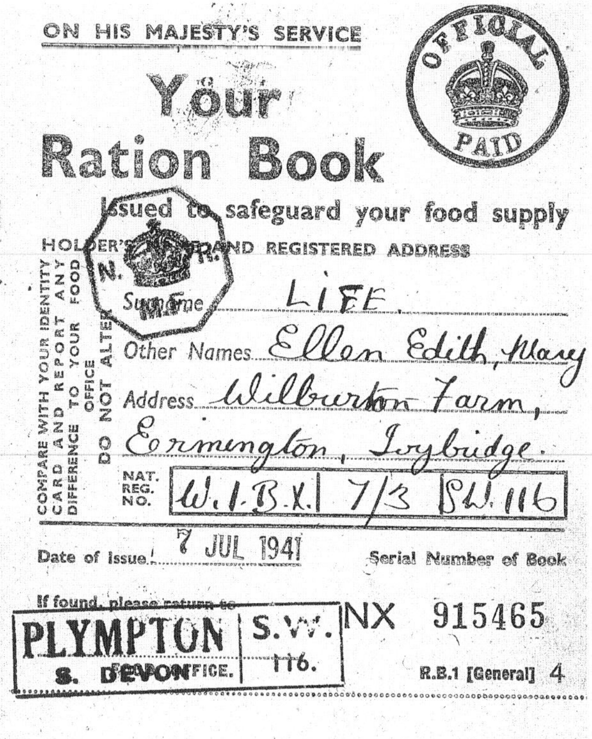

ON HIS MAJESTY'S SERVICE

OFFICIAL PAID

Your Ration Book

Issued to safeguard your food supply

HOLDER'S NAME AND REGISTERED ADDRESS

COMPARE WITH YOUR IDENTITY CARD AND REPORT ANY DIFFERENCE TO YOUR FOOD OFFICE

DO NOT ALTER

Surname LIFE.

Other Names Ellen Edith Mary

Address Wilburton Farm, Ermington, Ivybridge.

NAT. REG. NO. W.I.B.X. | 7/3 | S.W. 116

Date of Issue 7 JUL 1941

Serial Number of Book NX 915465

If found, please return to PLYMPTON S. DEVON FOOD OFFICE. S.W. 116.

R.B.1 [General] 4

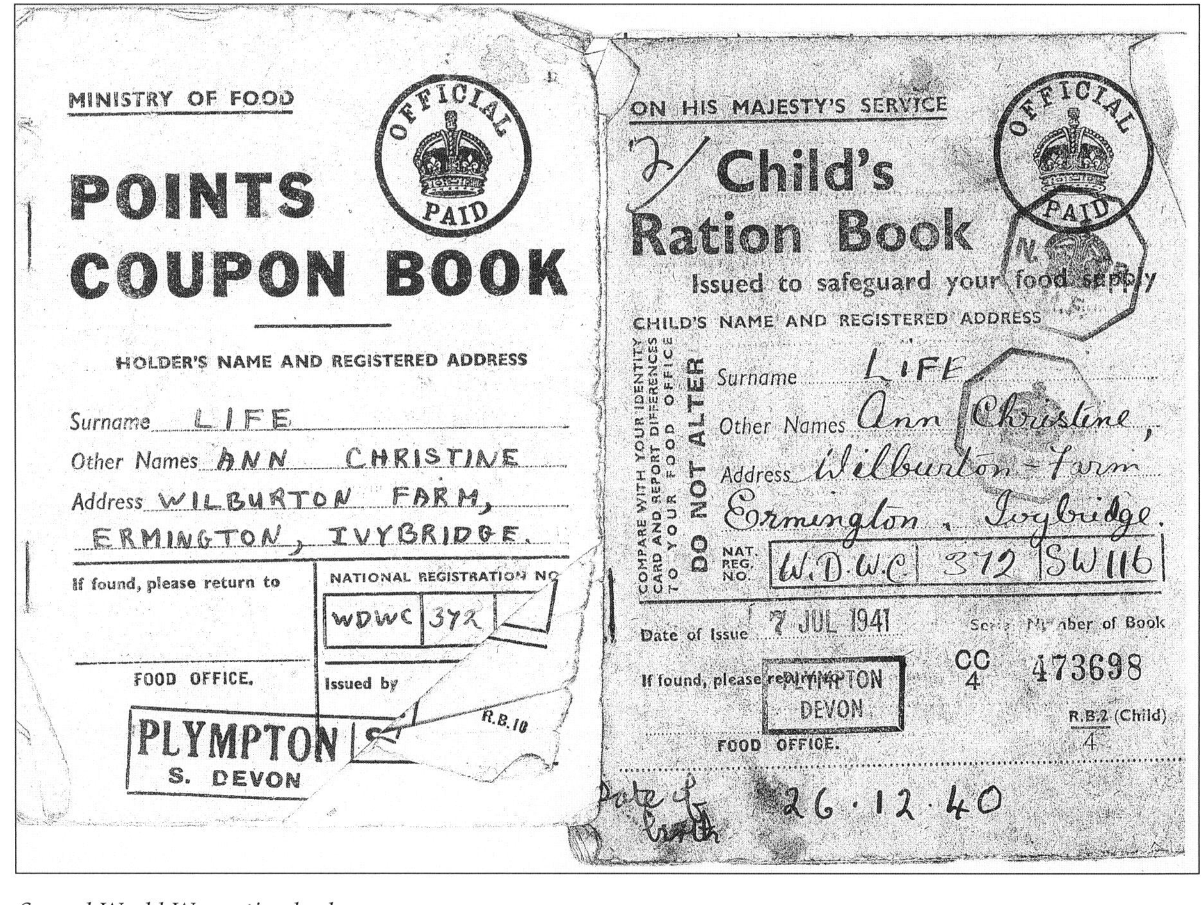

MINISTRY OF FOOD

OFFICIAL PAID

POINTS COUPON BOOK

HOLDER'S NAME AND REGISTERED ADDRESS

Surname LIFE

Other Names ANN CHRISTINE

Address WILBURTON FARM, ERMINGTON, IVYBRIDGE.

If found, please return to

NATIONAL REGISTRATION No. WDWC 372

FOOD OFFICE. PLYMPTON S. DEVON

Issued by

R.B.10

ON HIS MAJESTY'S SERVICE

OFFICIAL PAID

Child's Ration Book

Issued to safeguard your food supply

CHILD'S NAME AND REGISTERED ADDRESS

COMPARE WITH YOUR IDENTITY CARD AND REPORT DIFFERENCES TO YOUR FOOD OFFICE

DO NOT ALTER

Surname LIFE

Other Names Ann Christine,

Address Wilburton Farm Ermington, Ivybridge.

NAT. REG. NO. W.D.W.C. | 372 | SW116

Date of Issue 7 JUL 1941

Serial Number of Book CC 4 473698

If found, please return to PLYMPTON DEVON FOOD OFFICE.

R.B.2 (Child) 4

Date of birth 26.12.40

Second World War ration books.

checkmated him at the Isthmus and brought his last voyage to failure – 'One of the most famous men in his profession that have existed in the world, very courteous and honourable with those who surrendered, of great humanity and gentleness, virtues which must be praised, even in an enemy'.

Of Drake's voyage round the world, Dr A.L. Rowse states, in his book *The England of Elizabeth*, that the capital invested in the voyage was £5,000. The treasure brought back was £600,000, with the dividend to shareholders some 4,700 per cent! The queen was a shareholder and when the Spanish ambassador protested about Drake's behaviour, she replied: 'The Gentleman careth not if I disavow him.'

It is certainly a pity that in these dubious times the rising generation is being given a false impression of Drake and Elizabethan England. Then we were a nation of some five million. Elizabeth was queen, Drake the captain of the seas, and Shakespeare was its poet and playwright. With his gallant seamen, Drake had challenged the might of the Spanish empire, had given hope to all oppressed people, and had carved for himself everlasting fame.

Ivybridge at War

Dr Jack Dumoulin

The late Jack Dumoulin MBE was one of a small group of young British Army doctors recruited during the Second World War by the Special Operations Executive for work in enemy-occupied territory. He later enjoyed a disguised peacetime career as a consultant obstetrician and gynaecologist based in Plymouth.

He joined SOE in the summer of 1943 and was parachuted into German occupied Albania as medical officer with an SOE mission. There, in appalling conditions, the group worked with partisans led by the country's future dictator, the communist Enver Hoxha.

Dumoulin's task was to do what he could, with the scarce and basic resources he had to hand, to treat sick and wounded guerrillas and the shared sufferings of his colleagues. Dumoulin remained an excellent doctor who remained utterly calm and controlled in the most testing of circumstances.

Brought out from Albania in December 1944, Dumoulin volunteered for further SOE service. He was assigned to Force 136, the arm of SOE operating in the Far East, and parachuted into Malaya. There the task SOE was to organise guerrilla groups, mostly comprising Straits Chinese. After the end of the war in the Far East he was appointed MBE for his medical work with SOE.

In Albania, he had been assisted by a young local nurse, Drita Kosturi. When a card marked 'Captain J.G. Dumoulin RAMC' was found in her possession after the war, she was accused by Hoxha's regime of spying for the British. She was sent to a labour camp, where she remained for more than 40 years. As Albania was a closed country under Hoxha, Dumoulin did not learn of her experiences until he met her again on his first return visit in 1990. He immediately arranged for her to be flown to Plymouth for medical treatment.

Jack Dumoulin.

After school, he studied medicine at St Thomas's Hospital and qualified in 1942. Postwar he worked at Hammersmith and University College hospitals, specialising in obstetrics and gynaecology, before being appointed in 1953 as a consultant in Plymouth, where he practised until retirement in 1984.

He had a wide interest in the management of obstetrics at national, local hospital and speciality level, and particularly in research and training. A member of the Royal College of Obstetrics and Gynaecology in 1949, he became a Fellow in 1960. He subsequently served on the council of the college, where he was able to influence both training and the maintenance and improvement of standards of care.

There are many families in our area who have to be grateful to him for safe delivery of their babies and his work with difficulties pregnancies, etc. He died aged 88 in 2007.

Ivybridge at War

Reggie Hawker, killed in Mesopotamia in 1917. He was uncle to John and Michael Farr.

Right: *Trevor Withycombe during the First World War.*

Charles Hoare with his ambulance on the Western Front in the First World War.

NEWS+++NEWS+++NEWS+++NEWS+++NEWS+++

IVYBRIDGE is finally getting a memorial to Edmund Hartley, the only person from the town who has ever been awarded the Victoria Cross.

Col. Hartley was born in Ivybridge in May 1847 and was awarded the VC for bravery during a battle in Basutoland in 1879. Now a new apartment block being completed off Fore Street is to be named Hartley Court in his honour and a plaque will be erected on the building (above). Meanwhile the plaque on the left is in the Anglican Cathedral of St George in Cape Town, South Africa, where Col Hartley went to when he qualified as a doctor, aged 27.

Colonel Hartley's bravery is commemorated in a plaque on an apartment building off Fore Street, as reported in the Ivybridge Express *in 1997.*

Colonel Edmund Baron Hartley

VC CMC MRCS LRCP, Knight of the Order of St John, Mentioned in Despatches 1879, 1880, 1881, 1897, 1900

Edmund Hartley was born at Ivybridge, South Devon, on 6 May 1847, the eldest son of Dr Edmund Hartley, and, having been educated privately, took up an appointment with the Inland Revenue. He resigned the position in 1869 and entered St George's Hospital Medical School, becoming MRCS England, LRCP Edinburgh.

Following qualification Dr Hartley went to South Africa and from 1874 to 1877 was District Surgeon of British Basutoland, the first English medical man in that country.

When war broke out in 1877 he volunteered for service, being appointed Surgeon of the Frontier Armed Mounted Police (which later became the Cape Mounted Rifles). His first experience of action was in the same year, as medical officer to a mixed force operating against the Galeekas. The following year, 1878, came the Gaika campaign, Surgeon Hartley having been appointed Principal Medical Officer to the Cape Colonial Forces. In 1879, during the Moirosi Rebellion, Hartley carried out those acts of bravery which were recognised by the award of the Victoria Cross.

For conspicuous gallantry displayed by him in attending the wounded under fire at the unsuccessful attack on Moirosi's Mountain, in Basutoland, on 5 June 1879; and for having proceeded into the open ground, under a heavy fire, and carried in his arms, from an exposed position, Corporal A. Jones of the Cape Mounted Riflemen who was wounded. The Surgeon Major then returned under the severe fire of the enemy in order to dress the wounds of the other men of the storming party.

He was also Mentioned in Despatches and awarded the Campaign Medal with Clasp. Further Mentions in Despatches occurred in the Basuto Campaign in 1880 and in 1881. From 1882 to 1823 Hartley was PMO of the Colonial Forces under General Gordon (later of Khartoum). He was wounded in the Bechuanaland Rebellion (1897) whilst treating an injured soldier and was again Mentioned in Despatches.

Colonel Hartley served throughout the Boer War from 1899 to 1902 and was present at the Battle of Magersfontein and the Affray of Enslin, and as PMO of the Colonial Division was Mentioned in Despatches, awarded the Queen's and King's South Africa War Medals and Clasps, and was appointed a Companion of the Order of St Michael and St George.

Ivybridge at War

MINISTRY OF FOOD

SERIAL NO. BV 200767

RATION ALLOWANCE

Bacon & ham	4oz
Meat	To value of 1s.2d (6p). Sausages weren't rationed but difficult to get
Butter	2oz
Cheese	2oz, sometimes rising to 4oz or 8oz
Milk	3pts, sometimes 2pts
Eggs	1 shell egg, sometimes 1 every 2 weeks, 1 packet dried eggs every 4 weeks
Sugar	8oz
Margarine	4oz
Cooking fat	4oz, often 2oz
Tea	2oz
Preserves	1lb every 2 months
Sweets	12oz every 4 weeks

Second World War ration allowances.

Record of raids, damage and casualties IVYBRDGE

7 August 1940: Longham 3 high explosive bombs, 1 incendiary bomb.
2 August 1940: Cross Hands Cross 1 AA shell
1 March 1941: Field at Hall Farm, Harford, 1 high explosive bomb.
3 April 1942: Field near old toll gate 1 AA shell exploded.
February 1943: Field at Swainstone Farm 1 unexploded AA shell.
November 1943: Pithill Farm AA shell.

(Ermington)
August 1940: Cadleigh Farm 3 high explosive bombs, damage to Cadleigh Lodge and bungalow.
January 1941: Field at Westlake 2 high explosive bombs.
March 1941: Field at Farms Bridge 2 high explosive bombs slight damage to New Park house and shed.
August 1943: Penquit Farm 1 AA shell.
" ": Preston Hill 1 unexploded AA shell.
" ": Stitson Hill 1 AA shell.

A record of raids, damage and casualties at Ivybridge in the Second World War.

This scroll commemorates

Private J. D. Rogers
Devon Home Guard

held in honour as one who served King and Country in the world war of 1939-1945 and gave his life to save mankind from tyranny. May his sacrifice help to bring the peace and freedom for which he died.

RURAL DISTRICT OF PLYMPTON ST. MARY

Form L.R. 2.

Lodging Restrictions (Plympton St. Mary) Order, 1941

CONSENT TO GIVE LODGING

No. 1365

Name of Occupier Mrs Thompson.

Address "Sunnyside" 42 Western Rd. Ivybridge.

CONSENT is hereby given in accordance with the terms of the Lodging Restrictions (Plympton St. Mary) Order, 1941, to the lodging of the undermentioned person(s) at the above address subject to the conditions specified :—

Name(s) of Person(s) to be Lodged	From (Date)	Conditions (if any)
Mr J. Riley	22/10/42	
Mr G. Fentsakian	25/6/42	
Mr J. Pearse	30/5/42	
Mr R. [illegible]	28/8/42	

Date 2/12/42 (Signed) pp [illegible]
Chief Billeting Officer

N.B.—This consent may be varied or revoked by the War Emergency Committee.

Above: *Lodging permit from the Second World War.*

Left: *Commemorative scroll issued during the Second World War.*

Ivybridge at War

Local women and children making camouflage nets during the Second World War. This particular team, photographed at Station Road School, were so succcessful in their efforts that they received a letter of congratulation from the War Ministry.

Members of the Civil Defence Services at Ivybridge, 1944. Included are Arthur Freemantle, Mr Turner, Mr Ward, Esmé Patrick, Jean Pearse, Mollie Fry, Betty Harvey, Bo Hurrell, Lady Margery Edwards, Audrey Winston, Violet Bastard, Mrs Booth, Mrs Freemantle, Mrs Skidmore, Mr L. Nott, Mr Walker and Fred Hoare.

Ivybridge at War

Members of the hospital board and the ARP. Left to right, back row: *Mr Mansfield, ?, ?, ?, ?, ?, 'Jumbo' Williams, who drove for Hoare's Coaches;* second row: *Mr Walker (bank manager), Mr Freemantle (worked in mill office), Maud Gilbert (née Maddock), Mrs Maxwell Hyslop (Highlands), Mrs House (née Maddock), ?, Mr Thorne;* front row: *Lily Balkwell (ran the White House pub in Fore Street), Dosic Harvey (ran the draper's shop at No. 11 Fore Street, Mr Perry George, Mr Wilf Love (postmaster), Mr and Mrs Winston (Bridge Park) and Miss Love (schoolteacher).*

Trained firemen from the National Fire Service No. 7 Regional Training Establisment at Lee Mill

Ivybridge at War

Firemen of the National Fire Service.

Chief Petty Officer Carlyon, a telegraphist, served in China.

Blood donors in the masonic hall, 1948.

Auxiliary Territorial Forces - Churchill's Secret Army - at Slade House, Cornwood.

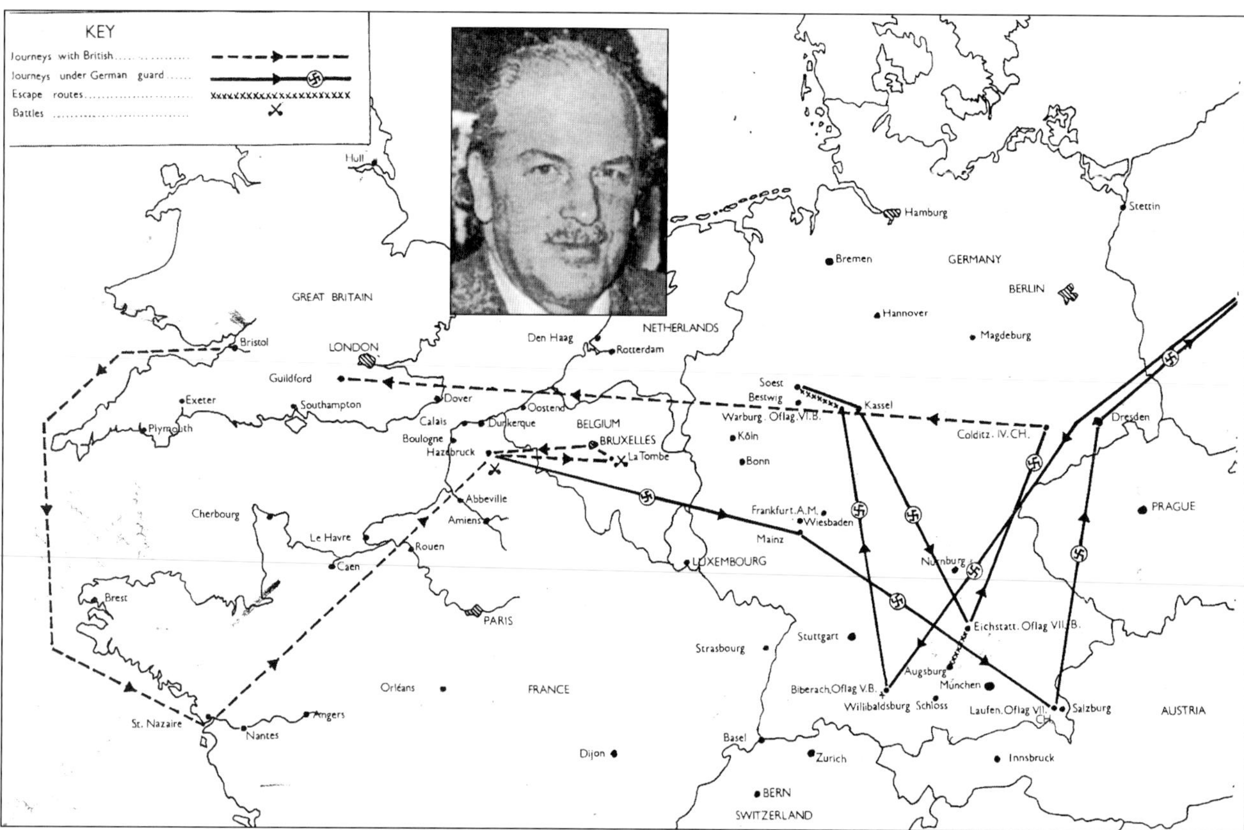

Captain Farr's escape routes. Inset: *Michael Farr.*

Colditz Castle.

He founded and commanded the Cape Medical Corps (later the South African Medical Corps). He was also a Knight of the Order of St John.

Later he returned to England, to Somerset, where he commanded six Voluntary Aid Detachments from 1910 to 1912. Throughout the First World War he was Secretary of the Voluntary Aid Hospital in Seaton, Devon.

John Hartley married Ellen, daughter of J. Ross-Innes CMC, Under-Secretary of Native Affairs Cape Town, in 1886, and he died on 20 March 1919, aged 72 at Ash, near Aldershot, Hampshire.

Captain Farr

Captain Michael Farr, one of Cornwood's most celebrated residents, escaped from a prison in Poland after being captured in 1943.

He got away only to be recaptured and sent to Eichstatt prison, where he tunnelled his way out to spend ten days on the run before being caught again.

The Germans sent him to Colditz, which was supposed to be escape-proof.

Bachelor Captain Farr, awarded the MBE in 1946 for his wartime exploits, was finally freed by the Americans.

The former Durham Light Infantryman was made a staff captain with the war crimes department after the war.

He later joined the wine business of J. Hawker & Son at the Barbican, Plymouth.

War Weddings

This list of war-time weddings gives the ranks and services of local and enlisted men and of those stationed in the area. It also shows where the men came from. The list is incomplete, as other similar weddings took place until the 1940s in chapels and the nearest registry office.

James Stickland, F/O RAF, Exeter, to Betty Harvey, Ivybridge, August 1940.

Alfred Louden, Ldg Stoker RN, Plympton, to Dorothy Avery, Ivybridge, September 1940.

Alexander Duncan, Pte RAMC, Stowford House, to Ivy Kingsland, Ivybridge, February 1941.

Henry Richards, Seaman RN, Plymouth, to Priscilla Thompson, Ivybridge, March 1941.

John Smith, Corp. RM, Ivybridge, to Nina Macdonald, Ivybridge, May 1941.

Ernest Smale, Stoker RN, Devonport, to Myrtle Davis, Ivybridge, June 1941.

Ivybridge at War

THE ERME STANDARD

1939
1945

IVYBRIDGE, TUESDAY, FEBRUARY 24, 1998. WEATHER: Dry and mild 34,953

IVYBRIDGE PREPARES

ALL around England citizens are preparing for war and Ivybridge is no exception.

Everybody is putting up blackout curtains and in Ivybridge people are preparing for evacuees.

The home guard has been armed with hand guns and rifles, literally anything they could get their hands on.

The land army has been doing a lot of work since last week, 2,000 fields have already been converted into vegetable fields.

Some children have already been evacuated two days before the war officially started, the reason being that they have family in Devon.

Citizens are putting crosses of tape over the windows to try to keep most of the glass in when bombing takes place.

Gas masks have been distributed to everyone in Britain in the fear that gas bombs will be dropped.

Bombs

So far no gas bombs have been dropped anywhere. We have no information of how many bombs have been dropped so far.

London and Plymouth had their first air raid last night. Politicians are predicting a blitz on Plymouth because of its naval dockyard.

Robert Myall and George Cole

INSIDE: An ARP's day.
How rationing affects you!
Land Army hits Devon.
Our poor city.

Operation Evacuate

SO far evacuation of city residents has been huge.

Children are leaving their parents and fleeing to the country to avoid the danger of war.

Some children are excited about going to the countryside but some are sad because they are leaving their parents.

Most children will probably see their parents again but some say they might like their evacuee parents too much and stay with them.

Obviously the children would want to have nice parents to live with but they will just have to wait and see.

Devon and Cornwall are two of the main places for children to be evacuated.

Flee

More children will flee from Plymouth if the expected bombardment takes place

This will further swell the over-bursting rural schools.

So if you get an evacuee child remember to take care of him or her because they are our future.

Reporters Jesse Bailey and Nathaniel Hunt

Blackouts to strike

IN Devon and most of the country people are rushing for suitable blackout curtains.

Marie Woodward wrote to us and said: "I refused a length of good black sateen at Binns for blackout purposes.

"I have, as a result, spent many tiring hours this week walking from shop to shop buying remnants of inferior sateen at higher prices.

"I have also spent many hours making up curtains for all windows and dimming lights."

Dark

And again she wrote to us and said: "Blackout restrictions, especially for cars and motor vehicles, are causing many fatalities.

"The restrictions are to be revised."

"I'm sure we'll all get used to the dark quite soon."

Robin Woodward

TONIGHT
GAS-MASK
DEMONSTRATION
At the
Ivybridge Council School
Learn how to use your mask properly.
3.30-4.00
BE THERE

Commemorative newspaper produced by the children of Erme School.

Ivybridge at War

Members of Ivybridge Home Guard, including Edward Moysey, Mr Mugridge, Basil Carey, Mr Salter, Jack Hurrell, Fred Andrews, Arthur Burnard, Arthur Johns, Jack House, Clarence Ryder, Edwin Osbourne, Bill Hodge, George Yelder, Bill Mortimore, Fred Priddle and Fred Bennett.

Bob Slaughter of Company D, 1945. Of the thousands who landed on Omaha Beach on D-Day, he was one of the few who survived to fight to the war's end.

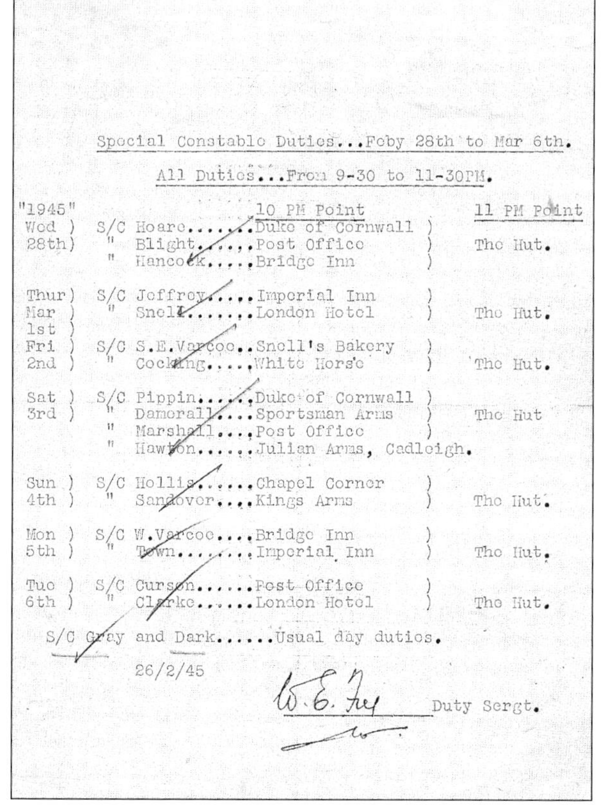

Special Constable Duties...Feby 28th to Mar 6th.

All Duties...From 9-30 to 11-30PM.

"1945"		10 PM Point	11 PM Point
Wed 28th	S/C Hoare......	Duke of Cornwall	
	" Blight......	Post Office	The Hut.
	" Hancock.....	Bridge Inn	
Thur Mar 1st	S/C Jeffrey.....	Imperial Inn	
	" Snell........	London Hotel	The Hut.
Fri 2nd	S/C S.E.Varcoe..	Snell's Bakery	
	" Cocking.....	White Horse	The Hut.
Sat 3rd	S/C Pippin......	Duke of Cornwall	
	" Damerall....	Sportsman Arms	The Hut
	" Marshall....	Post Office	
	" Hawton......	Julian Arms, Cadleigh.	
Sun 4th	S/C Hollis......	Chapel Corner	
	" Sandover....	Kings Arms	The Hut.
Mon 5th	S/C W.Varcoe....	Bridge Inn	
	" Town........	Imperial Inn	The Hut.
Tue 6th	S/C Curson......	Post Office	
	" Clarke......	London Hotel	The Hut.

S/C Gray and Dark......Usual day duties.

26/2/45

W. E. Fey Duty Sergt.

Duty roster for special constables in 1945.

Ivybridge at War

American soldiers of 116 Regiment at Ivybridge.

Captain Bedell (right) *in Germany, 1945.*

? Wingfield and John Schenk in Ivybridge, 1945.

John Wilkes and John Schenk.

Alan Huddleston outside Company A's recreation room, Ivybridge, 1943.

Ivybridge at War

Ken Lidstone.

Stoker Charles Maddock, RN.

Gunner Ronald Barnes, Pte Reg Vincent and Gunner Cecil Hodge photographed in Sicily, where they unexpectedly met in 1943.

John Elford remembers being swung by Pilot Staff Sgt Thomas K. Turner and mechanic technician Sgt William A. Franklin on the small grass airstrip at David's Cross, c.1944.

Left: *Geoffrey Rowe, a London refugee, at Bittaford, 1940. The girl's name is not known.*

Top left: *Wartime cartoon.*

Above: *Placing a wreath at the war memorial. In the background can be seen Vera Luckham and the Revd Cyril Short.*

Left: *Celebrating VE Day at the war memorial.*

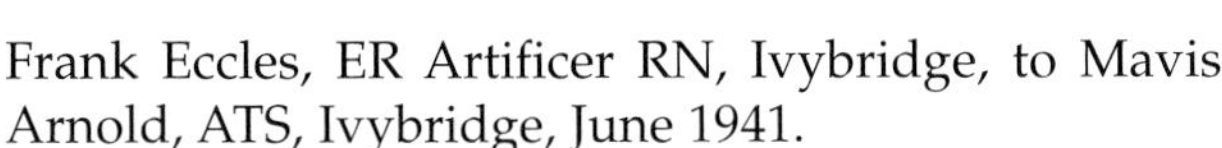

Frank Eccles, ER Artificer RN, Ivybridge, to Mavis Arnold, ATS, Ivybridge, June 1941.
George Issac, AB Ldg Seaman, Plymouth, to Gladys Hart, Ivybridge July 1941.
Frederick Goff, AC2 RAF, Ivybridge, to Lillian Davy, Ivybridge, September 1941.
Philip Corker, Pte, Devonshire Reg., Cornwood, to Joan Brownless, Ivybridge, February 1942.
William Davey, LAC RAF, Ivybridge, to Patricia Salter, WRNS, Ivybridge, March 1942.
John Partridge, Gunner RA, Ivybridge, to Margaret Hayes, Lee Moor, May 1942.
Desmond Hill, Pte Royal Ulster Rifles, Ivybridge, to Barbara Daniels, Ivybridge, June 1942.
Kenneth Leech, AC2 RAF, Ivybridge, to Margaret Jago, Ivybridge, July 1942.
William Bryant, Pte Army Catering Corps, Ivybridge, to Kathleen Geddes, Ivybridge, July 1942.
Mr Harvey, Sgt Devonshire Reg., Ivybridge, to Margery Vivien, ATS, Ivybridge, July 1942.
Francis Skelly, Sgt RA, Plympton, to Priscilla Barnes, Ivybridge, July 1942.
Granville Perkins, AC1 RAF, Modbury, to Betty Brookes, Ivybridge, August 1942.
James Yabsley, F/Sgt RAF, Ivybridge, to Mary Partridge, Ivybridge, August 1942.
John Fiott, L/C Hampshire Reg., Ermington, to Margaret Cane, Ermington, September 1942.
Arthur Terry, AC2 RAF, Bittaford, to Betty Carne, WRAF, Cadleigh Park, September 1942.
Ernest Lee, L/C RASC, Ivybridge, to Olive Tucker, Ivybridge, December 1942.
Kenneth Tebbatt, LAC RAF, Ivybridge, to Esme Patrick, Ivybridge, February 1943.
Charles Etheridge, CORP RM, Ivybridge, to Margery Avery, Ivybridge, May 1943.
Frederick Brown, Yeoman of Signals RN, to Thelma Ilingston, Ivybridge, June 1943.
Walter Manson, Ldg Sgt RA, Ivybridge, to Vera Cane, Ivybridge, July 1943.
William Morgan, Gunner RA, Sheerness, to Edith Carolyn, WRNS, Ivybridge, July 1943.
Alexander Sturgeon, P/O RN, Bittaford, to Crisular Kalpakis, Bittaford, September 1943.

William Pearce, P/O RN, Ivybridge, to Kathleen Stone, Ivybridge, December 1943.
Arthur Brown, Major (Army), Oxfordshire, to Anne Rule, ATS, Ivybridge, February 1944.
Clarence Wakelam, L/C RAC, Ivybridge, to Kathleen Carne, WAAF, Ivybridge, April 1944.
Alfred Mullin, F/O RAF, Sallop, to Audrey Downing, WAAF, Ivybridge, August 1944.
Mr Hunter, P/O RN, RN camp Sparkwell, to Winifred Leach, Ivybridge, September 1944.
John Ballard, Major Oxford & Bucks, Oxford, to Jean Rule, VAD, Ivybridge, November 1944.
Arthur Groves, driver RASC, on active service, to Margery White, Ivybridge, February 1945.
William Barnard, ERA RN, Ivybridge, to Gladys Thorne, Ivybridge, April 1945.

A Short History of Ivybridge

Although there have been dwellings in this district since remote times, the appropriately named village of Ivybridge was not developed until the eighteenth century. The old 'Ivy Bridge' which gave the village its name was constructed during the course of the twelfth or thirteenth century, when it had several farms and manor houses, but in 1692 all that remained were two houses and one or two cottages where in modern times is the centre of the village.

However, in 1789 the village had grown sufficiently to justify the construction of a chapel, since disappeared, just below the modern Parish Church. Until 1894, the village had been divided into four different parishes (Ermington, Cornwood, Harford and Ugborough) whose boundaries met at the old bridge.

At the beginning, the villagers worked on the farms or in the mines. In 1856 the last mine, at Filham, where silver and lead had been extracted, was closed. Following this, a paper works, opened in 1787, became our most important industry. To begin with, there had been several paper industries of different types, but today Stowford Paper Mills is the only one to remain.

In 1758, the main road became a turnpike (a toll road) where coaches could be seen on their way from Plymouth to Exeter and London. The London Hotel was built towards the end of the eighteenth century, and the other inns towards the beginning of the following century. In 1830 five coaches a day travelled in each direction. In 1848 the railway, South Devon Railway, was opened, and the line crossed the Erme Valley by means of Stowford viaduct above the village. Our railway station, alas, was abandoned in 1959. The primary school in Station Road opened its doors in 1856. Considerably enlarged since, the building is now used by infants of five to seven years. Children aged seven to 11 go to a new school, called 'junior', and the older ones to Ivybridge Community College, a secondary comprehensive school. There is also nowadays a school for children of five to 11 years at Stowford.

In 1882 the modern Parish Church was opened, the construction costing £4,000. The first Methodist chapel (now the Ivybridge community centre) was opened in 1812. In 1875 the Allen family, owners of the paper works, bore the costs of a second chapel as a replacement. In 1905 a power station was set up, at the invitation of the council, intended to generate hydroelectric energy from the river for lighting houses and streets. This station is no longer used, since the paper industry still produces energy from the river for its own use. During the first half of this century the inhabitants of Plymouth made their way in large numbers to visit Ivybridge. Thanks to the railway, the region was very easily accessible, and it was possible to walk in the Erme Valley or on Dartmoor.

In 1831 the population was nearly 1,056 persons: in 1901 it had increased to 1,575, and to 1,730 in 1911. Afterwards it remained more or less unaltered until the years following the Second World War. Since the '60s, the development of estates of private houses has been in evidence, with the result that the present-day population is reaching 1,600. It has been suggested that the figure ought to stabilise at about 11,000, a proposition which would present certain problems to the community.

Health in Sixteenth-Century Devon

C. Campbell

The course of human history is closely related to, and determined by, the history of its disease. Typhus was the third assailant in the Armada, the Napoleonic, the Crimean and the First World Wars, for instance, and usually came off best.

In the case of the Spanish Armada more men lost their lives from illness than from battle wounds or drowning. Sensibly, Phillip II of Spain recruited 98 physicians, surgeons and apothecaries to sail with the Armada, which included two hospital ships. Visitors to the Armada exhibition may recall the apothecaries' mortar and pestle, the fine-tooth comb of whalebone for removing headlice and the skeleton of a black rat, all recovered from a sunken galleon.

A sailor's lot was not a healthy one. Apart from the health hazards from enemy cannonballs or the bosun's cat-o'-nine-tails, 'ship fever' was common, and usually due to typhoid or typhus, both diseases of overcrowding and poor sanitation.

Typhus is caused by a germ transmitted by the bite of the body louse. This little fellow lived on underclothing, visiting his unfortunate host for a

Sports

Above and below: *The opening of Ivybridge Bowling Club, 1945.*

Sports

The opening of Ivybridge Bowls Club, 1945.

The earliest known photograph of the Bowling Club, 1930s.

Sports

Ivybridge Sports Committee, May 1944.

Ivybridge AFC, 1913–14. They played 28 matches of which they won 18, lost four and drew three.

Sports

Ivybridge AFC, 1911–12 season.

Cornwood AFC.

Sports

Ivybridge JuniorAFC.

Ivybridge AFC with trainer Stan Castle.

Sports

Above: *Mr Pethick wins the cup for the best garden or allotment at Ivybridge Show.*

Left: *Wiggins Teape sports day.*

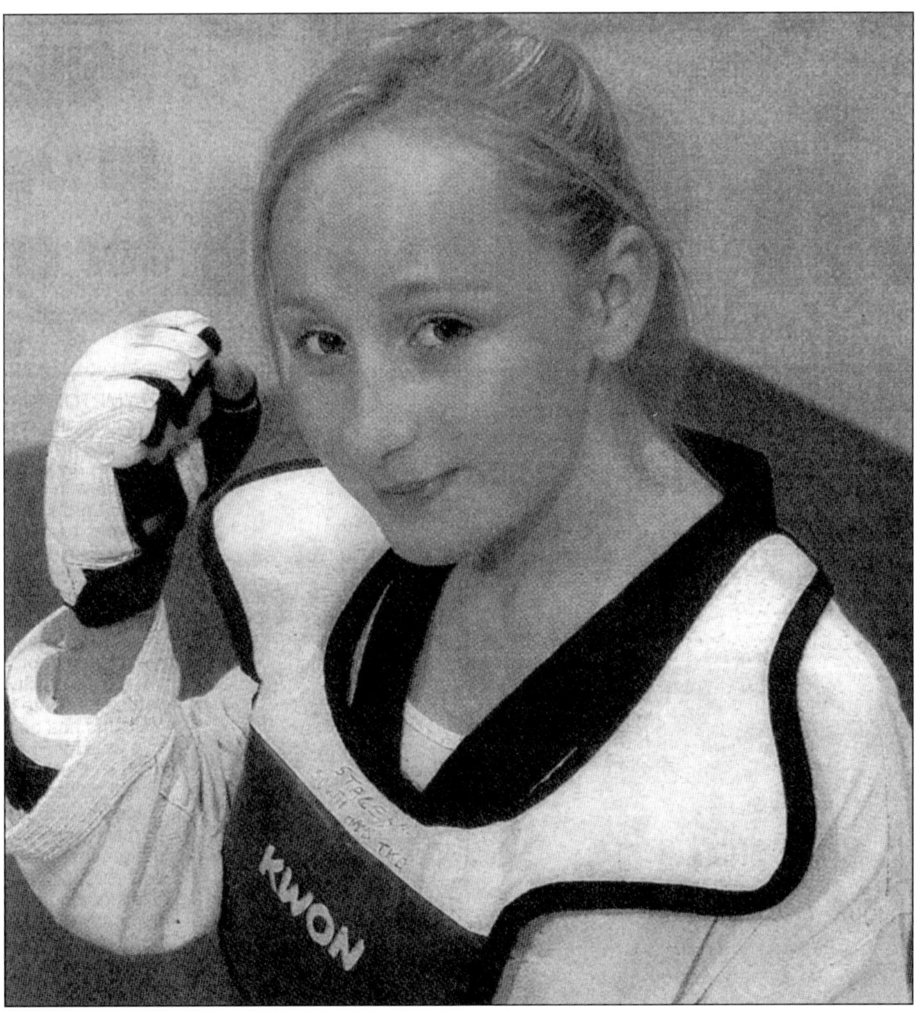

Stacey Jamieson of the South Hams Tae Kwon Do Club, who won a place at the European Cadet Championships in Budapest, her first international appearance.

meal of blood when hungry. These were good times for the louse, as bathing was out of fashion and undergarments were often worn the year round. (Indeed, children were often sewn into them for the duration!)

Ships' toilets were rickety wooden frames slung over the side of the ship. Even in good weather, not surprisingly, most sought relief between decks. Effluent would thus drip down into the hold (containing the galley food store, sick bay, rats, mice and sandy ballast), adding to the stench and squalor. This arrangement facilitated the spread of bowel disease: the 'bloody flux' or dysentery, gastroenteritis and typhoid. This hotbed of contagion ensured few seamen were older than 40. The overcrowded ships from Spain were described as wooden floating cesspits, many falling ill as the fleet made slow progress up the Channel. Their problems were compounded by contaminated water and rotting food due to leaky casks of unseasoned wood. Drake at Cadiz in 1587 not only singed Phillip's beard but set fire to his seasoned wood which, it seems, was less easy to replace.

When hospital ship the *San Pedro el Magor* foundered off Salcombe, 'so greatly diseased' were survivors that they were quarantined in isolated barns in the neighbourhood.

The English fleet also had its problems. The *Bonaventure* left Plymouth to patrol the Channel. Within a month typhus had done for 300 of the 500 souls on board. The captains of the queen's ships complained of bad crews, many of the men pressed into service being lousy vagabonds and drunken idlers, though Drake attracted loyal, tough young Devon men. Howard, Lord Admiral of the Fleet, was less fortunate. 'We have cast many overboard and a number in great extremity which we have discharged,' he wrote as typhus took its toll. Despite new crews and fumigation of the ships the outbreak recurred.

After the scrapping in the Channel the epidemics on board increased in virulence. Howard realised the rapidly spreading contagions were in part due to lousy clothing worn by the pressed men battened below decks in the foul weather of the Armada period. He wrote a pleading letter for provisions and clothes: 'so little shift of appareil, sickness and mortality begins wonderfully to grow amongst us'. Men sickened one day and died the next, which suggests food poisoning. Howard put much of the blame on bad food, and particularly on beer, a gallon a day being the standard seaman's ration, and which was often adulterated by unscrupulous landlords concocting cheap 'own brand' brews. Countless seamen died, many being sent ashore to lie dying in the streets of Margate without food, pay or shelter. Much distressed, Drake, Howard and the other admirals unsuccessfully petitioned the queen for help, she being advised by Lord Burghly that: 'By death, by discharging of sick men and suchlike there may be spared something in the great pay.' Such provision as was made was funded out of the pockets of the admirals themselves.

Aboard the Spanish ships typhus, and scurvy were common in all those that rounded Scotland, but seamen who regained land were well treated not only by their own countrymen but by Irish and Scots. Those unfortunate enough to surrender to the queen's soldiers in Ireland were sadly put to the sword or hanged. All in all, half the Englishmen and two-thirds of the Spanish perished, a handful from war wounds or drowning, the large majority from disease.

Sailors on long voyages to tropical climes faced the hazards of scurvy, 'the plague of the sea and spoil of mariners', and the tropical fevers malaria and yellow fever. So it was that Drake, despite his farsighted recognition of the importance of and his insistence on a clean ship and fresh food, lost nearly half his crew on his 1586 Central American expedition, malaria being the principal cause.

In 1589 Drake's ill-fated 'English Armada' sailed for Spain to set light to Phillip's beard, but had to limp home following the loss of 2,000 men in an epidemic caused by: 'Our slovenly pressed men whom the Justices have sent me as scumme and dregs of the country.' This was probably typhus, and on their return to Plymouth, was spread to its citizens, resulting in a further epidemic later that year and compounding the misery of the already rampant 1589 plague outbreak.

Both Drake and Hawkins were to succumb to a tropical fever (presumably typhoid) on their ill-advised last Caribbean adventure in 1594.

Devon people on land were also prey to infectious diseases, those great captains of death, pneumonia, gastroenteritis, smallpox, plague, typhus, TB and measles. Yet those that survived childhood stood a fair chance of achieving three score and ten, heart disease, cancer and bronchitis being rare. Malnutrition was a problem during the winter and spring months. In the absence of fresh fruit and vegetables scurvy led to great looseness of the teeth and bleeding of the gums in the spring. Tooth decay became more common as cane sugar arrived from the West Indies, and Queen Elizabeth's teeth were blackened ruins.

Plague appeared gradually throughout the sixteenth century, localised outbreaks leading to a great increase in the autumn deaths in parish registers instituted by Henry VIII in 1532. The epidemics died out in winter, as the plague-bearing fleas went into hibernation. In 1546 the plague made a dramatic appearance stage north in Barnstaple, killing 200 of its 2,000 population, spreading over a two-year period to the surrounding villages in turn. Later that year outbreaks were recorded in South Devon, spreading from Dartmouth to Totnes to Ugborough, which was particularly badly affected. Its closely clustered cottages must have helped the spread of thatch-loving black rats, together with their fleas and plague bacilli. There were 99 deaths, the average annual loss being 18 for that village.

Ports were particularly vulnerable to new virulent strains of plague spreading from the Continent, surrounding market borough towns (such as Totnes, Modbury, Ashburton and Plympton) becoming base camps for further spread. In 1563 such a strain of the plague spread from the Continent to London and then laid waste to East Anglia. The queen took the only good remedy of the time: 'To flee, and that quickly.' Retreating to Windsor Castle, she had erected a gibbet beyond for any that chose to follow from London! Plague-carrying vessels brought the disease to Paignton, Brixton and Stoke Gabriel in that same year. Plymouth was particularly vulnerable. The 'Black Book' reports:

> *A great plague in Plymouth whereof died about six hundred persons in 1579 the most of the inhabitants, both of the better and the meaner sorte, departing out of the town, leaving it defenceless .*

It is reported that provisions were made to the poor in times of pestilence, burials, quarantine, fumigation and removal of bodies being paid for. Some removed from gutters were negroes brought from Africa or the West Indies, John Hawkins having recently pioneered slave trading.

The pattern of sporadic outbreaks was to continue in Devon, as elsewhere, for a further century until after the Great Plague of 1665, when the wiry plague-carrying black rat was displaced in Europe by its sturdier, plague-resistant cousin, the brown rat, for which we owe it our eternal gratitude.

Typhus, poverty and overcrowding were common bedfellows, hence the pseudonyms 'trench fever', 'ship fever', 'gaol fever' and 'war fever', as well as the descriptive 'spotted fever'. The records of the 'Black Assizes' at Exeter in 1586 relate to how Portuguese prisoners languishing in a 'deep pit, and stinking dungeons' developed 'gaol fever', which spread to other prisoners, to the Judge at their trial, to 98 magistrates and thence to the citizens of Exeter and the 'Whole Shire'. Two of the five deputy lieutenants of Devon died, along with a number of leading gentlemen, all much involved with martialling local militia, leaving Devon bereft of military leadership at a critical time of Spanish hostility. They were to be sorely missed, the contemporary 'Dad's Armies' being small, undisciplined and often armed with no more than farm implements, or, in Cornwall, slings! They would have been little match for the war-hardened Spanish fighting men, even if they had been mustered to fill the hastily dug watery trenches around Plymouth.

In 1651 'the sweating sickness' swept around the country. A mysterious malady, the 'English sweat', or 'know thy master' brought 'a grete swetying and stynking and a continued thurst with grete heat'. It caused major outbreaks in Barnstaple and Uffculme, despatching many before disappearing from the face of the earth never to be heard of again. Catholic Queen Mary was carried away by such an 'ague', which was a great boon to the health of English Protestants. In 1558: 'A third part of the people of the land did taste the "General Sickness"', probably influenza, then pandemic in Europe. This led to an upsurge in deaths in Stoke Gabriel and other scattered Devon villages.

Famine stalked the land in 1596 following bad weather and failed harvests. Many in the country were particularly vulnerable, having been displaced from their smallholdings by the enclosures of the gentlemen sheep farmers. By 1597 North Devon was described as a disaster area, Plymouth, Plymstock, Widdecombe and Exeter also being badly hit.

As if this were not enough, Plymouth was a major breeding ground for 'the great pox', syphilis, a recent import from the Americas being bartered for smallpox and measles, which similarly wrought havoc across that Continent.

Medical facilities in these times were primitive and sparse, being described in a petition to Henry VIII in 1511:

> *For as much of the science of cunning of Physick and Surgery is daily within the realm exercised by a great multitude of ignorant persons of whom the greater part have no manner of Insight in the same or any other kind of learning. Common artificers as Smiths, Weavers and Women and accustomably take upon the great lives and things of great Difficulty to the Displeasure of God, great infamy to the Faculty, and the grievous Hurt, Damage and Destruction of many of the King's liege people most specially of those that cannot discern cunning from uncunning.*

Medical practitioners comprised physicians, surgeons, barbers, apothecaries and itinerant healers or quacks. Physicians practised in towns for the benefit (or otherwise) of the well-heeled citizens. They were in any case a largely ineffectual lot, following the teaching of the second-century Greek Galen. His concept of disease was one of unbalanced humours, blood, phlegm and bile, washing to and fro like tides through the veins and arteries. Release of excessive humours could be done by bleeding or purging, a theory that led to the premature demise of many patients, and to a delay in scientific medical progress of some 1,500 years.

More useful and accessible were the apothecaries or chemists, busy experimenting with extracts of recently imported cinchona bark (containing quinine, malaria still being common in England), cinnamon bark (India) and balsam (Peru).

Surgery was crude, a surgeon's worth being measured by his speed of working in those pre-anaesthetic days. Quick 'smash-and-grab' raids on the bladder for stones were common, as were amputations, alcohol and morphine serving as anaesthetic substitutes. Barbers would perform minor surgery, lancing boils or pulling teeth. They were also adept at the centuries-old practice of bleeding, employed for anything from bad breath to plague.

Alternative medicine was understandably much in demand and met by the quacks and other fringe practitioners who would ply their trade at the regular fairs and markets at borough towns such as Totnes, Plympton, Kingsbridge and Modbury. The quacks (named after quicksilver, or mercury, used as an effective toxic treatment for syphilis), in contrast to the physicians, claimed to cure a host of maladies, their stock-in-trade being purgatives, a glib tongue and a quick pair of heels. Also in the market-place would be found unqualified cutters for stones, hernia repairers and cataract couchers with varying degrees of expertise. Many tradesmen dabbled in medical matters. Grocers would sell patent remedies. Blacksmiths might pull teeth or set broken bones for man or beast.

Medicine being still a mixture of myth and magic with heavenly and astral influences, witchcraft had its place and was tolerated far more on the Continent. The execution of the three Bideford witches was exceptional.

Few hospitals existed following the privatisation and asset stripping of the monasteries by Henry VIII and his rapacious offspring, Edward VI. All monasteries had their infirmaries where the sick could find comfort, though prayer would be the principal remedy. Such units would have been attached to monastic foundations in Plympton, Plymouth, Buckfastleigh and Plymstock.

Hostels for leprosy were sited by the present George Inn at Plympton, and at Totnes, Plymouth and Modbury, but would have fallen into disuse following the disappearance of leprosy from the land after the Black Death of the fourteenth century, presumably an example of 'survival of the fittest'.

In the free enterprise culture of this earlier Elizabethan age, responsibility for health rested with the individual, and families would be largely self-reliant, making use of traditional herbal remedies. Herb gardens were common, and recorded in charitable bequests and feoffment deeds in Loddiswell, Kingsbridge and Modbury. Feverfew is one of the herbs used for headaches which has stood the test of time and scientific scrutiny to remain in common usage to this day. Herbs were important for medicinal purposes, for cooking, dying and as sweet-smelling bedding or floor covering. They were also used as perfumed 'nosegays' to ward off bad smells thought to carry contagious diseases. A primitive gas-mask was devised to ward off the plague, the cloth nose-cone being packed with aromatic herbs. It was hoped that such 'pocketful of posies' would ward off the 'ring of roses' rash, sneezing and the falling down that marked the progress of the plague bacillus.

On the Continent great progress was afoot. The famed physician Paracelsus aggressively debunked the standard dogma of Galen and his followers (comprising all the rest of the medical profession), while an Austrian Army surgeon, Ambrose Pare, was more carefully and quietly laying the foundations of modern surgery. Leonardo da Vinci and Farbriquus heralded the scientific era of medicine with their brilliant anatomical dissection and drawings, Leonardo commenting: 'A man is as old as his arteries.' While Sir John Hawkins was preoccupied with preparing the queen's Navy for war, Mrs Harvey was preoccupied with raising her son William, later to achieve pre-eminence as the physician who described the circulation of the blood.

It was to take some centuries before practical advantage to the common man would follow. Elizabethan England was an exciting and glorious age, Merrye for some, but for the man in the street or in the fields often uncomfortable in the extreme.

References

The Devonshire Association, 1977. 'Epidemics in Devon', Neville Oswald.

The Devonshire Association, 1982. 'A Review of Medical Care in the South Hams', Neville Oswald.

W.G. Hopkins, *Old Devon: Epidemics in Tudor Devon.*

J.S. Savery Letters

From Sir John Savery to Sir F.L. Rogers, 13 December:

Selden's Inn by Sir John's kind courtesy has, in consequence of the Hotel becoming untenanted, become a very valuable property indeed and does more business than even Rivers being quite in the Thoroughfare and really a very comfortable House. If Mr Dyer (although I doubt his means) would take the Hotel and fit it up as a Lodging House I cannot but think it would turn out a good Speculation, but I fear Mr Dyer neither in Purse or Character is a man calculated to thrive in such an Establishment.

J. Servington to Rogers, 4 December 1847.

The Village of Ivy Bridge has been in a sad state this Summer in consequence of a defective supply of water in the Back Lake many complaints I have had about it and on turning in the stream I found all the obstruction was in the under Gutter through Betty Phillips meadows (which I have no doubt will recur to you was covered in when Seldon rented it). On examining this

Gutter I found from the road leading to Pithill that the old leat was carried much too dead and it was consequently filled with roots, muck and sticks. I therefore suggested to Mr Horton of cutting the Gutter higher up the field so as to take the great drop in the Wood so as to make a greater fall through the Meadow by which we should divert the Gutter from approximately too near the hedge, which naturally leads all roots of hedge growth into it; this has now been done and the water has a good run through and the Village in consequence in a clean healthy state. This Back lake is an annual source of expense by our cleaning it, and it happens as I witnessed the Servants and occupiers throw everything into it, inasmuch as Crocks, Kettles and all manner of Earthenware is found therein, consequently I proposed to some of the lessees that we would put an Iron Grating to the extremity of each individual right so as to prevent its washing into the rights of others, and after which was done each lessee should be at any time called to remove all obstructions within their respective rights. This appeared to take well at first, but they considered that it would throw some expense on them and that you would receive... the benefit; this is the liberal consideration of the lessees – take everything and give nothing, and I really believe they would rather die of the plague than worst it by the outlay of a shilling.

From further letters by John Servington Savery:

5 March 1847. The Fire Engine has arrived at Ivybridge. John S. Savery suggests that the house should be in the garden of Gardener Philips, now Garden Cottage, leading from the entrance gate straight to the river. Stones from the viaduct refuse to be used – only small expense in carrying them. He has taken the measurements of the engine and has planned the house accordingly.

4 February 1847. J.S. Savery takes it upon himself to build the engine house. He suggests the Committee should pay a small acknowledgement annually by which means it would not become freehold.

The Erme from Head to Estuary

The Erme rises on Harford Moor at Erme Head, where there is a beehive hut – not a pixie's home but a former tinners' shelter. Here also are the remains of a blowing house, medieval workings, hut circles and an ancient oak wood, one of only three on Dartmoor.

The river then runs slowly down through Harford, gathering speed as it flows under Harford Bridge and on to Ivybridge, passing through Long Timber and Pithill Woods (now owned by the people of Ivybridge to use for recreational walks, nature studies, etc.). No hunting is allowed here in a bid to conserve nature. This was where the village reservoir once was, which later became a swimming pool for youngsters until it was condemned in the 1950s. It was also used by the American Army as part of an assault course.

Just a little further along on the left of the Erme was where in the early days water was extracted to power the mill machines for paper making. The water was then returned to the Erme by the entrance to the mill in Station Road.

Before this we come to the railway viaduct, still in use, with the pillars of Brunel's original railway still visible.

Now we come down to the Ivy Bridge, first mentioned in 1280 and widened to accommodate mail coaches in the 1700s. The bridge is built on a bed of blue elvin rock, a seam of which runs right up to South Brent. When the road was turnpiked the Royal Mail *Quicksilver* coach journey from London to Plymouth took just 24 hours.

This is where the Erme really starts to drop, and is why it is known as the second fastest flowing river in the country when in flood and looking angry. We now pass under our so-called New Bridge, dated 1825, on the new main road through our town. Here water was diverted to drive the equipment in Lee Mill (now a shopping centre), a corn mill which at one time also supplied the electricity for street lighting. It ran in front of the King's Arms (now the Exchange) in an open ditch into which customers, after a few drinks, would often fall. There was a long dispute and court cases between landlord and mill manager over this.

We now come to Julie's, where another leat took water to what is now Waterside House to drive a water-wheel for the Lower Mill. This aqueduct is also listed. All this work the Erme used to do! Now it just flows through the town doing nothing. It is well past time we again tapped its power in some way or another. We now pass a building on the right bank, also powered by a water-wheel, which used to be a store and then the offices of the *South Devon Times*. The Erme now flows through to Cleeve and

The River Erme in flood at the tennis courts.

A Journey Down the Erme

Erme Head, Ivybridge.

The Erme above Harford, near Ivybridge.

In the woods, Ivybridge.

On the Erme, Ivybridge

The Erme at Flete, Ivybridge.

The Ivy Bridge, 1907.

A Journey Down the Erme

Bathing in the Erme in Pithill Woods.

Swimming pool, Ivybridge.

Pithill Woods.

Above, left and right: *The Erme in flood. Note the old London Hotel* (above right).

then on to Keaton though to Ermington and under Erme bridge, then Fawns Bridge through Sexton, then Sequers Bridge and through Fleet Estate, winding its way to the estuary at Wonwell in Bigbury Bay. In prehistoric times the estuary came up nearly to Ivybridge. The estuary was once far deeper and was used to transport lime for agricultural use. Fish landed here were carried up the slip by donkey.

Now just a quiet summer beach for holidays and fishing with rod and line, the whole river is still full of salmon and trout. There were once competitions when the fishing was really good, and the fishermen would stay at the London Hotel.

Flower festival at the Priory.

THE PRIORY

In 1904 the French Sisters of the Sacred Hearts of Jesus and Mary came to Cornwall. They moved to Ivybridge in 1910 and began building a convent at Cadleigh, moving in on its completion in 1912. A school was then established and accommodation for a chaplain was built. When the nuns departed in the 1930s a new school was built in the grounds (still in use). While this was being built the school was housed for a while at Woodlands Farm, then owned by the Pearce family (ancestors of Nick Toms). In 1939 five evacuees arrived from London, although they had expected 14. The payment for the children was 8s.6d. per week (about 40 pence). The first marriage to take place here was on 19 April 1947 between William (Bill) Bowden and Mary Fry, the daughter of the corn mill manager. A Father Courtney seems to have been in charge for a considerable time and was a well-respected member of the community. I first met him in 1968 then gave him a lift and had a very long discussion with him on many subjects and the workings of his priory and such like. Running weekly bingo sessions in the Masonic Hall another thing that was very popular.

Nona Fry (left), *Mary Fry and Bill Bowden, 1947. Bill and Mary were the first couple to get married at St Austin's Priory. Nona and Mary were the daughters of the corn mill manager.*

STOWFORD MILL

The siting of Stowford Mill on the Erme in 1786 by William Dunsterville was not so much because of the purity of the water, as people are inclined to think, but rather because of the power it provided. Paper in those days was formed by hand, but the preparation of the rags by breaking them down into discrete fibres was a mechanical process normally driven by a water-wheel. Today they still have great involvement with the river; not for power, but because we need about 1.3 million gallons of water each week to run our process. It is certainly true that we are grateful for the high-quality water the Erme provides.

Another common misconception is that the mill makes banknote paper. Apart from odd makings of low denomination foreign currency, we have never been in this business. The mill is still referred to locally as 'Portals', and certainly for a number of years the specialist currency paper manufacturers Portals did own Stowford Mill. During this time other security papers were introduced where special features were incorporated in the paper to counteract forgery or counterfeit. These papers are still made today as part of the production mix and include such grades as passport, lottery, bearer bond, specialist

Stowford Lodge was built towards the end of the nineteenth century by the Allen family, who owned Stowford Paper Mills. The photograph was probably taken during the great blizzard of 1891. To the left of the house can be seen Brunel's original viaduct, built in 1848.

Glanville's Mill being demolished in 1978 to make way for the new shopping centre. It was in this building that weekly films were projected on the far wall.

cheque, share certificate and a number of government security papers where the document is of intrinsic value (pension, postal order, premium bond, etc). The other specialist area for the mill is in business stationery. They manufacture part of the Wiggins Teape 'Conqueror' range of papers, which is by far the leading brand of letterhead paper used by companies in the UK, and also finds extensive use overseas.

They also make special grades for organisations and companies which require their own specified quality. For example, an increasing number of companies are interested in incorporating their logo into their letter paper as a watermark, and the mill is well equipped to satisfy this part of the market.

By any standards Stowford is a small mill, employing 150 people and manufacturing annually 6,500 tonnes. They are the smallest unit in the Wiggins Teape UK organisation, the average size being in the region of 30,000 tonnes. Stowford was typical of the many small mills which existed in this country up to 20 years or so ago, but most of which have now disappeared. The mill continues to thrive because it has a niche in the market and a strength which is no longer very common. It can manufacture efficiently small quantities of high-grade paper which the larger mills cannot. Flexibility and efficient operation are therefore vital to survival.

Manufacture of paper at the mill today involves chemically prepared wood fibre (wood pulp), both hardwood and softwood, with cotton fibre coming from seed hair (linter) rather than rags, as in the past. The fibre blend is rendered down into a slurry with water and treated with a high level of mechanical power to refine the fibres. Various chemicals, dyestuffs and minerals are added and substantial dilution takes place. The dilute stock is spread onto a continuously turning porous belt, where the water

Silent films were shown weekly on this screen at Ivybridge corn mill, entrance 2d.

is drained through and the fibre forms a mat on the surface. The mat is removed continuously, dried first by vacuum then by squeezing between rollers and felts, and finally by steam-heated cylinders. Surface materials are then applied and surplus moisture is evaporated off. Surface finish and thickness are then controlled by calendaring between steel rollers. The completed roll of paper is then processed into reels or sheets and packed for despatch. During the course of manufacture substantial quantities of heat and power are needed. The heat is provided from a gas-fired boiler in the form of steam, and the steam, when passing through to the process, is used to generate about a third of the electrical power used in the mill.

In today's climate no one would, by choice, site a heavy shift-working process industry on a Class I river of highly variable flow. Also, a position so near domestic housing and the town centre would be carefully avoided. Yet their very position has led us to several successes in environmental terms. The most significant area relates to the river, where, over the years, the quality of the effluent we discharge has improved dramatically. In the early 1960s, following considerable local dissatisfaction, the mill installed a new effluent plant which made a step change in the quality of discharge into the Erme.. Since then, through a number of measures, the volume has been reduced and the purity has been increased to a point where we are able to keep trout in the effluent stream before it joins the main river. In this way, we can keep a close and continuous monitor on our effluent quality. In relation to other environmental factors, we avoid unsatisfactory flue discharge by burning mainly gas, but following a recent repair they have maintained their chimney height of 135ft for the rare occasions when we burn oil. Fortunately, our process is virtually odourless so we have no problems in this area. On the other hand, noise nuisance is something we try to avoid, and during night-time hours all operations are internal with the main pumps heavily silenced.

Papermaking has for many centuries been a craft industry. A rapid change is now underway, and while we have seen computers and video screens invade our offices in the past, we now have the prospect of rather similar change in our production areas. Computers gives the operators much tighter control of certain basic properties (thus improving the quality and reliability of the product), as well as showing much more clearly what is happening at any given time. These developments promise to add interest and knowledge for our employees rather than tending to 'de-skill' their work.

Over a number of years the company has invested steadily in the Stowford site, with the main emphasis on cost-saving projects. Whereas the future of any enterprise cannot be guaranteed, the long-term prospects of the mill look particularly good and we look forward to a further period where the town of Ivybridge and the mill co-exist in harmony one with the other. The mill has now been taken over by Arjo Wiggins but is still run under the same conditions and rules.

Mines and Quarries

Tin was worked in the Erme Valley during medieval and later times by streaming, and evidence of this can be seen in the river, and in remains such as those of the blowing-house on the Butterbrook at Harford. It is possible that the tenor bell in Harford Church may have included local tin, and it has been suggested that the church itself could have been for the tinners, since there has never been a village of Harford as such. There is evidence that there was a tin works on Henlake Down in 1596. In Ivybridge Woods, Tom Treneman's basin is a tinner's mortar stone.

In 1859 the discovery of a rich bed of alluvial tin about a mile above Ivybridge viaduct was reported. The deposit was said to be 4–5 feet thick with an area of nearly four acres. A proposal for working it came

The remains of the massive engine house of Filham Mine.

Members of Ivybridge Tennis Club celebrating its twenty-fifth anniversary.

to nothing for fear of fouling the water supplying the paper mills.

Apart from tin, silver and lead were worked in this area in the nineteenth century, by far the most important mine being that at Filham, known as Filham Silver Lead Mine or Ivybridge Consols. This was started before 1838 under grant from the Provost and Fellows of Eton College, closed in 1840 and reopened in 1843 under the same management, producing 20 tons of ore per month. The shaft had been sunk to 60 fathoms and by the time it was closed again in 1845 had produced sales of £4,500 with 30–50oz of silver per ton. There were two water-wheels (the largest 24ft in diameter), 190 fathoms of flat rods, horse-whim and drawing machine with crusher. Operations were suspended and equipment sold, largely because of the need to work under the land of an adjoining owner who refused permission.

The mine was reopened in 1852 under a new company with a considerably enlarged sett; by 1854 a 24in. steam engine had been installed and a new shaft, 'Beresfords', opened, upon which a 50in. engine was erected in 1855, the old engine being used for hoisting and crushing. An unusual feature of the engine house was that, because of the risk of fire, it was built without using wood anywhere except for the roof timbers and had slate floors and iron girders and stairs. During 1855/56 ore to the value of £3,446 was extracted.

The mine was financed on the cost book system, and because of the difficulties experienced in getting shareholders to meet their 'calls', an attempt was made to form a joint stock company. Legal difficulties proved insurmountable and operations were abandoned and machinery and materials were put up for sale in 1857. At the time, Mr Henry James was mine captain and about 60 hands were employed.

There is also a record of Caton copper and silver-lead mine on the banks of the Erme at the same time as Ivybridge Consols and of a prospectus for Wheal Francis (about 1820) in the valley of the Erme which, it was claimed, had been worked 102 years before.

A Geological Society memoir of 1920 reports 900 tons of 'Brown Haematite' (iron ore) from Harford parish and from Ugborough 258 tons lead ore, 171 tons lead, 2,688oz silver and 2,432 tons of iron oxides (brown haematite and ochre).

TENNIS IN IVYBRIDGE

Tennis has always been very popular as all old maps suggest. It does seem to have had courts in the grounds, even Harford Road car park used to be a court when it belonged to the old London Hotel. But now we are served by the Community College and by South Devon Tennis Centre at Erme playing-fields. Ivybridge Tennis Club was formed with help from various funds, including a loan from Ivybridge Council.

The club has gone from strength to strength, from four outside courts plus changing rooms, etc., to today, when it boasts indoor courts as well as meeting-rooms and outdoor courts with floodlights, all subsidised by funds from the National Lottery. The improved club was finally opened in May 2003 by John Crowther, chief executive of the Lawn Tennis Association. We have had a number of red-letter days. There have been visits by Sue Barker, Sue Mappin, Annabel Croft, the Duke of Kent, Jo Durie and the Cliff Richard Tennis Trail. In the summer of 1991, when the River Erme flooded, the tennis club was badly affected.

People and Places

Wedding party at Ermington c.1900.

Left to right: *Fred Hoare, ? Venn, Jumbo Williams, Percy Roberts.*

People and Places

Fred Hoare.

Football supporters ready for the off.

People and Places

Charabanc outings became all the rage as public conveyances such as this grew in popularity. Church and chapel groups, sports clubs and groups of workers made annual trips to the seaside or up on to Dartmoor, taking in a tea house, or perhaps a pub, for refreshment. This photograph, thought to have been taken in Cornwood, shows one such outing to Paignton in 1924.

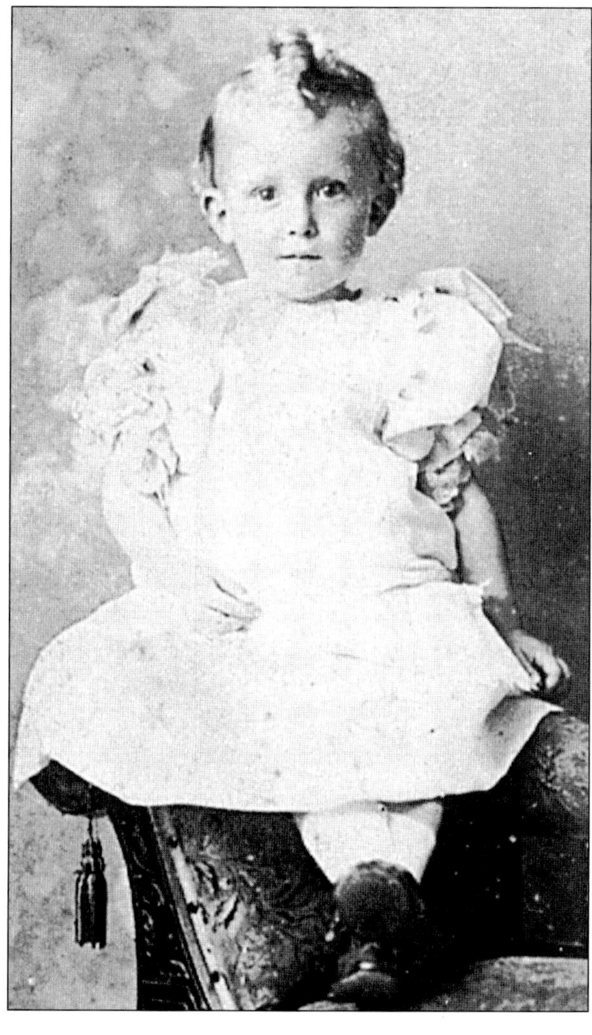

Above: *Cecil Holman, whose family owned Lee Mill. He emigrated to New Zealand.*

Above: *Cecil Holman as a child.*

People and Places

Edna Salter, née Holman.

Horace Salter.

Above: *Mr Bill Fry, Ivybridge lamplighter.*

Right: *Mr and Mrs John Pearse, who farmed at Piles Peek towards the end of the nineteenth century.*

Left: *Piles Peek Farmhouse, Ugborough, c.1890. The couple standing in the doorway are thought to be John Pearse and his wife, Annie.*

People and Places

Above: *The opening of the town hall, with Jay Vincent, Tony Barbour, Barry Thom, John Kelly, Joy Day, Ian Maddock, Mike Saltern and Jack London.*

Mr and Mrs Fred Gilley.

Left: *Joy Day, the mayor of Ivybridge with the winners of the road safety song competition.*

Above: *PC Slim Richardson helping Emma Wyatt to cross Fore Street on her hundredth birthday.*

Left: *Miss Emma Wyatt at the age of 100.*

People and Places

Vera Luckham, former landlady of the Sportman's Inn, on her 100th birthday in 2008.

Miss Veal on her 100th birthday.

Helen Carnell celebrating her 105th birthday

Jim Daniels, Ethel Nelder and Arthur Caseley, who were pupils together at Station Road School in 1908.

Charlie Leith and friends.

Mrs Clarice Bowker with her Maundy Money.

Muriel and Bill Davies and daughter at Buckingham Palace, where Bill was awarded the MBE in 1978.

Subscribers

Abbott Family, Ivybridge, Devon
Jill and Tony Barber, Ivybridge
Kevin Bennett, Crownhill, Plymouth
Edwin Bennett
Julie and Phil Briant, Ivybridge, Devon
John P. Browne, Ivybridge, Devon
Stan and Caroline Butcher, Ivybridge
Brenda S. Cansdale, Bittaford
John Marc Chapman, Ivybridge Town Mayor (2005-2007)
Martin and Fran Coard, Ivybridge, Devon
Rebecca Jane Cooper, Ivybridge
J. D. Cornish, Cornwood, Devon
Alison and Chris Daniell, Salisbury, Wiltshire
Roy Davey and Family, Ivybridge
C. and P. Davies, Ivybridge
Mr T. D. Eastley, Ivybridge, Devon
Ian Eastley, Ivybridge, Devon
J. W. Elford, Ivybridge, Devon
Don and Margery Evans, Ivybridge
M. Fraser, Oborne, Sherborne
Frank and Florrie Green, ran the village stores in Western Road
Fernley J. Harris, Ivybridge, Devon
Ned Hingston, Ivybridge
Desmond C. Hingston, Ivybridge
M. Hingston, Ivybridge
John and Jo Holcombe, Ivybridge, Devon
Lilian Holt, Ivybridge, Devon
Sidney John Ingram, Ivybridge, Devon
Michael A. James, Ivybridge, Devon
Margaret A. James, Ivybridge, Devon
Mrs S. Kerswill, Ivybridge
Keith A. Kiddell
Alan and Angela Knight
Tony Knox, Harford
Ellen M. Large, Ivybridge, Devon
Colin H. Leigh, Melbourne, Australia (formerly Ivybridge)
Joy and Ken Luke, Ivybridge, Devon
Michael G. D. MacLening, Ivybridge, Devon
Elizabeth Mason, Oaklawn Gardens, Toronto, Canada
Mr and Mrs N. Maythorne, Ivybridge, Devon
David McKee
Richard McKee
Jill McRae-Spencer, Corntown, Devon

Duncan and Gloria McRae-Spencer, Indiana, USA
Norah Miller (née Bowden), formerly at 'Belmont', Ivybridge
Gareth and Nancy Morgans, Charles Hankin Close, Ivybridge
Craig Alan Newcombe, Ivybridge, Devon
L. Owen, Ivybridge
Parkin Family, Pinehurst Way, Ivybridge
Ian, Kym, Naomi and Leanne Pearse, Ivybridge, Devon
Alan Pearse, Sparkwell, Devon
Celia Ralph, Ivybridge
Sylvia M. Rice, Ermington, Devon
Catherine M. Rogers, Weeke Farm, Modbury
Anne C. Rose, Ivybridge
Alison Rowlands, Ivybridge, Devon
Bill Salter, West Lake, Ivybridge
Nicholas and Michelle Scarr, Ivybridge, Devon
Mrs J. Skelley
Raymond Smith, Ivybridge, Devon
Jeremy R. Stabb, Ivybridge, Devon
Revd. Helene Stainer, Milverton, Somerset
Patricia H. Steer and Helen Carnell
Fred Stone, Ivybridge
Stowford Primary School
Patricia and Glynn Stringer, Ivybridge, Devon
John and June Thompson, Ivybridge
Russell Thomson, Esme's Cottage, Ivybridge
Brett Thorn, Ivybridge, Devon
Stacy Thorn, Ivybridge, Devon
Greg Wall, formerly Headteacher The Erme Primary School
Waterside House Residents, Ivybridge
Mr C. Willcocks, Cornwood
Nigel T. Williams, Ivybridge, Devon
O. C. Williams (Deceased), Ivybridge
Fiona Wilson, Ivybridge, Devon